Marianne —
I trust this will be thought-provok
for you. Thank you for all you do
in our community —
Namasté!
Donald B. Gill

- **Who was Jesus?**

- **What is heaven? Where is it? What about hell?**

- **Did God write the Bible? If he did, why doesn't everyone read it?**

- **Why do people sing about "The blood of the lamb?"**

- **Does the Bible really hate gay people?**

- **The only *true* Bible is the King James Version because that's the Bible the Apostle Paul used. Right?**

- **Your child asks: "When Mikey's mother says: 'Jesus died for my sins?' Did he? Why? What did she mean that I was born in sin? Did I do something wrong?"**

- **Does God really decide who is going to die and when? If he does, why doesn't he just kill the bad guys?**

- **Where is my soul?**

- **If I don't believe in Jesus, will I go the hell? Did Mahatma Gandhi, a Hindu, go to hell?**

Aren't all these questions supposed to be answered by the Bible? Yes, but most of us don't understand the Bible. If you believe that the Bible was somehow magically sent from God to men—verbatim—word-for-word—then this is probably not a book you will want to read. If the Bible wasn't word-for-word dictated to men by God as "his Word," then how can it be that the Bible is "… wholly accurate and trustworthy in every way," which is a favorite phrase used by Protestant fundamentalists and evangelicals or the fervent Christian Right?

There is a strong movement today for simplistic, literal, biblical beliefs and practices. Why? It provides a sense of safety and security – but it is fear-based and fear is the opposite of faith. This desire for literal biblical beliefs *is really a desire to control the knowledge of good and evil and, therefore, to be absolutely certain about what it is God wants.* This fear-based desire for security is not unique to our current times. It runs throughout the Bible, had its beginnings in the Old Testament, led to abuses in Israel's Temple-State system, and influenced what was included *and excluded* from the New Testament.

This fear-based desire for security lies behind many of the Protestant fundamentalists or fervent evangelicals and their desire to "overhaul" our society. As they use the Bible to buttress their position, they are *mis*using it.

Many of the Bible's writers edited existing, original material or wrote under the name of a familiar author. These latter-day editors/authors came from the perspective of a fear-based set of beliefs based upon purification and sacrifice. Upon reading this book you will understand how and why this occurred. You will also understand the *original* positive message of the prophets and of Jesus.

Perhaps you are one of the millions of "mainstream" church-going Christians who do not consider yourself to be a fundamental evangelical. Perhaps you have developed a deeply personal sense of spirituality as a result of your involvement in a Twelve-Step recovery program. Perhaps you have found an inner peace and calm through a form of New Thought religion, including variations of Eastern religions. Regardless, quoting scripture is probably not your "strong suit." Neither is a fully engaged religious discussion with those that do frequently quote scripture. Consequently, we need to understand how much we humans were involved in the process that produced the Bible and then apply some common sense, grounded in recent scholarly research, on these kinds of issues.

In short, there are three reasons for you to read this book:

- It's time you know the *real* story of the Bible for yourself.

- Many Protestant fundamentalists and evangelicals believe the Bible was almost literally "faxed" from God, and they are not shy about saying so. *What is it you believe about the Bible?* This book will help you answer that question.

- There are times when issues about gays or Jesus or miracles or abortion come up. You need to be able to offer yourself (and your children) a real answer – *your* answer.

Acclaim for O'Dell's book

The major strength of O'Dell's book is the commentary that relates the Bible and its history to our everyday lives. *Rev. Evelyn J. (E.J.) Niles, Embracing the Bible (ETB) Ministry, Manassas, VA. ETB is a sanctioned alternative ministry of the Association of Unity Churches.*

***

How the Bible became the Bible can put years of Bible study and Scripture reading suddenly into focus. It sharpens the big picture no matter how clear it seemed before.... The research and scholarship are excellent, yet it can be read as easily by those with little biblical knowledge as by those with [Bible study] experience. *Karen Harvey, historian, published author, and active member of the Memorial Presbyterian Church, Saint Augustine, FL.*

***

I visualize this book reaching out and touching the many people who may have settled for a ritualized and meaningless experience with God, or may have given up on their spirituality altogether.... I really appreciated the way the book concluded with a very practical spiritual message. *Rev. Elizabeth Claire, Center for Positive Living, a congregation of Religious Science International, Saint Augustine, FL.*

***

Even though I've had a lot of Bible study, I found it wonderfully informative and alive. *Ms. Amy George, Licensed Unity Teacher, Reston, VA.*

***

"The history and mystery of the Bible have been in the literary hands of only a few people compared to the millions who do not know the true meaning of the Bible – including what it *really is* and what it *really is not.* Mr. O'Dell has done insightful research to explain simply the pure intent ... of this greatly misunderstood book and how it came to be. I highly endorse and recommend O'Dell's exciting new work." *Dr. Tom Costa, Minister Emeritus and founder, Palm Desert, CA, Church of Religious Science and author of "Life: You Wanna Make Something Of It?"*

How the Bible Became the Bible

Donald L. O'Dell

**Florida Writers Association Royal Palm
Literary Award for Non-Fiction**

ISBN 0-7414-2993-4

Cover Design: Rik Feeney / Kurt Merkel

Published by:

INFINITY
PUBLISHING.COM

1094 New DeHaven Street, Suite 100
West Conshohocken, PA 19428-2713
Info@buybooksontheweb.com
www.buybooksontheweb.com
Toll-free (877) BUY BOOK
Local Phone (610) 941-9999
Fax (610) 941-9959

Printed in the United States of America
Printed on Recycled Paper
Published August 2007

Permission Notices

Contents

Tables, Exhibits and Maps

Tables

Exhibits

Maps

Acknowledgments

I would like to thank the Focus Group that read the initial, draft manuscript and made valuable suggestions for its improvement. Nevertheless, I accept full responsibility for the content of the book. The Focus Group included:

- **Rev. Elizabeth Claire**, minister, Saint Augustine Center For Positive Living, Church of Religious Science International;

- **Amy George**, perhaps my closest friend and, as a Licensed Unity Teacher, brings a perspective from Unity as well as from Twelve-Step Programs;

- **Karen Harvey**, historian, a published author, excellent writer, and active member in the United Presbyterian Church;

- **Rev. Evelyn J. (EJ) Niles**, minister, Embracing The Bible (ETB) Ministry, an alternative ministry of the Association of Unity Churches;

- **Harry Stafford**, a graduate of Columbia Presbyterian Seminary, who studied at Harvard Divinity School, taught biblical studies, is an experienced counselor and a well-respected local entrepreneur; and

- **Helene Sullivan**, a well-read and close friend with a deep understanding of our social/political fabric.

I acknowledge my family. In addition to reviewing the draft manuscript, they offered support and encouragement. **Christopher O'Dell**, my son and an attorney for an investment banking firm, interested and well-read in many subjects; **Leslie O'Dell**, my daughter and a teacher with a Masters in Special Education, committed to an alternative lifestyle; and **Marcia E. O'Dell**, my wife, who – more than anybody else – put events on hold, suffered through my discussions, and brought her distinct ex-Catholic perspective of very little biblical knowledge to the whole project.

I also am indebted to **Rik Feeney**, my content editor, publicist, and agent; **Beth Mansbridge,** an editor who proofread the manuscript; **Nancy Quatrano,** author of *Mayhem at Buckelew House,* who mentored me; **the Professional Writers of Saint Augustine**, a delightful local group, where I picked up more information than I realized I needed to know; and **Nadia Ramoutar**, a published author and professor of communications at Flagler College in Saint Augustine, who very early on was confident that this project had merit.

I need to acknowledge **Neale Donald Walsch**. He is the author of the "Conversations With God" series of books. As a guest of our church, he was here in November, 2003 for a lecture. During the lecture, he discussed the importance of religious tolerance and then reiterated the need for each of us to start doing something.

Lastly, I cannot begin to give enough credit to **Bill W.** and **Dr. Bob** without whom I would not have survived 1987, much less have written this book.

This book is dedicated to my three grandchildren: Christopher Elliot, Ian Christopher, and Jackson David.

By the time they are adults I hope our society will be more focused on an open and honest spirituality, bearing fruits of love, peace and truth, than in trying to prove itself to be right.

I believe this book is a step in that direction.

Introduction

There is an anonymous poster on the wall in the men's room of my church. It's located at just the "appropriate" place and height. I have read it often.

Life's Lessons

An elderly Cherokee was teaching his grandchildren about life.

He said to them, "A fight is going on inside me. It is a terrible fight, and it is between two wolves.

"One wolf is evil—he is fear, anger, envy, sorrow, regret, greed, arrogance, anxiety, self-pity, guilt, resentment, inferiority, lies, false pride, competition, superiority, and ego.

"The other wolf is good—he is joy, peace, love, hope, sharing, serenity, humility, kindness, benevolence, friendship, empathy, generosity, truth, compassion, faith, and laughter.

"This same fight is going on inside you, and inside every other person, too."

The children thought about it for a minute and then one grandchild asked his grandfather, "Which wolf will win?"

The old Cherokee replied, "The one you feed."

It's a wonderful sentiment, isn't it? In a simple, straightforward manner it communicates volumes—to adults as well as to children—about the nature of mankind. The observations of the old Cherokee are similar to the observations I believe were made by the author who first wrote the story of how Adam and Eve disobeyed God in the Garden of Eden in the Old Testament's Book of Genesis, Chapter 2:4–3:24.

Both authors struggled with a common observation: Ordinary people can do some truly awful, evil things. The two authors are dealing with the concept of evil. Where does it come from? Why is it there? The old Cherokee answers the question from the perspective of the "bad child" in all of us. He concludes: Evil just is and it will be strong or weak in us, depending on whether or not we feed it.

The first real biblical author (commonly referred to as the "Yahwist")[1], who wrote how mankind (male and female) disobeyed God, was dealing with the same issue as the Cherokee grandfather. The Yahwist concluded that mankind wanted to "… be as the gods." And so he tells the story that mankind wasn't content to be able to eat from anywhere in the Garden. Mankind wanted to eat from the forbidden Tree of the Knowledge of Good and Evil—the fruit of which would allow mankind to be as powerful as a god. Later he repeats the same theme in the story about the Tower of Babel (Genesis 11:1-10). The people wanted to build a tower so high in the sky that they could climb up and stand there and talk directly to the gods ("… make a name for ourselves …") and God was afraid they would be able to accomplish anything they put their minds to.

For the Yahwist this temptation to be as a god, to be in control of the knowledge of good and evil, was the root cause of evil. Given his Bronze Age understanding of life, two cornerstones of his belief were: (1) Each tribe/nation of people had their own gods; Yahweh was Israel's God; (2) gods, envisioned in anthropomorphic terms, rewarded or punished their people. Along with the belief that God punished mankind, this desire to be as God and its subsequent punishment explained to him why it was so hard to eke out a living around 1000 B.C.E., why life was so precarious, why women had such a hard time with childbirth, and other observations.

How would *you* explain the origin of evil? Try it! If your inclination is to talk about evil in terms of yourself or an individual, then you'll feel a definite affinity to the Cherokee grandfather. If your inclination is to talk about evil in more general terms, in terms of all of mankind, you'll feel a close affinity to the Yahwist. I think either is valid.

As a Presbyterian minister living in a church-owned home, my family and I were expected to keep the house reasonably clean. When my children were little they ate in a small room off our kitchen where their messes were easy to clean up. Originally the room had been a porch. It had been enclosed with sheets of paneling over the studs, very little insulation, easy-to-install aluminum windows, and a linoleum floor. We had painted the table and children's chairs in bright child-like colors—and enamel for easy cleaning.

One evening, as my former wife and I were eating our supper in the carpeted dining room, that unmistakable tinkling sound of breaking glass came from the children's room. On the tail of the sound waves of broken glass was my daughter Leslie's two-year-old voice: "Chris did it!" Instantly came my five-year-old son's reply: "She made me do it!" The classic "blame game."

You may smile as you picture the scene with my children, but we all still say these kinds of things: "He made me so mad that I said things I shouldn't have." [*Your loss of control is all his fault.*] "She woke up with a headache, snapped at me, and it put me in a bad mood. She ruined my whole day." [*Her headache's to blame for the bad mood you've chosen to carry around all day.*]

You can read that same dialogue, the classic blame game (Genesis 3:11-13), when God confronted Adam and Eve after they ate the forbidden fruit: Adam: "She made me do it!" Eve: "The serpent made me do it!" However, please notice that although they ate the forbidden fruit from the Tree of the Knowledge of Good and Evil, they didn't die or receive any lasting flashes of God-Smarts!

My Spiritual Awakening

I went to Alcoholics Anonymous to stop drinking, but I found myself continuing to sit on small chairs in damp church basements because I was learning, for the first time in my life, how to take responsibility for myself. Also, while in those church basements and for the first time in my life, I truly experienced the redemptive power of God, as I understand God. Even having been an ordained minister, I experienced a sense of spirituality, for the first time, on a visceral level, not simply on an intellectual level. While I was still drinking, I would begin to get a knot in my stomach every afternoon around four. By the time I'd get home from work, usually about seven, it would take a nice, tall vodka to make that knot begin to unravel.

During my first six months in AA, the knot would continue to appear around four, right on schedule. However, rather than going straight for the house after work, I'd head for a seven o'clock AA meeting. Just by touching the doorknob to the church basement, the knot would start to disappear. For me it was a miracle that defied rational explanation. It wasn't magic. It wasn't an answer to my prayers. It was visceral, experiential, and real.

Some of you also may have found the spirituality of a Twelve-Step Program mind-boggling and life changing. Like me, perhaps you began a Twelve-Step Program to conquer an addiction and ended up with a new sense of life and spirituality, along with newly-learned skills for living it.

As a member of a Twelve-Step Program, I was learning how to live as a responsible adult. After all, nobody made me take a drink. My feelings and moods were my own. I could allow them to take charge of me or I could choose to simply treat them as feelings. Old habits: "She made me so angry that I blew my top, said things I didn't mean, and had several stiff drinks" slowly became new skills: "I got angry at what she said. Since I can't handle anger very well, I drank to anesthetize my feelings." New habits: Adulthood. Responsibility. No more blame games like Adam and Eve.

The Connection

Perhaps you are one of the millions of "mainstream" churchgoing Christians who does not consider yourself a Fundamental Evangelical. You do not believe that the Bible contains the exact, almost dictated, words of God. You support a congregation with your time and money. You attend Sunday school as well as Sunday morning worship. Your children attend with you, go to some of the youth group activities, and attend a summer church camp or vacation Bible school. You understand enough to believe that the first eleven chapters of Genesis consist of local (to the Genesis writer) myths, fables, and allegories. At a party, if someone begins to extol the virtues of some political movement or condemn certain societal actions and uses quotations from Scripture to support their argument, you will generally smile, remain quiet, and be respectfully polite. After all, quoting Scripture is not your "strong suit," and the last thing you want to do is become engaged in a religious argument. But it bothers you to listen to someone like that. Isn't there something you can say? Or should say?

Whether or not you're a Twelve-Stepper or a mainstream churchgoer, you may consider yourself a nontraditional believer. Perhaps you've found New Thought religion—Religious Science (Science of Mind), Unity, Christian Science, or blends of Eastern/Metaphysical thought—intellectually stimulating and spiritually comforting. These approaches simply make sense to you. Questions about God, the meaning of life, the moral foundations of good and bad personal behavior, meditation, the afterlife, and prayer are not only relevant, but the answers you are getting are actually intelligible and usable.

Writings about spiritual paths, inner peace, stress reduction, creativity, addictions, health, holistic and alternative therapies seem to be right on the money for us. They all talk to us about essential spiritual things—the mind-body-spirit connection—in a language we can understand.

Marianne Williamson, Neale Donald Walsch, James Redfield, Don Miguel Ruiz, Deepak Chopra, Wayne Dyer, Louise Hay, and others are writers whose books will be found on your bedside tables, dog-eared and heavily highlighted. The same is true with writers of self-help books, be they books on substance abuse, codependency, eating disorders, compulsions, gambling, or shame. These are familiar authors, such as M. Scott Peck, John Bradshaw, Earnie Larsen, and Melody Beattie.

All of us—mainstream churchgoers, Twelve-Steppers, and New Thought spiritualists—read our favorite self-help books and we feel good. We look forward to going to a religious service or to a Twelve-Step meeting. We simply just feel "right" about it all—until our child comes home from school and asks: "Do angels really fight with devils over my soul?" Following the vacuous stare and onset of dry mouth comes that frightening thought: *"Does the Bible really say that? Am I supposed to believe that?"*

What does the Bible really say?

We don't need to have children to raise these kinds of questions. We ask that kind of question all by ourselves. We hear someone quote Billy Graham or Pat Robertson (or any other evangelist) about demons, angels, Original Sin, or the condemnation of a movie we're looking forward to seeing, and we catch ourselves thinking: *"Am I supposed to really believe that?"*

We listen to a newscast of some heated legislative debate dealing with cloning, an abortion clinic bombing, the right-to-die movement, "evil" empires, a hate crime, stem cell research, prayer in school, or some gay/lesbian issue. Many of the arguments are bolstered by very Scripture-laden phrases, and we catch ourselves ·thinking: *"Does the Bible really say that?"*

Those of us who are discovering our spirituality in a Twelve-Step Program or in New Thought religion are *not* in a mainstream, Bible-based religion. Those of us who are mainstream churchgoers usually are not involved in a Bible-quoting, Jesus-is-my-very-best-friend denomination. However, we live in a society that appeals very heavily to Bible-based religion for all sorts of support.

As an example, I would imagine in the Bible Belt it's easier for a good, solid Southern Baptist to get elected to the local school board than it is for a member of a Unitarian congregation. Will that election affect the materials used in your schools, the priorities established within the budget, the openness of the district to hire an excellent teacher who may be Hindu or may be gay? Do those school board decisions affect your community? *You bet they do!*

State and national politicians campaign on Bible-based moral slogans. They make promises, backing them with Biblical quotes, to gain the support of very conservative, "Bible believing" groups or coalitions sometimes referred to as the Religious Right or the Christian Coalition. Many of these promises or campaign platforms can be quite divisive and polarizing. Can this affect you? Can this sway you (either positively or negatively) for a candidate or issue? *You bet it can!*

Who reads the Bible today?

Most of us don't read the Bible. If we do, it's a verse here, three verses there. The Bible is not in a language we easily understand. It's dull and seems irrelevant. Besides, every time we've tried to read the Bible, we were confronted with all sorts of emotional baggage associated with the Bible/church/religion that muddles the issue. We start to read the Bible and the chatterbox in our mind begins replaying images of:

- The local pastor who deserted his family and ran off with your best friend's mother

- The Sunday school teacher who embarrassed you publicly over a sexual question you asked, but was later run out of town, having been caught with young men

- Sister Martha, of the convent school, spanking your hand with a ruler

- Arguments you've had over the Bible. Some of the ideas in the Bible just didn't make any sense to you then and they still don't now. So you've just walked away, gone on with the rest of your life, and endured the tolerant but condescending "tsk-tsk" from family members.

- The constant references to your sinful nature, so graphic and frightening that you've ended up a personal wreck. After all, you're so worthless!

- The church treasurer who absconded with congregational cash—the same person who was wonderfully skilled in the art of making you feel guilty about your seemingly paltry contribution

- The minister who kept at you about loving God as you did your father. You said you couldn't. He said the devil had already gotten you. You tried to explain, without revealing the life-threatening secret of your family, that often your father physically abused your mother.

So, we don't read the Bible.

How we can relate to the Bible

I believe if we understand what the people of the Bible are trying to communicate, we can begin to see beyond their words, cultures, or history. When we've done that, we can see ourselves in them or, conversely, them in us. Then they become very real people and their experiences can relate to our experiences.

Just as I witnessed my own children use the same blame game defense attributed to Adam and Eve, I have seen how I used that same defense to insulate myself from my drinking: "If you had my boss, you'd drink too." or "If you had my ex-wife (or my ex-wife's lawyer), you'd drink more than I." There are other dramas besides the blame game: explaining death; explaining the fine line between joy and sadness; trying to understand why bad things happen to good people; comprehending the power of love. If we look, we begin to observe these same kinds of basic human dramas playing out over and over.

We see Kahlil Gibran, the Lebanese poet, touching on these common human threads in The Prophet. We see these threads in the Hindu classic The Bhagavad-Gita, in Ernest Holmes' The Science of Mind, and in Emmet Fox's writings. We see them in the Gospels and many Letters of the New Testament. We see all sorts of people in a variety of cultures and times making similar observations and trying to communicate them—all in language and culture comfortable to themselves.

Equally, we observe proponents of these writings still clamoring and shouting: "Our interpretation is the only right one!" Why is that? Why is that so important to them? For example, why will people hate and deride and fear and kill those who disagree with their interpretation of the Bible or the Quran? Why? It provides a sense of safety and security. As such, it is a fear-based response, and fear-based beliefs elicit aggressive behaviors.

Just as mankind (personified in Adam and Eve) was tempted by the idea that the "forbidden fruit" would provide all they needed to know to understand God—to be as God—I believe many think of the Bible in the same way. There is an attitude of worship and protection that surrounds the Bible itself, as if it were some form of magic book.

[One could probably say much the same thing about the Radical Islamists or the Jewish extremists, although I will not be discussing that.]

I believe the Yahwist's observation is still relevant: *The desire to be as God—to be as absolutely sure you are as right as God—is still very much alive, causing as much pain now as it was believed to have caused then.*

Making sense of the Bible

This book will give you an overview of how the Bible developed. It will provide you with historically accurate "broad-brushstrokes" of biblical history and the sources of scriptural writings as well as the context in which these writings were created.

What do I mean by broad brushstrokes and by sources?

If I were to educate you in broad brushstrokes about the Impressionist style of painting (*pun intended*), I would make two points: Impressionist painters tried to capture the use of color and light. Many times their brush movements were simply dabs of color instead of strokes.

Secondly, they painted their impressions of real life. Until the Impressionists, most painters painted portraits, religious scenes, or depictions of epic historical events. Impressionists used common, everyday scenes as the subject of their works: people drinking coffee, taking a bath, or brushing their hair. Does this explain all there is to know about Monet, Manet, Renoir, or Van Gogh? No. Wouldn't art historians roll their eyes at the simplicity of my description? Probably. Nevertheless, it's a pretty good beginning.

As to what I mean by biblical sources: The Bible didn't have authors with protective copyrights, like we do now. Without oversimplifying too much, there are essentially six primary sources of much of the written Old Testament: The Yahwist, the Elohist, the Deuteronomic Reformers, the priestly writers, David's court historian, and the major prophets. Likewise, there are five primary sources for the New Testament: the writers of the four Gospels, including Acts, and the Apostle Paul.

I will be illustrating throughout the book that these principal sources of biblical writings were people just like us. If we cannot see ourselves in them, then we are forced to conclude that they truly were different and that God spoke to them in ways differently than he speaks to us (if he speaks to us at all).

If that is the case, then the whole biblical record really is of another time—irrelevant to us. The best we can do under these circumstances is to vicariously adopt the personal faith of these biblical characters. We achieve that by being mesmerized by the very words of scripture, which therefore must not change—cannot change. That's the essence of the children's ditty: "Jesus loves me, this I know, for the Bible tells me so." If we take this position, it puts us in a very dangerous place—a spiritually unhealthy adoration of the Bible itself. I call this unhealthy adoration *Bibliolatry*.

What you will learn

After reading this book, you will be knowledgeable in basic biblical themes and will be able to develop answers that work for you. You will be able to develop answers that fit comfortably within your beliefs, while allowing you to understand those that may be more fundamentalist. You no longer have to remain quiet because you feel inadequate. This book will help ease the fear that can be present when those of us who don't interpret the Bible literally are around those that do. You can offer your children (or provide yourself) helpful, positive guidance, even though our society is becoming more polarized by the rhetoric of the Religious Right masquerading as political initiatives.

I believe biblical wisdom and truth do help me actually live a fuller day-to-day life, but I also do not read or interpret the Bible literally. To understand my position, it is important to truly appreciate what's in the Bible—namely, to see down-to-earth people who came to know, believe, and trust in a Supreme Being. I believe real "flesh and blood" people wrote the Bible in response to their very real history. Some of them overreacted, while some of them misinterpreted events. Still others chastised or corrected them. I can relate to all that and so I tell you some of my story in the hope that it will help you relate to these Biblical authors as well.

The down-to-earth people who wrote these Biblical texts had a sense of God that was a knowing/believing/trusting consistent with their understanding of the way the world worked. It was also consistent, from their anthropomorphic point of view, with the way God *should* work. They told their story the way they saw it, using language familiar to them. As I tell you of the reality of a spiritual presence in my life during my journey to sobriety, I think you'll come to understand *it is very difficult to verbalize spiritual realities.* Consequently, we'll journey through the background of the Bible from the standpoint of its history and how it was written and, within that history, meet the principal sources or authors of scriptural writings and understand the principal conflicts or tensions that influenced what they wrote.

This is not a book written for academicians, although I have done significant research. For a book this size to cover the massive scope of history involved, I provide only general descriptions. I am certain that knowledgeable scholars will wince as they read how, from their points of view, I have summarized, oversimplified, and determined what to highlight. But I didn't write this book for them.

Part 1

Part 1 discusses the development of the Old Testament, briefly tracing the history of Israel and the sources that formed the Old Testament from Abraham, Isaac, and Jacob (the Patriarchs, circa 1700 B.C.E.) to the start of the initial millennium of the Common Era. Besides the basic elements of who did what to whom and why, we will explore the continual tension that existed between the priestly class of Israel and the prophets: the priestly class wanted to codify or institutionalize a form of "national" righteous or moral behavior; the prophets kept insisting they were on the wrong track. Also, we will get to know the people behind the principal sources of the Old Testament writings—who they were and what they were trying to communicate.

Part 2

Part 2 continues this thread with a discussion of Jesus and the New Testament. Part 2 could also be titled: *How Christianity and the New Testament Grew and Matured.* Here you will begin to understand why the letters, Gospels, and other writings that make up the New Testament are in the Bible *as well as why other writings are **not** in the Bible.* This is a very important issue because I believe some of the ideas and concepts that didn't make it in the New Testament should have. What we can learn about Jesus from the early Jewish Christians of the Jesus Movements, *who were pretty much "out of the loop" in the formation of the organization we know as the "Early Church,"* is terribly relevant today. The theology of freedom worked out by the Apostle Paul, and generally misunderstood by later Biblical writers, isn't the only theological platform available to us. Jesus of Nazareth repeated (and lived!) the messages of the Old Testament prophets. However, much of his message dissolved as the organizational aspects of the emerging Church began making the same kinds of mistakes made by Israel's priestly class during Old Testament times.

If you want to skip around

I believe the Old Testament is fascinating, but I understand not everyone shares this fascination. If you are not particularly interested in the development of the Old Testament, I would recommend you read the Introduction to Part I followed by Chapter 1, the section entitled the *Patriarchal Narrative* in Chapter 2, and Chapter 5. This will provide you with enough general information to allow most of the Old Testament references in Part II to make sense. If you just want to get an overall scope of the book, read Chapters 5, 9 and 12. Then you can focus on whatever aspects of the Bible (or biblical history) that most interest you. Of course, since this is a high-level overview, the design of the book is that you read it from cover to cover. Following this initial reading, you can concentrate on those sections that have sparked your interest, using the Notes at the end of each chapter as well as the Bibliography as guides for further, more in-depth reading.

A potential path

I believe it will make a significant difference if people begin to say, "This is the path I have chosen in order to know and experience God, as I understand God" rather than "This is the only path to God."

Enjoy.

Think.

Grow.

And ...

Walk with God, as you understand God, in a manner that disciplines you to see the love of God in others and allows others to see the love of God in you. This will bring peace on earth as well as a personal peace to you—a peace such as the world cannot give.

Namaste.

Donald L. O'Dell
2006

Donald L. O'Dell

Introduction Notes

[1] Known as the Yahwist because the author routinely used the word, Yahweh (Hebrew: YHWH), as the word for God, as opposed to Elohim, the primary word for God used by a later author. The Yahwist is regarded as the first principal author of the Old Testament, writing about 950 B.C.E. The Yahwist is also known as the "J" writer. The first scholars to discover this literary strand in the Old Testament were German and they used the German "J" (Jahwist or JHWH). American and English scholars use the English "Y."

Part 1

The Development of the Old Testament

𝔚hat images come to mind when you think of the middle-to-late Bronze Age? What about the early Iron Age? Something a little more sophisticated than early cave men? Early, primitive farmers? Well, this is the era of much of the early Old Testament: from Abram (later Abraham) in the Middle Bronze Age (circa 1700 B.C.E.) to the century that was the height of Israel's glory (circa 1000 B.C.E.). Israel became a legitimate political nation in the Late Bronze Age or early Iron Age (1020–922 B.C.E.), first under King Saul, followed by King David, and lastly King Solomon.

Introduction to Part I

The Old Testament is stupendous in scope. As we progress from the simple nomadic family and its tribal religion of the patriarchs to the highly developed cult of Judaism centered on the temple rites and festivals, we will advance almost one and one-half millennia. In the Old Testament, just as the "devil is in the details," so the knowing of God is in the knowing of history.

I've tried to make the history of the Old Testament read like a story. I want to show you the dangers involved when people try to make certain that their religious convictions (many of which are based on the *mis*use of the Bible) get codified into State or federal law. Their assumed rationale? To help us become a more godly nation. This desire to achieve a righteousness that is pleasing to God, through formal, legal means, has been going on since 600

B.C.E. in the Old Testament. It wasn't a good idea then and it is not a good idea now.

So, to understand the Bible and how it came about, we start with an overview of the Old Testament. *Chapter 1* will discuss the meaning of the term "biblical sources." *Chapters 2 and 3* will discuss the major historical threads of Old Testament Israel in order to put into perspective how, when, and why most of the Books of the Old Testament came about. *Chapter 4* will focus on the principal sources of the Old Testament, including some of the influential prophets. *Chapter 5* will summarize critical events and movements of the Old Testament that I believe are most pertinent for us right now.

As you read Part 1, please notice that Israel made some of the same mistakes over and over and the prophets kept admonishing and correcting over and over. As history unfolded, their understanding of God became fuller and more mature. All along the way their concept of God kept getting more and more personal. More facets of God appeared. Through the prophets it began to become evident that God wanted a personal—not simply a legislated—sense of righteousness. Yet all along the way as well, the growing influence of the "formal" priestly class kept insisting on preserving emerging religious customs and rituals. For the prophets, personal righteousness—or doing the next right thing— was an individual response to an individual situation. That personal decision of how to respond was made over and over as different situations kept popping up. For the priests, personal righteousness was exhibited in maintaining the purity of ritualized behavior. If one followed all the customs to the letter, then, by definition, one was righteous.

The mistakes Israel made? The shift away from oral recitations based on tribal remembrances to written literature made it easier for Israel to focus on the codification or institutionalization of the Law, of rigid ritual instructions, of an overall "legalism." What does this mean—codifying or institutionalizing? *It means trying to make legal and explicit the external behavior that will signify the kind of person that will please God.* This happened, perhaps most dramatically, with the writing of Deuteronomy after Israel, Jerusalem, and the temple were crushed and destroyed. It happened again, with the Priestly

Code, during the 400 years after the Exile. This institutionalization also happened during the development of the New Testament.

From the standpoint of the Christian Bible, the Old Testament leads to the New Testament. The Old Testament is the story of the nation of Israel and its covenant with her God. Within that story—that history—Israel slowly began to see God revealed more and more. By the end of the first century (C.E.), Christians were beginning to think that maybe the emerging Church was the "new Israel," the continuation of that very special covenant. Christians believe that in Israel's history and in the world at-large, God is making his will and purposes known. "God (Yahweh) called his children out of Egypt, a holy God made for himself a holy people, a covenantal God chose an "elect" people, a righteous God called a responsible people, and a faithful God fulfilled his promises to a waiting people." (Cited from my seminary notes.)

For the Christian the reality of the people of God finds its complete fulfillment in the living expression of the Church, the new Israel. It is Paul, the Christian apostle, who wrote that the church can dismiss the Old Testament only at the cost of its life and gospel: "They are Israelites, and to them belong the sonship, the glory, the covenants, the ... law, the worship, and the promises; to them belong the patriarchs, and of their race, according to the flesh, is the Christ. God who is over all be blessed forever. Amen." (Romans 9:1ff)

Paul accurately sums up the relationship of the Church to Israel, the New Testament to the Old. Paul goes on, however, to try to satisfy—himself mostly—the difficulty of integrating what he had experienced as a result of his transformation with what he knew of Jewish law as an educated Pharisaic Jew who was also a Roman citizen. The Church, however, has gone on to construct its theology and belief system chiefly around this expanded Pauline theology. In doing so, I believe they misunderstood Paul. *Is this understanding the only understanding available to us?*

Well, that's the subject of Part 2.

Chapter 1

The Sources of the Old Testament

There is a place for literary criticism of the works of Shakespeare. The same is true for the Old Testament. There are literary questions we must face if we are to understand the Old Testament, which is full of irregularities and inconsistencies. We must be able to acknowledge these. For instance: There are two "creation" stories: Gen. 1:1-2:4; and Gen. 2:5-25; the future father-in-law of Moses is called Reuel (Ex. 2:18). But in Exodus 18:1ff, the same man is called Jethro; and there are two versions of the Ten Commandments. One is in Exodus 20; the other is in Deuteronomy 5.

For the last 200 years biblical scholars have concluded that there are four main literary strands that make up the first six books of the Old Testament. These strands have been given the symbols J, E, D, and P.

- J, the earliest source, comes from the time of the monarchy, circa 975-950 B.C.E. The J notation comes from the author's consistent use of the Hebrew word JHWH or YHWH (Jahweh or Yahweh) for God.

- E, a closely related source, comes from about 750 B.C.E. The E notation comes from the author's consistent use of the Hebrew word Elohim for God.

- D comes from about 625 B.C.E. The D stands for Deuteronomic. It is primarily the Book of Deuteronomy.

- P, so called because of its priestly interests, comes from a period (circa 450 B.C.E.) after the fall of the nation in 587 B.C.E. Priests are believed to have been the principal authors.

Some of the very earliest material of J and E were merged rather quickly to the point that we cannot separate them any longer. That material has traditionally been referred to as JE. When we add the narrative material furnished by David's court historian (much of the material for I-II Samuel and I Kings), the material of all the prophets, the wisdom literature (the Psalms, Proverbs, Job, Song of Songs, etc.), and apocalyptic literature (Daniel and much of the Apocrypha), we have accounted for most of the Old Testament.

Think of this analogy:

Person A in 1850 writes a history of the United States. It is the first written history. It begins with the pilgrims at Plymouth Rock in 1620, goes through the efforts to subdue the country and the Indians, moves on to the problems with the British government, discusses the Revolutionary War and how the colonists defeated the English, discusses the Constitution with its built-in checks and balances among the three branches of government so it cannot overwhelm the individual person or the individual State, lightly touches on the War of 1812, and closes as the history approaches the author's present time—1850. The history is there. The theme is the indomitable spirit of the new America and how it subdues its foes—human or nature. Obviously the writer uses nineteenth-century language: verbs such as 'slaying,' or 'doeth,' for example; modes of transportation are all horse powered, with no mention of steam railroad trains; mail delivery that doesn't mention the Pony Express.

Person B, writing in 1920, also writes a history of the United States. The author is involved in the early labor crisis of the time, fighting for better working conditions, and fighting for the rights of women in the workforce and for the right of women to vote. In this history the author mentions the Spanish colony at St. Augustine (founded some seventy-five years before Plymouth), as well as Jamestown in 1607, and mentions the Federalist Papers and the Declaration of Independence in addition to the Constitution. The history discusses the Civil War from the standpoint of the economics of the South and the industrial impact of the North. The history mentions taking the train to Trenton, New Jersey. It mentions the wonder of four-day mail service to Philadelphia. It mentions trolley cars and big city tenement buildings. Throughout the history, Person B is hammering away at the fight for human, individual rights—not against England, like Person A—but against monopolistic conglomerates and slum-ridden, overcrowded cities.

In 1990, Person C weaves these two histories together without changing much of the originals. But person C wants to emphasize improving racial relations. So, as these two histories are intertwined, Person C adds a few things, such as a discussion of the biased treatment of the American Indian and a constant castigation of the U.S. Congress for treaty breaking. Person C discusses the Civil War from the standpoint of the slave and underground railroads, the Jim Crow society, segregation during World War II, and the civil rights movement in the 1960s.

It wouldn't be too difficult to separate out Person A's and B's narrative, nor would it be too difficult to ascertain their respective points of view or themes. That accomplished, you'd be left with the account of Person C.

Is the earliest version (Person A's) the most accurate? Is the latest (Person C's)? Should you discount the narrated history of each of the authors because they each had a built-in bias? How do you answer the question: Which person wrote the most accurate history? It's an impossible question to answer because it's an improper question. They are all correct interpretations of history, yet they are all flawed accounts, in the sense they each have "an axe to grind," which may have twisted their narratives or unduly influenced what they included and what they excluded. Even though B wrote after A, B included material (St. Augustine, Florida) about an earlier historic fact than A did.

Even though someone was writing later, they may have been including material that was earlier. In later periods other historians took up anew the task of reinterpreting the past in such a way that it could speak to their own situation. *Sometimes when writers add material— even if some if it is new—it really ends up telling us more about the writers and their times than it does about the times they are writing about. The writer, as a person, is interdependent on the history that is occurring.*

Several examples of this interdependence come to mind. The first is the novel by Harriet Beecher Stowe, *Uncle Tom's Cabin*. When she wrote this prior to the Civil War, it was influenced by and in response to her perceived horror of slavery in the South. In turn, her book made an enormous impact on the movement to abolish slavery ("The Abolitionists") in the northeastern United States. Similarly, the first "full-length" movie, *The Birth of a Nation*, made in the early 1900s by D. W. Griffith, was a history of the United States from the perspective of white supremacy. It too was influenced by and in response to the perceived history of the times. It frightened viewers and led a "call to arms," emotionally, at least, for continued enactment of segregation legislation throughout the South until the 1950s.

These are the kinds of issues that biblical historians, linguists, archaeologists, and the like have struggled with for the past several hundred years. This is the world of the Old Testament scholar. The major strands of literature that have been uncovered and analyzed—J, E, D, and P—are similar to uncovering and analyzing Persons A, B, and C, or to understanding the "mind and times of the writer," like Harriet Beecher Stowe.

Historians used to notate dates in terms of B.C. or A.D.: B.C. referred to times before Christ. A.D. referred to times after Christ. That has changed. Books use the same concept but now refer to the time before Christ as B.C.E. (Before the Common Era) and the time after Christ as C.E. (Common Era). I will use the B.C.E./C.E. convention.

Also, let me mention a word about biblical references. Verses 8-11 of Chapter 34 in Exodus will be noted as (Exodus 34:8-11). A reference to a body of work in Chapters 3, 4, 5, and 11 of the Book of Job will be noted as (Job 3-5; 11).

I've developed Table 1 (below) to summarize some of the events, personalities, and major religious themes that we'll be talking about in Part I. However, in *Appendix A* I've developed a chronological timeline that is more complete than we can discuss here.

Historical Event(s) [Dates are b.c.e.]	Key Personalities	Key Religious Issues
The Patriarchs (1700–1500)	Abraham, Isaac, Jacob, King Hammurabi of Babylon	The Canaanite influence on Pre-Mosaic Israelites; family/clan gods; purification and sacrifice; personal monotheism; the Code of Hammurabi
In Egypt and the Exodus (1500–1250)	Moses, Miriam, Egyptian Pharaoh Rameses II	The Exodus; the Covenant; the law and the Yahweh cult; God in history
The Judges and the Conquest (1250–1020)	Joshua, Samson, Deborah, the prophet Eli	Renewed monotheism; sanctuaries; cultic personnel and tribal confederacy
The Monarchy (1020–922)	Saul, David, Solomon, Bathsheba, the prophet Samuel, David's unknown court historian, the Yahwist	The epic of the Yahwist
The Divided Kingdoms (922–586)	The Elowist; the Prophets (Elijah, Elisha, Amos, Isaiah, Micah, Hosea; Jeremiah, Ezekiel, et.al.); Deuteronomic reform	Role of the prophets; the Reformation of 621; sin and repentance
The Babylon Exile (586–538)	The Prophets (Habakkuk, Jeremiah, 2nd Isaiah); King Nebuchadnezzar	The impact of the fall of Jerusalem: revision of history; individual piety and prayer; hope in a messianic age; the Messiah and suffering servant
Postexilic Judaism (586–167)	The Prophets (Haggai, Zechariah, Malachi), Deuteronomic redactor; the synagogue, the Prophets (Ezra, Nehemiah), the Priestly Writers (P), the Chronicler, Alexander the Great	Emerging images of Judaism: the synagogue and growing use of oral interpretation; growing sense of exclusionism; the apocalyptic prophet; the personal experiences behind wisdom literature

Historical Event(s) [Dates are B.C.E.]	Key Personalities	Key Religious Issues
The Maccabean Age and following (167 B.C.E.)	The Maccabees, Pompey, Caesar, Mark Antony, Cleopatra, Herod the Great	From prophetic to apocalyptic

Table 1. *Summary of the Major Historical Events of the Old Testament.* *The Old Testament covers a span of history from the Middle Bronze Age to the Roman Empire—an awesome time period of almost 2,000 years.*

Chapter 2

From the Patriarchs to the Kings

𝔄 short history of the Old Testament, up through the Monarchy, can be summarized as follows:

> "Shortly after the turn of the second millennium B.C.E. (circa 1900–1700), Israel's ancestor, Abraham, migrated from Mesopotamia in the land of Canaan, stopping first at Shechem. These patriarchs, or ancestral fathers of Israel, were migrants and moved about in the hill country of Canaan, with Abraham, Isaac, and Jacob succeeding one another. Eventually, during a time of famine, Jacob's family migrated to Egypt. There, after enjoying initial favor, they were subjected to forced labor by the Egyptian pharaoh, Ramses II. Under the leadership of Moses (circa 1300 B.C.E.), however, and favored by an extraordinary series of events, these Hebrews escaped into the surrounding desert, where they were forged into a community, under Moses, with a single religious allegiance. Later, under the leadership of Joshua, they successfully attacked Canaan and claimed the land as their own. During this time, they had to wage ceaseless wars of defense. Enemy pressure became so intense that a monarchy was established under Saul, and in the time of kings David and Solomon (1000–922 B.C.E.), Canaan was an Israelite empire."[1]

However, for our purposes, that's a little too short.

The Hebrews in Egypt

We begin our history of how the Jewish Scriptures became the Old Testament with the story of Moses. The emergence of Israel as a cultural (not yet a political) nation—with a common history rooted in a common God—all begins with Moses. Moses led the Israelites out of Egypt, established a covenant with God on Mount Sinai (J) or Mount Horeb (E), culminated by the declaration of the Covenant (*"Yahweh is our God; we are Yahweh's people; He has a job for us to do; He will protect and bless us."* Exod. 6:6–8) and the issuance of the Ten Commandments (Exod. 20; Deut. 5).

"Behind all and within all is the historical consciousness of Yahweh's mighty deeds in history (the Exodus); the man Moses; the understanding that the Twelve Tribes were the chosen people with a great commission; the prospect toward a future in which the meaning of the Covenant will articulate itself and Israel will trust and hope in its promises."[2]

But who were the Israelites? How did they get to Egypt? When were they there?

The tablets of Mari in Mesopotamia (circa 1700 B.C.E.) contain references to Semitic peoples, including a term, "'Apiru" or "Habiru"—that in the judgment of most scholars is the earliest reference to "Hebrew." There is good reason to suppose that the Hebrew clans entered Egypt during the period of the Hyksos occupation. Hyksos means "foreign rulers" in Egyptian. As an aggressive, hybrid people of Semitic backgrounds—who had chariots!—they were able to overthrow the Pharaohs of the Thirteenth dynasty about 1750 B.C.E. The Hyksos ruled Egypt in the Fifteenth and Sixteenth dynasties for about 200 years, and were friendly and open to other Semitic migrants including the Habiru.

About 1570 B.C.E. (200 years later) the Hyksos were overthrown by Ahmose I, and the dynasties of "true" Egyptian Pharaohs were reestablished. These "new" Pharaohs, including Thutmose III, felt uneasy with all the non-Egyptian peoples in their country. What if they wanted to rebel? After all, these Semitic peoples had been in Egypt for over 180+ years by now. *That's a long time. Not many years ago I did some genealogy work on my family history. What I found from fellow researchers was that if I could go back 150–175 years (to 1825 or 1850), I was doing extremely well.* Under these new Pharaohs the status of the Semitic peoples changed suddenly; they were relegated to slave status and menial duties. They didn't like it and many wanted to go back to the lands of their fathers.

This is highlighted in the traditional Oriental method of storytelling (using a person or two to represent a people) in the stories of Joseph (Gen. 37–50) getting to Egypt, moving up in the world, and finally rising to an important imperial post in the government. Interestingly, the coming of these new Pharaohs, who were threatened by the Semitic migrants, is summed up by the little verse in Exod. 1:8: "And there came a time when the Pharaoh didn't know Joseph." Ahmose I expelled the Hyksos ruling classes and began a long oppression of the immigrant Semites in Egypt at the time.

The Exodus

The idyllic story of Moses' birth and the romantic stories of the great contests between Moses and the Pharaoh all follow the Oriental imagination in these accounts, but the overall historicity of Moses is rather certain. "While we have no extra-biblical material corroborating the story of the Exodus, such materials as we may glean from the ancient Near East concerning the periodic invasion of Semitic Tribes into Egypt, the reference to Israel in the Merneptah stele (circa 1229 B.C.E.), the earlier witness of the Tell el-Armana letters (fourteenth century B.C.E.), and the important results of excavations in Palestine (e.g., Bethel, Lachish, etc.), as well as extra-Palestinian sites, help us to see the events in a convincing context and setting. As to the historical existence of Moses there can no longer be any serious doubt. He is as well authenticated as the founder of any of the great world religions."[3]

Most scholars today believe the Pharaoh during the Exodus was Ramses II (1290–1224 B.C.E.). What we know of the Exodus, with all due respect to Charlton Heston and Cecil B. DeMille's *Ten Commandments*, we know from the book of the Bible that bears that name. Moses was of Hebrew origin, born in Egypt. He was raised as an educated Egyptian, however, and even had an Egyptian name. He had an experience with the Lord God on Mount Horeb, where God Almighty of the Mountain (El Shaddai) revealed himself to Moses in a burning bush and instructed Moses to lead the Hebrews out of Egypt and into a land flowing with milk and honey. When Moses asked "When I talk to the Pharaoh, who am I supposed to say sent me?" The bush answered: "Tell the Pharaoh YHWH sent you." YHWH is an unpronounceable word loosely related to the Hebrew root-form of the verb "to become." The best translation of the Hebrew probably is "Tell the Pharaoh that I AM WHO IS sent you."

Hebrew is written in consonants. Vowel "sounds" (small markings) are added around the consonants to help with the pronunciation. The name of YHWH was considered unpronounceable because Jewish theology states that to "name" something is to take lordship over it. You can't do that with God. That's why Adam was asked to "name" the animals in the story of Creation. To remind the readers of the Hebrew text not to pronounce the name YHWH during synagogue readings, the Hebrews inserted the vowel markings of the word Adonai (Lord) onto the Hebrew consonants YHWH. It was to remind them to audibly say "Lord" whenever they saw the word YHWH. Early non-Jewish translators, unaware of this, attempted to make a real word from the consonants YHWH that had the vowel sounds of Adonai embedded. Their best transliteration: Jehovah.

Exodus Event	Biblical Reference
Call of Moses at Mount Horeb. It was here that the tribal god of the patriarchs, El Shaddai (God Almighty of the Mountain), revealed himself to Moses as YHWH	Exodus 3:1–17
The Plagues	Exodus 7–11
Passover	Exodus 12:1–13, 16
Song of Miriam	Exodus 15:1–21
Visit of Jethro, the Midianite	Exodus 18
The Ten Commandments & the Book of the Covenant, also known as the Mosaic Law (Exodus 20:22–23:19; 23:20–33).	Exodus 20–23; 24:7
Golden Calf	Exodus 32

Table 2. *Summary of the major events of the Exodus*. From Moses to the beginning of the Conquest, the Exodus was the defining moment of Israel's history.

Moses enlisted his brother Aaron to go before the Pharaoh. Together, they argued with the Pharaoh to "Let my people go." The two brothers challenged the Pharaoh's priests to a series of contests to demonstrate the power of their respective gods. Finally, a series of ten plagues descended on Egypt that convinced the Pharaoh to let the Hebrews leave. These plagues included frogs, swarms, boils, locusts, hail, and lastly the deaths of a household's firstborn. The Hebrews believed they were spared the consequences of this last plague because they spread lamb's blood over the lintels of their doors. The plague thus "passed over" the Hebrew houses, the source of the Jewish celebration of Passover. As the Hebrews massed to leave, the Pharaoh changed his mind and pursued the motley band of people. At the Sea of Reeds the Hebrews made their final escape.

The crossing of the Sea of Reeds (The Papyrus Marsh), where the Hebrews crossed on dry land and the following Egyptian army was mired in mud and drowned in suddenly rising waters, was captured by the Song of Miriam, a hymn of deliverance and redemption—one of the historically oldest fragments in the Old Testament: "Sing to Yahweh, for he has triumphed mightily. The horse and its rider he has hurled into the sea." (Exod. 15:21) Seven centuries later her song was expanded into the poetic form that appears in Exodus 15:1–18.

Freed from the pursuit of the Egyptian army, the Hebrews were faced with famine, thirst, and loss of direction. The people moaned and groaned. The Lord provided manna as a form of bread. He provided a pillar of fire to guide them during the evening hours and a cloud of dust to guide them during the day. Nevertheless the faith of the people waxed and waned. They whined until some new problem seemed to have been solved by the Lord, then their faith was restored. Then it would wane. They wanted to build idols and worship Baal, the god of other familiar Semitic peoples. Then they would whine some more; then be restored once again.

Not until the experience of the Exodus, almost two generations (about forty years) in the making, did this collection of Hebrew wanderers, with a loose tradition that bound them together, emerge as the People of Yahweh. Moses encountered Yahweh again and the result was the Ten Commandments—the basis for the Law that was to guide them—and a new covenant, whereby Yahweh promised to lead the motley band into the land of "milk and honey" originally promised to Abraham, generations earlier. Moses, however, never saw the Promised Land. He died, Joshua became their leader, and the Conquest into the Land of Milk and Honey began.

The Conquest and the Judges

Second perhaps only to the Exodus from Egypt, the Conquest of Canaan is one of the most important phases of Hebrew history. Occurring between 1250 and 1020 B.C.E. and authenticated by archaeology and other historical records, the occupation was not as swift, complete, or permanent as some of the later-written Hebrew remembrances would like us to believe. Although occurring about 1200 B.C.E., the records of the Conquest were written down on the basis of historical oral narratives over a period from 950 to 200 B.C.E. However, the main theme remains unchallenged: A part of the Hebrew people went down to Egypt; suffered bondage; were marvelously released by Yahweh; and finally entered the land that had been promised as early as the time of Abraham.

Many scholars believe there were three waves of immigrants who entered Canaan and settled there in the period known as the Conquest: from the north, near Lake Huleh; from east of the Jordan River, led by Joshua, into central Palestine; and from the south, a composite group which comprised the later Judah. The Hebrews never did wholly conquer or expel the native Canaanite population from the coastlands, their fortified cities, or the Jordan River valley, nor did they fully expel the Amorites from the highlands. Nonetheless, by the time of Solomon (961–922 B.C.E.) the Canaanites, as a distinct force, had all but disappeared.

The general "tone" of the religion of Semitic people in Canaan was similar to the contemporary religions in Babylon and Egypt. It was a nature religion and clearly exhibited cultural interchanges among the existing empires. In Canaan the cultic worship dramatized the relationship between the storm god Baal and his consort Ashtart. In Egypt the Isis cult focused on Osiris and the female counterpart Isis. In Babylonia the cultic worship centered on the god Tammuz and the goddess Ishtar.

The Ras Shamra tablets from northern Syria are dated from before 1350 B.C.E. and were discovered in 1929. They paint a clear portrait of Canaanite religion at the time prior to the Conquest. It was a sophisticated cultic religion, far more complex than the simple fertility rites we (and Cecil B. DeMille) had thought they were.

The "chief" god of the Canaanite cult was *El,* the "Father of the Years." The principal goddess was Asherah. The second pair in line were Baal and his sister, Ashtart (Anath), who was known for her violent sexual passion. Other warring gods, those controlling drought, for instance, in the Canaanite pantheon, defeated (maybe murdered) Baal. Ashtart searched for Baal, found him, and killed his captors. Finally, the violent lovers, Baal and Ashtart, were reunited. The death and resurrection of Baal has continuously played itself out in the annual cycle of the four seasons. Thus, there is a rhythm in nature: life and death; spring and summer; fertility and drought. The Canaanite cultic religion allowed mankind to attempt to persuade the gods to control nature and ensure the fertility of the soil. Through rituals and rites the Canaanite worshipper was able to relate to what was believed to be divine—the cycle of nature's seasons.

This was tempting to the assimilating Hebrews from Egypt and to those Hebrews already in Canaan. Many scholars believe the common Hebrew farmer or shepherd was able to make a distinction between their belief in Yahweh and a belief in Baal. The belief, faith, and practice of Yahweh worship was for more official public consumption and for tribal protection. The Baal cultic worship was for the assurance of fertile soil, ample rain, and good crops. *Even today, we make such distinctions. We can fully believe in God's power to heal through prayer and, at the same time, believe and trust in science and medical technology.*

This cultural interchange occurred during the several hundred years of the Conquest. Admonitions that "Yahweh was a jealous God" came from this period as attempted warnings to keep the faith in Yahweh pure. However, the pervasiveness of this cultural interchange was evident. Both Kings Saul and David, the "Anointed Ones," gave Baal-like names to their children. (The Hebrew suffix *"bosheth"* is a substitute for *"baal"* in a name, as it was edited by later redactors, e.g., 2 Sam. 21:8 where Saul's child, Mephibosheth, would have been called, originally, Mephibaal.

31

Although the priestly editors of the material wanted us to believe that the Conquest was complete and final, other textual evidence, for example, Judg. 3:5ff, indicates "the children of Israel dwelt among the Canaanites, Hittites, Amorites, Perizzites, Hivites, and Jebusites." Additionally, there were others—not of the Twelve Tribes—who were also part of the migrating Hebrews, e.g., the Kenites, who were wandering, gypsy-like metal smiths. The father-in-law of Moses was a Kenite. That Kenites, as well as Amalekites, were at times affiliated with Judah is evident as Saul advises the Kenites to separate themselves from the Amalekites (whom he is about to attack) because he recalled kindness to his forebears during the Exodus (1 Sam. 15:6). These various people joined with the Hebrews in their first entry into western Palestine during the Conquest (Num. 10:29–32). *The smithing skill of the Kenites was a very important skill. It is critical to note that the Canaanites were a formidable foe. This was the period of the later Bronze Age and the beginning of the Iron Age. The Canaanites had chariots and weapons of iron (Judg. 1:19).*

It must also be remembered that not all of the Twelve Tribes of Israel went to Egypt in the first place, and therefore did not experience the Exodus. *We'll be talking about the patriarchs and the Twelve Tribes of Israel later on.* For example the Tribe of Judah did not go, nor did the Tribe of Levi, nor others who were found already occupying central Palestine at the time of the Conquest. These did not need to be subdued, but merely amalgamated. Manasseh and Ephraim, part of the Joseph Tribe, went north after Jacob's funeral and probably remained in Palestine (Gen. 50:6-7). These tribal kinsmen, already rooted in Canaan, blended right in with those who entered at the Conquest.

One of the earliest accounts recorded in the Old Testament concerns the Conquest. It is the Song of Deborah, which is dated about 1125 B.C.E. It narrates a battle between allied forces of Israelites under Deborah, a prophetess, against the Canaanites under Sisera. There are two versions of this account—a prose version (Judg. 4) from the Elohist, and a poetic version (Judg. 5) considered to be one of the earliest monuments of Hebrew poetic literature.

The reality of the Conquest could best be stated as follows: The settlement in Canaan and the displacement of the Canaanites was a slow process covering two centuries between Joshua (circa 1250 B.C.E.) and the establishment of Saul (1020 B.C.E.), and the

wives and consorts to worship their own local gods and have their own private chapels, shrines, priests, and court patrons.

Israel was beginning to feel like a nation. They had stories about ancestors they could remember and recite: stories that went back to Egypt, to their deliverance, and to their inheritance as promised by Yahweh, of the land that now was their country. This sense of a common history was now about 350 years old. *This time span is similar to our sense of American history: the Pilgrims, the Colonists, the French and Indian War with Benedict Arnold, the Revolution and Declaration of Independence, George Washington, and Benjamin Franklin. All of that is about 350 years of history.*

By the end of Solomon's reign both Egypt and Assyria were stirring again, trade was declining, and taxes had been increased. After Solomon's death his successor and son, Rehoboam, was implored by Israel's tribal elders to reduce the taxes. He refused. The beginnings of the schism—the dividing of the Monarchy— had begun. Later priestly edits and additions to the texts would indicate the Monarchy collapsed because of Solomon's disobedience to God in terms of monogamy and his laxness with foreign deities. *The truth of the matter was, just as it is in our recent presidential politics, "It's all about the economy."*

The Yahwist Epic and the Court Historian

The Yahwist's Epic was written toward the end of the Monarchy or shortly thereafter. This was the first integrated, cohesive written account of the beginnings of the Bible. The Yahwist is the author and he[4] is known as such because YHWH is the name he consistently used for God. This Epic is also referred to as the J source because the pattern of using YHWH was initially discovered by German scholars, who used JHWH—the "J" in German being the equivalent of "Y" in English.

It integrates the story of Abraham, Isaac, and Jacob—from remnants of all the tribal oral history of the past 700+ years—into the emerging "national" traditions of the Exodus and Conquest. Beyond integrating the story of the patriarchs, the Yahwist expanded his written epic by adding a prologue, Gen. 1–11, which was constructed from well-known local (mostly Babylonian) myths and legends. This discussion of "prehistory" by the Yahwist articulated, for the first time, the monolatry or monotheism—

Donald L. O'Dell

although after the fact—that underlay Israel's loose but common heritage. The Yahwist is discussed more fully in Chapter 4 - *The Primary Sources of the Bible.*

This was also the time of the written history of the court of Saul, David, and Solomon, incorporating material from David's court historian. Scholars presume much of 1–2 Samuel, as well as the opening chapters of 1 Kings, to have been written by Ahimaaz, son of Zadok, a contemporary of the time (2 Sam. 15:27, 36). It is considered to be virtually unsurpassed, notwithstanding the earliest masterpiece of historical writing in ancient texts.

The Yahwist's Epic was a tremendous accomplishment. For the first time the Hebrews could "see" the behind-the-scenes tribal stories, traditions, and memories from the northern tribes (Israel) and the southern tribes (Judah) coalesced into a common narrative. Since the Yahwist's record, which included the patriarchs, has now appeared on the scene, it is appropriate for us to take a historical look at the patriarchs and the tribal roots of Israel's history.

The Patriarchs

The patriarchal narratives begin with Abraham, move to his son, Isaac, and finally to Isaac's son, Jacob. In the interwoven passages of the Yahwist and Elohist, Jacob is an individual, but in later passages "Jacob" often designates the nation Israel, of whom Jacob is considered the father. Jacob had twelve sons by his two wives, Leah and Rachel, as well as their handmaidens, Zilpah and Bilhah, respectively.

Leah	Zilpah	Rachel	Bilhah
Reuben, Simeon, Levi, Judah, Issachar, Zebulon	Gad, Asher	Joseph (aka Ephraim & Manasseh), Benjamin	Dan, Naphtali

Table 3. *The Twelve Tribes of Israel. The Tribes of Israel sprang from the two wives, and their handmaidens, of Jacob (later referred to as "Israel").*

There was a loose oral tradition that created the sense of kinship of these nomadic "tribal" cults. These "tribes" shared a common father (Jacob), grandfather (Isaac), and great-grandfather (Abraham). They shared their cultic sacred shrines: Hebron,

40

Shechem, Beer-sheba, Bethel, and Penuel. As we have discussed, this loose confederation of tribes became one people—Israelites who worshipped YHWH—during the Exodus under Moses. We'll take a closer look at Abraham, Isaac, and Jacob, and then at the Patriarchal Age, as a whole.

We have to keep reminding ourselves that the Patriarchal Age is the Bronze Age; that's 3,700 years ago. Not only is it fascinating, but it's important as well. We'll spend a little more time than normal on the Patriarchal Age—the Middle Bronze Age—because there are some fundamental aspects of the religion of the Hebrews that begin here, namely the concept of sacrifice within their ideas of worship. Some of these concepts are very relevant to how some "religious" people still want to run countries today: the reactionary Islamic supporters who want to make Middle Eastern nations Islamic states; conservative Jewish groups, like the Hasidim, who want the same for Israel. A case could be made for this concerning the Religious Right here in America.

Abraham

He was a son of his age—the Middle Bronze. Archaeologists refer to the "Age of Abraham" as being the era of transition from the last kings of Sumer to the First Dynasty of Babylon, whose greatest king was Hammurabi, the Amorite codifier of laws resembling both many of the early Hebrew customs and practices, as well as of Canaanite (and their god Baal) practices. Abraham married Sarah and they had difficulty having children. Consistent with Hammurabi laws of inheritance, Abraham had a son, Ishmael, by Sarah's handmaiden, Hagar. Finally, in their old age Abraham and Sarah had a son, Isaac. Also consistent with the Code of Hammurabi, at Isaac's weaning ceremony, Abraham banished Hagar and Ishmael (Gen. 21:8–21) with some flocks. *Ishmael is considered to be a patriarchal ancestor of Islam and reputedly is buried, with his mother, in Mecca.*

The tribal God of Abraham called him from Ur (now thought to be in Sumer) and promised he would build a nation of Abraham's descendents (Gen. 12:1–4a, 7). However, the defining moment in Abraham's life is the sacrifice of Isaac. In a religious ceremony for Baal long practiced by his Canaanite neighbors, he was about to sacrifice Isaac as a test by God of his loyalty. When Providence intervened and provided a ram caught in a thicket,

Donald L. O'Dell

Abraham's faith was exalted and the promise of God ensued (Gen. 22). This intervention registered deeply in Hebrew consciousness as an early beginning of YHWH's promises to Israel.

Isaac

Isaac does not get as much "press coverage" as Abraham or Jacob. It is possible that the Isaac stories were stripped by later editors in favor of the Abraham stories. After reading the prophet Amos and his reference to The House of Isaac (Amos 7:9–16), it becomes clear that the prophet thought of Isaac as the poetic equivalent of "Israel." In the story of Isaac's sacrifice, the submission and obedience of Isaac to paternal authority are as emphasized as Abraham's faith.

Isaac married Rebekah and eventually they had two sons, fraternal twins, Esau and, just minutes later, Jacob. Although persecuted by Philistines, Isaac was blessed by God and prospered both in agricultural pursuits as well as in raising cattle. At Isaac's deathbed, Rebekah helped trick him into believing he was passing on his inheritance and blessing to his firstborn son, Esau, when in fact it was Jacob who was receiving the inheritance.

Isaac's material is centered around the shrine of Beer-sheba, where he had made a peace covenant with Abimelech the Philistine (Gen. 26:23–33). This was also the site of his earlier, younger days (Gen. 21). A great deal of the contradictions and duplications in the Isaac stories are due to a blending of the J, E, and P sources without much editorial effort to harmonize them.

Jacob

The written portraits of Jacob are much more complete than those of Isaac. Nothing in Near Eastern literature surpasses the descriptions of Jacob's grief over Joseph and Rachel. No effort is made to gloss over his weaknesses. Though the ancient sagas portray him as a shrewd and crafty man, it also stresses his deep love for Rachel and his scrupulous attention to the complicated business of owning large flocks and protecting his many children. In his old age he deplored his early sins and emphasized the grace of his god.

He had a vision and wrestled with an angel of the Lord at Bethel, where he made his vows to God (Gen. 28). He erected a

42

boulder there, the first step in establishing the Bethel sanctuary, the cultic shrine most related to him.

Jacob wanted to marry Rachel and was willing to work for her hand. Eventually he had to take her older sister, Leah, first, and then work for his father-in-law, Laban, seven more years until he could have Rachel as well. Between the two sister-wives and their handmaidens, Jacob had twelve sons. (See table above.)

The Patriarchal Narrative

A very interesting description occurs in Gen. 15. Abraham has cut animals in two and placed one of their halves over against the other. As a mystic darkness falls over the site, the presence of a deity (described as a smoking fire pot and a flaming torch) passed between the pieces. This account preserves an ancient ritual of covenant-making: the practice of entering into a personal relationship with that particular deity.

This kind of personal relationship is a principal characteristic of patriarchal religion that was in existence throughout the Fertile Crescent. (The borders of the Fertile Crescent can be defined as slightly northwest from the Persian Gulf, as bounded by the Tigris and Euphrates Rivers, almost to the southern end of Asia Minor [now Turkey], and then bending back southward along the Mediterranean Sea almost to the Nile River in Egypt). The Fertile Crescent has been identified as the cradle of ancient civilization where, along with Egypt, it was the scene of human activity for centuries before the appearance of the initial Hebrews.

Abraham, the Father of the Hebrews, Islam (via his son, Ishmael), and Christianity, was said to be from the city of Ur. When Ur was excavated by archaeologists near the southern end of the Euphrates River, its remains bore a great witness to the ancient glory of a kingdom known as Sumer. Also, there was a rival kingdom, a little farther north, called Akkad. The Sumerians established a brilliant civilization there during the first part of the third millennium. They are believed to have been the first people to have developed a written language. About 2400 B.C.E. the Akkadians, under Sargon I, defeated and captured the cultural treasures of Sumer. *Sargon I has often been referred to as the first empire builder of history.* Several hundred years later the Sumerians recaptured their homeland and held it until the mountainous Elamites (from an area which is now modern Iran) brought their renewed empire to an end about 2000 B.C.E.

In the resulting political confusion a semi-nomadic people, known as the Amorites, flooded the coveted Mesopotamian plain. These Semites came from the Arabian Desert, the cradle of all Semite peoples. Another wave of peoples came as well from the Caucasian Mountains of Armenia. They were Hurrians (the Old Testament calls them Horites). They came not as an army, but simply as opportunistic migrants. Within several hundred years the Amorites and Hurrians had taken control of Mesopotamia and established the first Babylonian Dynasty, whose last and greatest king was Hammurabi (1728–1686 B.C.E.), author of the famous Hammurabi Code of Laws. Each of these Semitic tribes worshipped their own variation of the god Baal.

The Fertile Crescent.[5] *This area is often thought of as the Cradle of Civilization.*

A vivid picture of this era was provided by recent discoveries: The recent discovery (about 1935) of some 20,000 tablets at Mari (an ancient city near the border of modern Iraq and Syria); and the discovery of thousands of clay tablets at Nuzi.

Mari was conquered by Hammurabi (circa 1700 B.C.E.) and some of the tablets represent correspondence between the king of Mari and Hammurabi himself. These tablets illuminate the cultural background of the early Patriarchal Period and are of extraordinary interest to us. The tablets contain many "biblical" names (for example, Benjamin and David) including a term 'Apiru or Habiru—a term that in the judgment of most scholars is the earliest reference to "Hebrew."

The tablets found at the Hurrian town of Nuzi have shed light on the story of Rachel's theft of household gods (Gen. 31:19, 30–35). According to Hurrian custom, a man's possession of the household idols ensured his leadership of the family clan and his claim to the family inheritance. Now we can understand why Laban was so angry—with some justification—at what he construed to be Jacob's attempt to ruin his family—stealing Laban's daughters, his best livestock, and even his household gods.

Scholars have placed the migration of Abraham into Canaan with the Amoritic invasion of Mesopotamia and Syria. His hometown was Haran, an Amorite settlement at this time. Towns around Haran, such as Peleg, Serug, and Nahor, are credited in the biblical tradition with Abraham's relatives. Other Amorite names, such as Jacob-el and Abram, point to a common Semitic background. Throughout the Genesis stories of Abraham, we also can see remnants of the Code of Hammurabi. For instance, the laws of inheritance for Abraham's son, Ishmael, by Sarah's handmaiden, Hagar (Gen. 16–17); the customs surrounding Abraham's willingness to deliver his wife (Sarah) to desirous strangers, telling them she was his sister. The Code indicated that it was common to simply take a sister, whereas to take a wife, one would have to first kill her husband (Gen. 12:10–20).

When the migrating Semites left Mesopotamia, they brought with them a sense of religion which was very similar to the nature religion of the Fertile Crescent. There the father of the gods was known as El. Each major clan or family head had experienced a personal relationship with the god(s) of the area.

The God of Moses and the Exodus—recited in the oral history of the tribes—was the same god as the cultic or patriarchal gods of their tribal affiliations: names such as El Shaddai, El Bethel, El Elyon, and El Olam. It was Moses who first united all these patriarchal tribal gods under the Lord God YHWH. Joshua reminds the Hebrews that their fathers, who once dwelt across the Euphrates, had served "other gods" and he urged them to put away the remnants of their ancestral polytheism (Josh. 24:2). With each of the patriarchs there is a special vision (theophany, or private encounter with God) in which the god reveals himself in a very personal way. These were family or clan gods with names and associations in which the intimate relationships of the family were applied to the gods. They were personal gods and they bore the names (which is obvious in the original Hebrew) of those to whom they first appeared: the God of Abraham (the Shield of Abraham, Gen. 15:1); the God of Isaac (the Kinsman, or Fear, of Isaac, Gen. 31:42); and the God of Jacob (the Mighty One of Jacob, Gen. 49:24). The names of these gods were directly associated with the patriarchs. Family kinship was prominent in all the Semitic religions of the time and the Hebrews employed exactly the same terms to describe kinship as their neighbors did.

Among the patriarchal Israelites, as among all contemporary ancient nations, worship of their gods meant domestic service, providing their gods with whatever they needed—most notably, food and shelter. The following is a quote from the Hittite *Instructions for Temple Officials* written long before Moses and roughly parallel to patriarchal times.

> "Is the disposition of men and gods at all different? No. ... When a slave stands before his master, he is washed and wears clean clothes; and he gives him something to eat and something to drink. And his master eats and drinks something, and he is refreshed in spirit and gracious toward him. If, however, the servant is neglectful and not observant, his disposition toward him is different. If the slave annoys his master, they either kill him, or injure his nose, his eyes, his ears...."[6]

Lying under this patriarchal Israelite concept of worship was the primitive concept: Do what your god wants and he'll bless you; don't do what he wants and he'll punish you. As this ancient Hittite text illustrates, there was a negative and a positive aspect to worship. The slave (*or the human*) is to be washed and clean and he gives some nourishment to his master (*or the deity*). The patriarchal tribal religions of Israel, like all the others, had these same negative and positive phases: Avoid what is perceived to be displeasing to the deity, e.g., dirt and impurity, and please the deity. The negative phase consisted of purifications, while the positive included sacrifices and offerings.

Purification, often referred to in the Old Testament as "sanctifying oneself," required baths, washing garments, wearing special garments, and often removing one's sandals when near holy ground. *Vestiges of these rites of purification remain with us today. Baptism is a symbolic cleansing. Shoes, or sandals, must be removed before entering an Islamic mosque. I have a favorite aunt, almost ninety years old now, who will not go to church without wearing her "Sunday best," which, for her, must be a dress.*

Although human sacrifice was rare among the primitive Hebrews, it did occur. However, the story of Abraham's intended sacrifice of Isaac was an indication that the Hebrews very early had substituted an animal sacrifice to "redeem" the firstborn (Exod. 13: 13–15). *Sacrifice and offerings—and their associated rituals—were at the heart and core of Hebrew worship.* Over time, more and more animal substitutes became more and more common. Eventually, through rituals, it was accepted that clan "sins" could be imparted to an animal and then killed (or banished) with it. The Hebrews developed the concept of a "scapegoat" as an offering to Azazel, the demon of the desert (Lev. 10:8-20). This was an actual goat who would be dispatched into the wilderness carrying the sins of the people. In various Old Testament passages the lamb had conveyed the idea of persecuted innocence, of vicarious suffering expressed in the burnt offering, and of deliverance, as at every Passover (Exod. 12:3–14).

The Hebrews had the conception that differentiated between Sin and sins. People were in Sin when they did not possess the faith in and obedience to Yahweh sufficient for God to work through them. For example, God was able to work through Moses not because he was sinless, but because he had this wholesome relationship with God—a relationship marked by faith and obedience. The results of a character like Moses are loyalty to one's covenant vows, just dealing, and humility of attitude and action before God. When one commits sins (lowercase "s"), those are individual acts of error, misjudgment, or hurt. They are correctible. They occur because we are human and less than perfect. To be in Sin (capital "S"), however, is to have the attitude of "wanting to be as God," as the Yahwist defined it, or egoism, where everything always ends up about self. The committing of sins can be dealt with through religious acts of contrition. The attitude of Sin in one's heart requires a true repentance—a turning around of one's self in regard to faith and obedience—and, sure enough, Yahweh will be there.

For Israel's patriarchs, *very unusually*, their conception of God was monotheistic. Additionally, their God, who was altogether righteous in nature, was in marked contrast to the more fluid personalities of the gods of Egypt, Mesopotamia, and Canaan. These gods changed their natures and names and often were portrayed in animal form. The early Hebrews of the Patriarchal Period apparently thought of their singular God as possessing human (though often unseen) form and as having the capacity for emotions such as love, hate, and sympathy— although typically anthropomorphic—but on a universal scale. There was some "sense" that their tribal god was the God of all mankind, but he had a unique and distinct relationship with the patriarchal tribesmen. Other cultic gods of other tribes or nationalities, although also emotional, were simply their very own tribal deities.

In Genesis, in addition to this sense that the patriarchal God was singular (monotheistic) and bigger than just their clan, there was a historical "germ" there from the beginning. The patriarchal tribal god was personal, yes, but not totally agricultural, or nature-based, as were so many of the other Semitic gods. Remnants of ancient Hebrew clan tales present us with a concept of God that was quite different from Canaanite worship. The Canaanites were agricultural and the interests of their gods reflected their interests: nature, fertility, and the cycle of crops. The Hebrews were more nomadic and, for some reason, their focus was far less on agriculture or nature and more on the history of their tribal clans. Their knowing of God was part of their history; the two couldn't be separated. You couldn't have a discussion about what Yahweh was like without talking about your history. *"I know my Yahweh is a faithful god because he delivered up Isaac from the sacrificial pyre."* You couldn't talk about your history without talking about Yahweh. *"It was interesting when the universal famine hit all of us, because that's when Yahweh opened the door for us to go to Egypt, where there were friendly distant cousins, Habiru, willing to share their excess grain."*

The Hebrews understood that part of Yahweh's nature from the beginning was that their God was only one God and was bigger than just a patriarchal tribal god. Equally, this historical interest cannot be attributed to the later authors or compilers. These features: the role of history within the Hebrews' tribal/clan religion; the role of purification and sacrifice in worship; and the monotheism and universal nature of Yahweh are all important. These concepts, many of which we recognize today, all came from these Bronze Age patriarchs.

Consequently, from the beginning the gods of the patriarchs (Abraham, Isaac, and Jacob) had these seeds of "personal-ness." These common seeds enabled Moses to coalesce these ancient beliefs in tribal deities into a common vision of an all-encompassing Hebrew YHWH. David and Solomon took Moses' common vision a step further—centralizing the cultic practices in Jerusalem, developing some elaborate worship ceremonies (still based on the principles of purification and sacrifice to please God), and supporting an emerging priestly class of citizens.

Summary

We have reviewed how the tribal patriarchs each had developed a primitive sense of monotheism (really a form of monolatry) under their various tribal gods—the god of Abraham, the god of Isaac, and the god of Jacob. Through the historical events surrounding the Exodus and the Conquest of Canaan, this tribal monolatry, under Moses, became a monotheistic belief in YHWH. Israel began to "feel" like a nation even though it was still governed by a tribal leadership of people referred to as The Judges. Under the united monarchies of Saul, David, and Solomon (as well as the emerging priesthood David established), the early concepts of sacrifice and purification became the principal pillars of worship, and the time when the role of the temple and the city of Jerusalem became central to this emerging sense of nationalism and faith.

Donald L. O'Dell

Chapter 2 Notes

[1] Anderson, Bernhard, *Understanding the Old Testament*, pp 3–4
[2] Muilenburg, James, *Interpreter's Bible*, Vol. 1, p 305
[3] Muilenburg, James, *Interpreter's Bible*, Vol. 1, p 298
[4] Bloom, Harold and Rosenberg, David, in *The Book of J*, make the case that the Yahwist may have been a woman.
[5] From Anderson, *Understanding the Old Testament*, p 17
[6] *Harper's Bible Dictionary*, 7th Edition, p. 824

Chapter 3

The Schism and Beyond

𝕌nder the Monarchy of Saul, David, and Solomon, the tribal, cultic sense of religion that was predominate among the Hebrews had begun to be coalesced into a national sense of "Israel" under the care of Yahweh. The new temple of Solomon, the ceremonial rituals and rites introduced by David, the emerging professional priesthood, and the emergence of the Yahwist's Epic all played a significant part in this emerging sense of a national religion.

Just as we did with the Patriarchs, we're going to take a closer look at events during the Schism and the Exile. These events, too, have a direct bearing on trends that are occurring today.

The Schism, Shattered Dreams, and Exile (922–526 B.C.E.)

We began the last chapter with a quote from Bernard Anderson that was a short history of Israel up through the Monarchy. The remainder of that short history follows.

"After the death of King Solomon this united kingdom [of Israel] split into the two kingdoms of north and south—Israel (Ephraim) and Judah. These kingdoms, by virtue of their strategic location in a buffer zone between Mesopotamia and Egypt, were drawn into the power struggle of Near East. The northern kingdom, Israel, fell under the aggression of Assyria in 721 B.C.E. After more than a century of vassalage to Assyria, the southern kingdom, Judah, fell victim to the Babylonians, who wrested world rule from Assyria. Jerusalem fell to the Babylonians in 587 B.C.E. and the people were carried away into Babylonian captivity. But under the benevolent rule of the next empire, Persia, the exiles were permitted to return to their homeland, where they rebuilt Jerusalem and resumed their way of life. The restoration took place chiefly under the leadership of Nehemiah and Ezra (circa 450 B.C.E.).

"After more than two centuries of Persian (Iran) rule and significant Persian influence—[*most notably the concepts of demonology, angelology, and the dualism of good and evil*]— Palestine came within the orbit of Greek control as a result of the world conquest of Alexander the Great (322 B.C.E.). Alexander's policy of imposing Hellenistic cultural uniformity upon the world was continued by those who inherited his divided empire, especially by the Seleucid rulers of Syria. When this policy was forced upon the Jewish community by one Seleucid king, open revolution broke out under the leadership of the House of the Maccabees (168 B.C.E.). The literature of the Old Testament breaks off at this point. History tells us, however, that the Jewish nation achieved a century of independence, which was finally eclipsed by the next world empire—Rome."[7]

Although Israel's national religion would continue to grow and be defined, it would not do so under the umbrella of a united Israel. By the end of Solomon's reign, both Egypt and Assyria were stirring again and travelers needed to worry again about war, which affected trade routes. Reduced traveling resulted in reduced tribute paid. With tribute from trade declining, taxes had been increased to keep up the treasury. After Solomon's death, Israel's tribal elders pleaded with Rehoboam, Solomon's successor and son, to reduce their taxes. He refused and the beginning of the schism—the dividing of the Monarchy—was under way.

Israel regrouped along basic tribal lines. Seceding from the unified kingdom were ten of the twelve tribes. They referred to themselves as Israel (sometimes Ephraim). This left the tribes of Judah and most of Benjamin, which referred to themselves as Judah.

This division was not new to the Hebrews. After Saul's death in 1000 B.C.E., Samuel anointed David king of the southern portion of the nation and he ruled for six years from Hebron. The northern tribes had selected Saul's son, Esh-baal (or Ish-basheth), as king. When he was murdered (2 Sam. 4:7), David was made king of all Israel.

A Confusing Time

To be sure, it was a confusing time. Each little nation—north and south, Israel and Judah—had its own king and court. At times the northern kingdom and the southern kingdom were operating independent of each other, at times they were active commercial and/or military allies, and at times were almost at war with each other. At times biblical authors or editors (scholars call them *redactors*), especially the Deuteronomic and Priestly writers (600–400 B.C.E.) writing hundreds of years after the fact, sometimes referred to "Israel" as the unified Hebrew people and at times "Israel" referred to the northern kingdom only.

Adding to the confusion was the fact that this era became the great era of the Prophets—almost reminiscent of the era of the Judges. Although the Prophets didn't exercise any political control or influence as did the Judges, they were instrumental in defining (or redefining) the continued revelation of the character of Yahweh and his demands on his people. For the prophets this continued revelation of the character of Yahweh usually took the form of: "Hear the word of the Lord..."

These two small independent nations agreed as much as disagreed. Yahweh was the God of both, however much they might have vacillated in loyalty to him. As the two kingdoms became more urbanized, both kingdoms fought against Baal-worshipping nations who were trying to influence them. In the north, the traditions of the Tribal Confederacy were kept alive. Yahweh had remained the Yahweh of the Exodus desert, of the tribes, and of the sheep from the tribal remembrances of the Exile. In the south, since David had made a new covenant with Yahweh (2 Samuel 7), God promised to preserve this Davidic line and spare the Davidic kingdom. Yahweh had also become the God of David, of the farmer, of grain and crops, social/temple festivals, and wholesome family life. However, for both the Jerusalem-based Judaeans in the south, as well as tent-based Israelites in the north, Yahweh was the abiding reality. The desire of both nations to be loyal to Yahweh was at the core of the codes of sound social, ethical, and religious laws, which were slowly being developed. So while Judah gloried in her new temple, built by Solomon, and

Donald L. O'Dell

the beautiful rituals centered in Jerusalem, initiated by David, Israel maintained a determined loyalty to the Yahweh who had delivered them up from Egypt.

The Northern Kingdom – Israel

The Northern Kingdom, Israel (922–721 B.C.E.)—had twice the population and almost three times the geographic area of Judah. It was generally more productive than its southern neighbor—in terms of culture, power, foreign relations, and commerce. This productivity also included the religious aspect; virtually all of the prophets came from these northern tribes. The exceptions were Amos, Isaiah of Jerusalem, and Second Isaiah. The Elohist presented his epic during this time as well. He wrote about 750 B.C.E. and referred to God, not as Yahweh, but as Elohim. Unknown editors soon intertwined his epic with the Yahwist's earlier Epic. Much of what we now know as Genesis, Exodus, Joshua, Judges, 1, 2 Samuel, and 1 Kings was beginning to take shape around 750 B.C.E.

The northern kingdom of Israel lasted for almost 200 years. Israel basically aligned herself politically with Samaria, which helped the stability of the new nation. Eventually Samaria was invaded and destroyed by Assyria. Israel's leading citizens were deported to various places within Assyria (2 Kings 17:5–6).

The ten tribes comprising Israel would never have a homeland again. After Judah fell 150 years later, and was eventually restored only to become a vassal state under the Persians, Greeks, and Romans, *the nation of the Hebrews became synonymous with Judah—called Judaea under Roman rule.*

The people were scared and confused. Yahweh's "promised land" was disappearing right before their very eyes. What had happened? What had they done? Why didn't Yahweh like them anymore? *Just like ourselves, when things begin to change rapidly—as the Information Age and the resulting global technology/economy is forcing changes on us—we begin yearning back to simpler times: Times when kids could be kids and play in neighborhoods without fear of lawsuit or abduction; when people went to church and attempted to treat their neighbor as themselves; abortion was not talked about; drugs were not obvious; the term "queer" meant "odd"; and the term "gay"*

54

meant "cheery." When there were no cell phones, e-mails, and Internet dating—instead, people actually conversed with each other. Responding just like we do, there were movements to restore the righteousness or holiness of Israel by turning back to the ways, rites, and rituals of yesteryear—the rituals of purification and sacrifice.

This was the time of the Deuteronomic Code (D). The code was written by priests and consisted primarily of what we now recognize as the Book of Deuteronomy. Written as an attempt to revitalize the faith of the Hebrews, it focused on institutionalizing external practices of many of the customs and beliefs. Times as disturbed as those that produced the fall of the northern kingdom were now threatening Judah. This naturally inspired a great longing for a return to tradition. The writers of Deuteronomy doubtless intended to present a transcription of the Mosaic faith, as they understood it, for their own times. As well, it focused on the growing role of the emerging professional priesthood—the formal priesthood jump-started by King David—who had the ritual of purification and sacrifice, as a method to pacify Yahweh, pretty much institutionalized.

As the northern kingdom was crumbling, Judah was prospering under King Josiah. He attempted to expand Judah's influence in the former northern territories (now Assyria). He stepped up a sense of a unified nationalism and nationalistic reforms. An unknown *Book of the Law* was found when the temple was being renovated, and Josiah was very moved by it (2 Kings 22:1–11). This *Book of the Law* is the Deuteronomic Code. In the Deuteronomic Code (Deuteronomy 12–26, 28), although Jerusalem is not mentioned as the central sanctuary, Josiah identified it as such for his own reforming purposes. More than likely the original Deuteronomic writers had Shechem in mind— the scene of the covenant renewal under Joshua. Deuteronomy clearly depends on old northern covenant traditions that had been recast to fit the seventh century B.C.E.

The message of the Deuteronomic writers? Israel is a chosen and covenant people. Being chosen by Yahweh gives a historical character to the idea of holiness—Israel didn't "earn" her right to be chosen—it was an act of divine mercy. The covenant relationship to Yahweh demonstrated God's love and mercy. Israel must respond with utmost holiness. In fact the holiness of Israel should describe her character and meaning of life. If you are to be holy, you really had to work to keep yourself pure.

However, there were some severe theological flaws in the rediscovered *Book of the Law*. When these flaws began to appear, early "supporters" of these reforms inaugurated by Deuteronomy began to rail against it, like the prophet Jeremiah. The new law was too heavily influenced by a defiant nationalism and an external, codified piety. According to Bernhard Anderson[8] the general tone of the Deuteronomic writers put God in a theological straitjacket. YHWH's divine justice was now totally predictable: Follow the codified piety and God will bless you; Fail to follow it and you will experience hardship. *Sounds a lot like the early primitive concepts underlying the sacrificial aspects of tribal worship, doesn't it? That's because it is very much like the underlying aspects of tribal worship.*

Although the belief in divine reward/blessing and divine punishment/judgment was fundamental to Israel's beliefs, it was always prefaced with a personal commitment to be willing, loving, and obedient to Yahweh in one's heart. The Deuteronomic writers had added something: A strong belief that obedience and disobedience in one's heart could be measured by a code of rules set down in a book—the *Book of the Law*. The new danger, railed against by Jeremiah and the prophet Habakkuk, was that the Hebrews would obey the ritual code of law simply to "get the goodies"—or in Deuteronomic prose, "in order that it may be well with you," or "in order that your days may be long upon the land which Yahweh your God gives you."

We know faith doesn't always bring what we expect, but the Deuteronomic Law didn't really address that. So, new questions confronted the Hebrews. What do you do then? What do you do when the "magical" formulas don't seem to work? This faith issue began shortly after the Deuteronomic Book of the Law: *If men obey the laws of God and are "rewarded" with suffering or hardship, how can God be just?* The prophet Habakkuk took that question head-on and concluded: It is faith in God, not the sacrificial rites, that matters to Yahweh.

Okay, I think I understand that the prophets said it's what's in my heart, not what I do, that matters. But do I just ignore trying to "do good" and trying to define what that means to me? Of course not. Does this mean that I shouldn't have any "rules" about my moral actions? Of course not. But whatever definitions or "rules" you come up with are just that—they are your rules. They fit your sense of spirituality—your sense of what it means to walk humbly with your God. Your job is to define what's moral in your heart, in gratitude to God, and then follow it. Yes, share your sense of morality, if asked, and how you arrived at it. No, it's not your job to convince people that your solutions—your sense of morality— are the "right" solutions for everybody.

This tension between the message of the prophets and the message of the priesthood is beginning to brew. The prophets are saying that Yahweh wants an inward, personal sense of righteousness and justice. The message of the growing power of the priesthood is that to gain (or maintain) the favor of Yahweh we must present ourselves as holy before the holiness of God. To do that we must obey the cultic rituals of the Temple Law to the last letter. We are going to see this same tension, in a variety of situations and flavors, pop up over and over throughout the rest of this book.

The Exile (587–539 B.C.E.) or the Fall of the Southern Kingdom (Judah)

In general the Exile refers to the period of captivity when Hebrews were deported into supervised living conditions under alien powers in Mesopotamia or Persia. When the northern kingdom was overrun by Tiglath-Pileser III, the leading citizens were taken to Assyria. The Ten Tribes would never again have their own country. "There was none left but the Tribe of Judah." (2 Kings 17:18) This was certainly part of the "consciousness of the Exile" of the Israelites.

Technically, however, the Exile refers to the similar fate of the southern kingdom of Judah because the same thing occurred to them. Following the defeat of Assyria, the Babylonian Empire and Egypt were in conflict. These two powerful neighbors fought and Judah was caught in the middle. Judah allied herself with Egypt, who named Jehoiakim as king of Jerusalem (2 Kings 23:34). The Babylonian king, Nebuchadnezzar, defeated the Egyptians. Jehoiakim refused to pay him tribute, so Nebuchadnezzar marched on Judea. Jehoiakim was killed and his son took over. Judah surrendered in 597 B.C.E. (2 Kings 24:8–12). The biblical record suggests that only the poor and incompetent remained in Jerusalem. However, that was an oversimplification.

Nebuchadnezzar had appointed Zedekiah as king of Judea. Zedekiah rallied the remaining inhabitants and moved them into the abandoned estates and homes of those recently exiled. They developed a false sense of security over the next several years and, in spite of Jeremiah's warnings, their sham sense of nationalistic pride fed Zedekiah's ego and he rebelled against Nebuchadnezzar. Following a siege, Jerusalem fell for good in 587 B.C.E. The temple, with its altar, and palaces (of Solomon) were plundered and burned. The entire population, except the farmers and vineyard keepers—the "poor of the land," according to 2 Kings 25:4-21—were taken to Babylonia. From other records we know that some escaped to Egypt.

These exiles were usually located in colonies. The treatment they received and their reaction to it proved to be a mixed bag. Some suffered greatly with deep despair. *That's not hard to imagine: Just think of recent television images of Bosnia, Somalia, Rwanda, Kosovo, and Afghanistan where there's been a wholesale uprooting and/or flight of villages or territories.* Others, however, did quite well. They married, possessed houses, started new careers, made money, and achieved high standing—some even in high state positions—in their newly adopted country of Babylonia. *Personally, I think of Cubans who repatriated to America, principally to Miami, Florida, where within several generations they prospered.*

The Hebrews were there for about two generations until the door was opened for them to return to Jerusalem. In 539 B.C.E., Persia, under their king Cyrus, overthrew Babylon. Cyrus permitted Jews to return to Jerusalem in Judea. The nation Judah (Judaea) would never again, however, be a free and independent nation. It continued as a Persian (Iran) vassal state, then—grouped collectively with Palestine and Syria—as a part of the Hellenistic empire of Alexander the Great, the Ptolemies of Egypt, and finally as a part of the Roman Empire.

It is difficult to describe and visualize the pervading uncertainty that occurred during these various deportations. For over a thousand years the history of the Covenant had been: God promised a nation to Abraham's descendants—the nation, the country, of Israel. Now it was as if Yahweh's history had to be rewritten: God promised a nation to Abraham's descendents—but it would be a "nation" only in terms of ritual worship, complex laws, musty old scrolls, and circumcision.

But things had already begun to change. By the time the Hebrews could choose to leave Babylonia, a lot of them chose not to. Others, though, had used their time in Babylonia to refocus. The temple priests—high social, hereditary positions since the time of David that were reserved for the wealthy, influential, and educated—began to reduce the temple laws and rituals to writing. Some of these codified laws and rituals appear in what is called the Holiness Code (Lev. 17–26). Although they dreamed of the past—wanting to restore the temple, for instance—they developed the institution of the synagogue to serve as a substitute for the temple while in Babylonia. This priestly class, formally begun under David, also began to edit and incorporate their own literature into the existing body of "scriptural" writings. This was to become what we know as the P writings. These writings include most of what we know as Leviticus and Numbers, as well as many editorial additions in Genesis, Exodus, Deuteronomy, and the historical scrolls of Joshua, Judges, Samuel, and Kings.

Worshippers, cut off from temple rites, rituals, and sacrifices, continued to pray, continued to circumcise their sons, and they began to write. Writings we have of this post-Exilic period show the beginnings of new themes that were common in Babylonia and Persia (Iran). The influence of Babylonian ideas and cultural influences—especially astrology, dualism, and demon mythology—became more and more commonplace within the exiled Hebrew culture. *This is not too hard to understand. Two generations can make a big difference. For example, if Grandpa and Grandma move from New Jersey (*New Joizie*) to Mississippi, two generations later their grandchildren will speak and think (*thank*) like Mississippians.* Hebrew writings from this period began to incorporate many of the Babylonian and Persian ideas of mythology, especially angelology and demonology. After the Judeans were allowed to return to Jerusalem, they would remain a Persian vassal state—and exposed to Persian culture—for several hundred years until Persia was conquered by the Greeks. It should be noted that the same had been happening with people from the northern kingdom's Ten Tribes that had been in Assyria and Persia for almost 200 years by the time Judah fell.

After the Exile: Post-Exilic Judaism (587–150 B.C.E.)

The faith of the Jewish people, the Hebrews, centered on the temple rituals, festivals, and rites that celebrated the historical roots of their patriarchs: the Exodus from Egypt and the Conquest of Canaan. With the fall of the northern kingdom, followed by Judah's fall and the destruction of Jerusalem and its temple, those symbols were shattered. Temple worship in Jerusalem was how the Hebrews had defined themselves as Israelites. That was now gone. In exile in Babylon and parts of Assyria, Hebrews were having to exercise their faith for the first time without the use of the temple.

The synagogue, or meeting place, allowed for the reading of the Law and the commandments. It became the seat of a rational worship without sacrifices and offerings. Its central feature was instruction in religion and eventually it became the model of both Christian and Moslem worship. The synagogue service included the Hebrew reading of a portion of the Torah (the first five books, or the Pentateuch), its translation into vernacular language, a brief homily or sermon, and eventually a reading from a scroll of one of the Prophets.

Although the Persian king, Cyrus, allowed Hebrews to return to Jerusalem, it was never quite the same. Many of those living in Babylon elected not to return to Jerusalem. Being dispersed and living apart from Jerusalem, these Hebrews were referred to as being in the Diaspora, a term still in use today. They had lived in Babylon for about forty years and had established families, roots, and businesses. They were settled, comfortable, and flourishing. Their sense of "Hebrew-ism" was coming from weekly gatherings in the local synagogue. This became a time of redefinition. New structures and rites within their religion began to appear, e.g., the role of the rabbi, the growing body of written religious material, and especially the re-emergence of a distinct priestly class from the Tribe of Levi—bent on wanting to have their Kingdom ruled, not by one like David, but by priests. Priests were the only ones, they argued, who could "guide" the Hebrews into becoming "holy" enough to win, once again, Yahweh's favor.

Little was being done in Jerusalem, however, by those who had returned to their holy city. The walls and gates were still piles of rubble. This was brought to the attention of an influential businessman named Nehemiah. In 450 B.C.E., almost 100 years after Cyrus allowed the first exiles to return to Jerusalem (circa 539 B.C.E.), Nehemiah approached the Persian King Artaxerxes I for help. Artaxerxes concurred and named Nehemiah as governor of Judea. He gave him guarantees of safe conduct along with letters instructing Persian authorities in Syria to provide the necessary materials for the city's reconstruction.

About the same time, Ezra, a high-ranking priest, returned to Jerusalem carrying blessings and instructions from Artaxerxes to rehabilitate the temple and the religious life of people of Jerusalem. It was written that Ezra also had a book of the law (Neh. 8:1–3). What was it? Scholars believe the references were to the almost completed Torah—the Pentateuch or the first five books of the Old Testament: Genesis, Exodus, Leviticus, Numbers, and Deuteronomy—as edited and completed during the Exile. That being said, Ezra in his reforms during the rebuilding of Jerusalem with Nehemiah, is said to be the "Father of modern Judaism."

Together Ezra and Nehemiah began the reconstruction of Jerusalem's walls as well as its temple. Beyond the physical reconstruction, they attempted to revitalize Judaism. Simultaneously, the priestly writers had begun their additions and edits of the growing body of written religious scrolls. The Priestly Code (found essentially in Lev. 17–26) is a concise, dogmatic history of God's organization of his holy congregation through Moses and in Canaan through Joshua. It was written by priests in Jerusalem about 450 B.C.E., perhaps as a part of the reforms of Ezra and Nehemiah. Much of what we recognize as Leviticus and Numbers is the result of these priestly writers.

Many of the people were clamoring—or if not clamoring, then yearning—to get once again that confidence in their "expression" of a faith that would resonate with Yahweh. They wanted assurances that their God hadn't abandoned them. They wanted the security that the path they were on was the "right" path and Yahweh would smile on them and make everything all right again. The desire of the professional priestly class was ever too willing to accommodate these common frustrations.

Emphasis on ritual legislation is the essential part of P, designed to ensure that Jews could maintain their identity—their separateness from the Gentiles—as God's own people, even though they were without a state and country of their own. For example, it was during this time that the P writers added the second account of Creation, the story of the six days of Creation, in order to emphasize the seventh day, the Sabbath, which was crucial for the survival of the emerging concept of the synagogue (Gen. 1:1–2:4).

The insecurities and frustrations of the people "fed" the priestly class to continue in their reforming efforts by tightening up the rituals and the spelled-out codes of right behavior. These new ritualistic reforms satisfied the desire of the people to have easy-to-understand methods to regain Yahweh's favor.

The more the priests emphasized how "holy" God was, the more elaborate the temple and priestly rites appeared—because the holiness of God kept him virtually inaccessible on a personal level. This ritual legislation, with all its complicated system of worship and excessive qualification of the Law (as in Ps. 119) assured God's remoteness and provided job security for the priests, who were classified as scribes or Sadducees.

Scribes had their origin in the legalistic development of the Exile and were the "official expositors" of the vast body of the Law—the Torah—that controlled Jewish life and activity. Their chief reverence was for the written word and its traditional meaning. In general terms, the scribes had completely lost that living spirit of the Law that was so evident in the prophets. For the scribe there could be no new truth. Only tradition had any authority.

The Sadducees were the dominant priestly party. As such, they were much more conservative in matters of legalistic and ceremonial interpretations of Scripture. They were not usually averse to other cultures and there is evidence that they had developed markedly worldly interests. They encouraged the traffic within the temple precincts and benefited from the prices charged and profits made.

Collectively, these priestly classes used the Deuteronomic Book of the Law and Priestly Code of Leviticus to reverse the teachings of the reforming prophets (750–600 B.C.E.). These prophets included Amos, Hosea, Micah, Isaiah of Jerusalem, Habakkuk, and Jeremiah. They had denounced the corruption connected with the ritualized worship of the various sanctuaries, including the efficacy of sacrificial rites to gain God's favor. "… Yahweh was revolted by [the Hebrews' gorging at festivals] and refused to accept their sacrifices." (Amos 5:21–24) "For Yahweh preferred loyalty to sacrifice and knowledge of God to burnt offerings …" (Hos. 6:6) "When He delivered Israel from Egyptian bondage, He demanded of them obedience and not sacrifice." (Jer. 7:21–23) "[YHWH does not require numerous sacrifices, rather] … to do justly, and to love mercy, and to walk humbly with thy God." (Mic. 6:6–8) These reforming prophets were not opposed to worship rituals or sacrificial rites. They were opposed to the misuse of sacrificial worship. They were convinced that the whole religious ritual was offensive to God if it was not accompanied by honesty and mercy for the outcast and needy. If the ritual, in and of itself, was expected to induce God to overlook one's iniquities, then the ritual offerings and sacrifices were nothing more than what amounted to a bribe to God.

This is exactly the situation that confronted Jesus when he drove out the money-changers in the temple. The practices and traditions that so angered Jesus began during these post-exilic times. The sense of Jewish Law that so preoccupied Paul began during these post-exilic times. The railing of the prophets was a lot like what Martin Luther went through during the Reformation about 1500 C.E. The Catholic Church, among other things, was selling penance—forgiveness, if you will—and Luther, a priest, posted ninety-five questions on the door of the church at Wittenberg, Germany. This was how one announced issues one wanted to debate with other church priests/scholars. The Church thought he was crazy, then a heretic for refusing to obey the hierarchy, all of which, when coupled with a healthy dose of political opportunism on the part of Vatican-hating German royalty, led to the Protestant Reformation.

Living under the liberal rule of the Persians, this priestly class created for the Hebrews a spiritual commonwealth to which the Persian authorities did not object. The Priestly Code (Lev. 17–26) was the charter of this holy commonwealth of Israel under the rule of God. *Thus, the Priestly Code created a virtual holy state within the Persian Empire. It was the first organized "church" in human history, chiefly by controlling, through a combination of religious and civil rules, the exact ritual of public and private devotions.*

With all the new codes and the growing, formal institution of the priestly class, the emphasis shifted again from the personal morality called for by the prophets to the blind ritual worship espoused by the priestly class. This whole ritual system was based on two inviolate principles: (1) physical holiness because God owned everything and (2) arbitrary divine enactment, which enabled mankind to use what was needed without "robbing" God. This ritualized religion was the logical man-made extension of the tribal concept of purification/sacrifice. This ritualized religion was the embodiment of the recognition that God owns the property, the time, the land, and the very persons of the Israelites. Consequently, the people needed to blindly obey the enactments of their divine sovereign, whether the "rules" seemed sensible or incomprehensible, under penalty of personal exile (excommunication) or death.

According to the Priestly Code, God had said (and I paraphrase), "This land is mine (Lev. 25:23) but it's okay for you to use it if you pay me the firstlings, the first fruits, and the tithes as sort of a 'rental' fee." The festivals and the Sabbath fees were expounded by the priests as a tax paid to God for the use of time. In short, since God redeemed them from the Egyptians, the Hebrews really were a "slave" to him. Since the Law (many of which were old, resurrected tribal customs, e.g., the "scapegoat" rite for Azazel incorporated into the Day of Atonement or Yom Kippur) required human/animal sacrifice or agricultural produce, the priests substituted monetary values for these. During the period from about 450–100 B.C.E., the whole sacrificial system, except for a few optional (and personal) offerings, was transformed to a schedule of monetary fines and fees. The sacrificial worship in the Priestly Code was conceived in part as payment of what was due God and in part for the expiation of sin. Since God had made Israel a holy nation, it was imperative for her to observe the ritual enactments exactly, even when incomprehensible, lest God destroy his people.

The original idea of paying "rent" to God was grand and led to astonishing changes in the ancient common law when it was adapted as the basis for the Israelite economy. Because of the concept behind the law there was no such thing as a natural and private right to the exploitation of property. Each tribal clan—not the individual—had the right to redeem any property that was sold. The land, after all, belongs to God, who gave it to the community or tribal clan. If the clan didn't exercise its right to redeem the land, the property would automatically resort to the tribe in the 50th or jubilee year (Lev. 25:13–17). This prevented a person from buying, and thus dispossessing, Israel's common citizens from all forms of economic slavery, since the land was the basis of all wealth.

Requirement	Original Sacrificial Offering (for which many cash equivalents had been established)
Required "taxes" be paid to God as a general "thank you"	• First-born (or 5 shekels) • Annual tax of 1/2 shekel
Required "taxes" be paid to the priests, in lieu of God, for the peoples' use of their property	• Heave offerings; • Meal offerings; • First fruit offerings; and • Tithes (which went to the Levites, although the "best tenth" went to the high priest
Fines for the expiation of "national" sins	• A he-goat on the new moon and at festivals • A bull for a sin offering at the consecration of priests • A burnt offering of a ram
Fines for the expiation of "personal" sins	• A sin offering; • The trespass offering (which consisted of restoration PLUS 20% to the priests; • The meal offering; • The burnt offering

Table 4. *Examples of Fines and Offerings.* *The sacrificial worship system was transformed into a schedule of fines and fees.*

The Protestant English did this in absolute reverse in Catholic Ireland in the seventeenth and eighteenth centuries. They amended the law, exclusively for Roman Catholics, which allowed an estate to pass to the eldest son. In Catholic families the estate of the parents had to be equally divided among all the children. Consequently, with each passing generation the heirs' portions of landed estates would become smaller and smaller, ensuring the eventual poverty (and lack of political power) of Catholics in Ireland.

Initially the priests' intentions were probably honorable. They had desired to develop ways to preserve the identity of the Hebrew "nation" when it was without its own state and country. Over time those intentions simply dissolved and the remaining residue was accepted at face value. This honorable intention went awry, however, due to the greed, egos, and the incessant desire of the temple priests to appear to the people as being as knowledgeable of the "rightness" or wishes of God as was God himself.

There were some tensions within Judaism itself during the period of this great priestly reform. The reconstruction along the lines of an exclusive community—with the temple as its center and the Torah as its constitution, moved forward with great gusto (primarily because the ruling Persians had blessed the reforms, which they thought would add some stability in the region). There were dissenters, however. We have mentioned the Book of Ruth, written to protest the ban on mixed marriages and the welcoming of Gentiles into the faith. Another was the Book of Jonah. The story described how Jonah was trying to escape Yahweh's calling—to preach to the city of Nineveh. The moral of the story was aimed at the ruling priestly class. *Just as Jonah was avoiding God's call, so were the priests. The Jews were retreating into the "walls" of their exclusive community and trying to close the doors behind them.* That was a denial of Yahweh's commission to them, which was stated so eloquently in the poems (e.g., Isa. 41–42) of the prophet Second Isaiah, where Jews were castigated for letting their pride believe that Yahweh's purpose was only for the preservation of the Jewish community itself, even at the cost of the destruction of Israel's enemies. They were reminded that other people—even enemies—were embraced by Yahweh's mercy.

By circa 400 B.C.E., following the addition of the Deuteronomic code and the additions, edits, and rewrites of the priestly writers, the first five books of the Old Testament (called the Pentateuch, which means "Five Scrolls") were pretty much as we know them now. Some scholars also add the Book of Joshua, forming Six Scrolls, or the Hexateuch. When you add the growing body of prophetic writings, finalized about 200 B.C.E., the Old Testament, in the form of the Law and the Prophets, would look very familiar to us.

Mythologies of the Apocalyptic (the Last Days)

Between the end of the Exile and the beginning of the "common" era—almost 450 years—there were significant cultural changes occurring within the Judaistic communities. Many of the writings that began appearing had a "flavor" or "tone" that was "unearthly": demons, final conflicts between good and evil; between God and evil; the coming of a messiah, sometimes warlike, sometimes not. The roots of this kind of Hebrew literature began when patriarchal tribal cultures began meeting the full-blown mythologies that had existed in Babylonia and Persia.

These Babylonian and Persian ideas began showing up more formally in Jewish literature. We see it in some of the Wisdom literature, as well as in the Book of Daniel and the Book of Enoch in the Apocrypha. These writings about the end of time (with warring demons and angels; good finally triumphing over evil— although in an afterlife)—were filled with a sense of ultimate hope also but did much to fasten animism to the popular thinking of later Judaism and early Christian times.

Babylonia, Assyria, Persia: An aside about geography and names—Mesopotamia (literally meaning "between the rivers") is a geographical region encompassing the Tigris-Euphrates river valleys and a little beyond. This area was controlled by Assyrians, Babylonians, the Chaldeans (new-Babylonians), and Persians. As I use it, Babylonian/Persian influence generally refers to all of the above. That being said, Babylonia and/or its capital, Babylon, probably influenced the Hebrew mind, culture, and life more than any other culture outside Palestine.

Babylonian/Persian Influences and Greek Philosophical Ideas

The Babylonian/Persian influence of demonology was almost as significant as the intense refocus of temple law and ritual (now in written form) in terms of the long-term impact of the Exile on the religion of Israel. From earliest primitive mankind there had existed a simple form of demonology, and Assyria and Babylonia developed this into a fully formed dualistic (Good versus Evil) mythology. *At the risk of being overly simplistic, to primitive mankind it was the animism or "alive-ness" of malignant spirits that was accepted as being the causes of disaster, disease, and evil. You and I are a tad more sophisticated, but we do the same thing each time we get on our "pity pot." We ask, "Why did God do that to me?" or "Why doesn't God let things work out for me? He lets really bad people get good jobs, promotions, or win the lottery. Why not me?"*

Donald L. O'Dell

Primitive mankind had the same reactions. At first they blamed it on their tribal god, who was punishing them for something they had (or hadn't) done. Now they just blamed it on demons or devils. The Hebrews had primitive strands of this as well, from their earliest tribal cultic worship centers. However, the fully developed mythology of demons from the Persians and Babylonians made its fullest impact on the Jews during the period of the Exile and after. Then the influence of the Greeks—the Hellenistic culture—came into play following the defeat of the Persians by Alexander the Great. The mythology became more fully developed. This Assyrian/Babylonian/Persian demonology began to be married with the Hellenistic concepts of immortality and fate.

The result, as dictated by mankind's logic? If God made the world and demons exist, then God made demons. If the world God made was indeed good, then demons must have been good, too—at least in the beginning. So what happened? These initially good demons were really angels. They made bad choices and became bad angels or demons.

Consequently, in one theory based on Jewish tradition, demons (of whom Satan was chief) were created by God before the world. In another theory, certain angels forsook their allegiance to God in order to marry attractive daughters of men (Gen. 6:1–8) and their offspring were demons. From an early, primitive, tribal custom, Azazel was the demon of the desert and he made traveling dangerous for the unaccompanied pilgrim. Thus, early mankind's fear of being lost and alone in the desert was incorporated into a worship ritual of Judaism. This offering is similar, perhaps, to the ancient Semitic shepherds' feast of sacrifice (Exod. 5:1–3). Eventually, the idea of the "scapegoat" influenced other temple rituals, including the blemish-less lamb—the Paschal Lamb—which became a later analogy for Jesus among early first-century Jewish Christians.

Images of angelology grew out of despair and self-pity over human conditions—the "Why me?" syndrome. Early Hebrew writings are difficult to translate and understand when it comes to angels. In many of the passages it is difficult to distinguish whether an angelic reference is to God, personally, or to a distinct representative of God. When prophets would discover that their warnings or predictions of a reward for the righteous had failed to

68

have its desired effect, they were led to extend the operation of a just, righteous, loving God to realms beyond the earthly plane of time. Here, angels and demons were very real and the overriding thought was that the just would indeed get their due, although maybe not in this lifetime—perhaps in an eternal or in a temporal messianic kingdom. Likewise, the evil would be punished, if not here on earth, then in some form of eternal realm.

Concepts of the "Eternal"

The angelology and demonology of the Persian/Babylonia connection had an element of "the eternal" associated with them. However, the Old Testament concepts of eternal always had a "now" element to them. *Eternal, as in endless, only seemed to apply to the nature of God.* There really wasn't a Hebrew concept of eternal, as in time. Mostly in older Old Testament writings, man's eternal-ness could be discussed in terms of his progeny. Abraham would live on through his children, and his nation, Israel, would enjoy the promised (by Yahweh) land of milk and honey. The soul—in Hebrew: Nephesh or Breath—was something different from the "flesh" but nevertheless was a living thing. It could be cut off (Num. 15:30), could be fasting (Ps. 35:13), could be cast down in despair (Ps. 42:5), or could have friends (1 Sam. 18:1).

About 350 B.C.E. the Greeks defeated Persia. Judah, now grouped with Palestine and Syria, fell under Hellenistic control and influence. Judah was mostly referred to as Palestine, although sometimes Judea. This was also the Golden Age in Greece: Pericles (460–429); Socrates (470–399); Plato (428–348); Aristotle (384–322). Books, libraries, and ideas all abounded. The same trade routes that had made David and Solomon wealthy now brought new ideas. *In terms of the impact of Hellenistic culture we must remember, for writers from 350 B.C.E. on, that people could not have avoided the "spirit" of Greek culture or thought any more than we can avoid the influence of the scientific or technological "spirit" of the twentieth century.*

Among these ideas were concepts from the philosophical schools of the Greeks. These ideas impacted the Hebrew concept of the "eternal." The Greek concept of immortality blended nicely with the eternal-ness of the Babylonian/Persian mythology. Following their return from Exile, the Jews had absorbed demonology and angelology from their surrounding cultures and they were beginning to add the concept of "eternal" to them.

Slowly, as the Babylonian/Persian mythology was augmented by the Greek concept of immortality, the belief began to mature that the soul was mankind's immortal "part." The whole Greek concept of philosophy and rational thinking was a big influence as well; the desire to "get it down on paper" in a logical, rational progression of ideas began to build a framework of coherent thought and doctrine. Hebrew writings began to mention an "eternal" hell or an "eternal" heaven as a reward for the "immortal" soul.

Before this, the Hebrews had the concept of Sheol, the place of the dead, all dead. Neither good nor bad, necessarily, just the dead. Most of the time in the Old Testament the word Sheol in Hebrew can be translated as "pit' or "grave."

A thought on death: The death of the individual was not a serious problem in early Israel, for it was believed that an individual's life was given meaning by involvement in the covenant community. This is very much as we have discovered about the beliefs of Native American Indians. Within the culture of the Indians the true, organic individual is the tribe. It is the tribe, not any one person, that is the key to survival. Think of the passions we feel today as we fight (either for or against) the legal right to die or the intense legal battles concerning "pulling the plug" on someone. That same passion directed the survival of the tribe by the Hebrews for well over 1,400 years (1700–300 B.C.E.).

Images of Hope

This was also the time when images of hope began to dominate the religious landscape. Life in "the promised land of Abraham" or in the land of the "Covenant of David" was so far removed it was almost unrecognizable. Prophetic messages and images concerning a messianic hope for restoration back to the Holy Israel became more and more prevalent. The verbal images of the coming messiah varied: sometimes the messiah was a person; sometimes Israel, as a holy nation, was the messiah; sometimes the messiah was a warring, angry messiah; sometimes a quiet servant messiah. Regardless how these messianic images were painted, they all shared the same hope: "Yahweh, please return this land

and our customs to us, your chosen people." This hope, as we have seen, was wedded to the priestly desire for the kind of holy nation that could only be achieved through absolute perfection in obedience to all the laws and rituals of the Torah.

Following the death of Alexander the Great, his awesome empire was divided into three emerging ones: Macedonia, Syria (under the Seleucids), and Egypt (under the Ptolemies). Each of these in turn would eventually fall to one another or to Rome. Palestine was a vassal state of the Ptolemies (Egypt) for almost 150 years, until Syria (Seleucids) defeated the Ptolemies of Egypt about 200 B.C.E.

Just as Israel—besides political struggles—had to "battle" the worship of Baal when they were settling Canaan (and for a long time thereafter), now they had to "battle" the culture-creep of Hellenism. The result? Again, a growing revival of Israel's sense of nationalism as expressed in her combinations of temple ritual and rites, coupled with her awe and reverence of the Torah. This revival, like that of the Deuteronomic Reforms or the priestly revival of Ezra-Nehemiah, was a simultaneous push by conservative religious groups to return to the Torah as well as by a nationalistic fervor to reestablish the Davidic Kingdom. A little-known conservative sect, known as the Hasidim (the "loyal, pious ones" and forerunners of the Pharisees) became full-fledged "fire-fanners" in this movement. Although Hellenism had been invading the Jewish upper classes, the Hasidim were from rural, poorer stock.

Pharisees, or separatists and offshoots of the Hasidim, much like our original use of the term "Puritan," came into existence in the third century B.C.E. They were the champions of a complete Jewish exclusiveness. The stage for a revolt based on this revival was set. The dramatic turn of events occurred when the Seleucids of Syria defeated the Ptolemies of Egypt about 200 B.C.E. Palestine was now in the political "family" of the Seleucids, ruled by Antiochus the Great and his successor, Antiochus IV.

Antiochus IV ruled with absolute authority and stopped at nothing in imposing Hellenistic culture throughout his total realm. He believed he was divine and had coins minted that said so. Although he did allow people (including the Hebrews) to continue to worship their local gods, the political test was the worship of

Zeus (the supreme Greek god), of which Antiochus was a representative or Son. Obviously, this violated the very foundation of the Hebrews' essential tenet—Yahweh was their God and there was no place for additional gods.

The Maccabean Revolt

Since Antiochus needed monies after the wars against the Ptolemies, he raised taxes and, essentially, "auctioned off" the Office of the High Priest to the highest bidder. Believe it or not, people did make bids—primarily two brothers. One won, the other deposed him, and the original winner appealed to Antiochus for help. He responded by entering Jerusalem, ousting the usurper, but in so doing, the temple was plundered and local citizens were killed. In order to keep these "rebels" under control, Antiochus outlawed the Jewish religion and ordered the complete Hellenization of Jewish life. According to the edict:

- Mothers could be put to death for circumcising their sons;

- Copies of the Torah were to be burned;

- Observance of the Sabbath was a capital offense; and

- Possession of a copy of the Torah was a capital offense.

The people fully revolted under a leader called Judas Maccabeus (the Hammerer). They fought against the Syrians as well as Jewish elements who were willing to assimilate the Hellenistic program of the Seleucids. Judas did win a surprising victory and sued for peace. On the 25th of Kislev (December), 165 B.C.E., Judas Maccabeus began rebuilding the altar of the temple and restored the service of Jewish worship with a service of rededication. *Today, the Hanukkah feast (Feast of Rededication or Feast of Lights) is still celebrated around Christmastime.*

The following generations of Maccabees continued the war with the Seleucids of Syria, who were severely handicapped in their efforts because a pesky neighbor—Rome—was increasing its intervention in eastern affairs. The Jews thus enjoyed almost a century of relative independence, even though still a vassal state of Syria, until Pompey, one of the Triumvirate of the Roman Empire, came to Jerusalem in 63 B.C.E.

During the Maccabean Wars, the Book of Daniel, composed by a zealous Hassidim, was written to rekindle the faith of Israel in the face of the danger to the Hellenistic encroachment. He also wanted to summon the Jewish people to an unswerving loyalty to Yahweh, even in the face of persecution. The religious faith of the Hasidim, *still one of Judaism's most conservative parties,* demanded a loyalty to the Torah at any cost. As we read his stories in Dan. 1–6, we need to keep in mind that he was writing in a form of allegorical code because it was in a time when simple possession of the Torah was a capital crime.

This unknown author released his writings under the name of someone well-known (a common practice)—in this case Daniel, a traditional pious Jew (Ezek. 14:14), a legendary hero of the Ras Shamra literature, and an oral folk hero of early Israel. The message? There is light at the end of the tunnel! Regardless of the current persecution, God will prevail, eventually.

Both the post-exilic period of Israel's history as well as the history of the development of the Old Testament come to a close here. There were all types of literature coming from this period: wisdom, history, short stories like Esther, many of the Psalms, and the apocalyptic. The most popular was the apocalyptic. *This has always been true. When times are really troubled—when the result of our faith seems to be without reward—when we're asking ourselves "Does it really matter? Does it really work? Is this really the right way? Are we sure this is what God wants?" we begin hoping for vindication ... eventually.* Apocalyptic literature resonates with that yearning.

Since, during the time of Ezra, when it became accepted that the time of prophecy in Israel was over (unless, of course, an older text was found), writers had to ascribe their writings to an accepted, older author—like Adam, Enoch, Noah, Moses, or to a figure like Jeremiah, Baruch, Daniel, or Ezra. That's what the writer of Daniel did. Many others became known to us in the body of work we refer to today as the Apocrypha.

The Septuagint

This was also the time of the *Septuagint,* the Greek translation of the Hebrew Scriptures in the third century B.C.E. Accomplished in Alexandria as part of the overall Hellenization process, the

Septuagint got its name from the supposed seventy plus scholars who worked on the translation. The *Septuagint* was the "Bible" in the Greek-speaking world in the time of Jesus and the apostles. When the New Testament writers quoted from their Scriptures, it was from the *Septuagint*.

During the last hundred years or so before the beginning of the Common Era, that time between the outbreak of the Maccabean Wars and the Dawn of the Christian Era (165 B.C.E.–50 C.E.), Judaism continued to evolve. The result was the continuation of various "party" movements within Judaism, depending on how one believed a devout Jew should interpret the common tenets of faith in daily life.

- *Sadducees*: They were extremely strict in their view of the Torah—so strict that they would not accept any teaching from the prophets or wisdom literature. Consequently they rejected the concepts of resurrection, apocalyptic thought of angels and demons, and predictions about end-times. Their view was that the Torah outlined the divine plan which would come to fulfillment for Israel when a priestly theocratic community would come into existence based on strict regulations concerning sacrifice and priestly prerogative. However, on social issues they were quite moderate, advocating policies of tolerance and compromise—an understandable position since they were from families of prestige and political influence.

- *Pharisees*: Although stricter than the Sadducees in terms of practicing the customs that separated Jews from Gentiles (dietary rules, circumcision, fasting, prayer), they were more liberal in terms of the Torah. They accepted other teachings from Books of the Old Testament outside the Torah. They began codifying the opinions of the prophets, for example, into a book called the Mishnah (circa 100 C.E.). This led to an expanded edition, eventually known as the Talmud.

- *Zealots:* Closely aligned to the Pharisees theologically, they had political views, however, that were more in line with the Maccabean revolutionaries.

- **Essenes:** Known most recently from the Dead Sea Scrolls at Qumran, these were a sect(s) that separated themselves from the world to practice a more monastic devotion to the Torah, while awaiting the end of Yahweh's historical drama.

The Apocrypha

The Jews didn't "set" the scriptural canon until 90 C.E. in the coastal town of Jamnia. They had no reason to have a "set" canon. After Christianity became more prevalent, people became confused between Christian and Jewish writings—between what Christians and Jews meant when either would refer to the Scriptures. The many Books of the Apocrypha were in circulation during the growth of the Christian Church. Simply because Judaism later chose not to include these Books as Holy Scripture, but relegated them to the status of Apocryphal Writings (works that are not held to be equal to the sacred Scriptures but are good for instructional reading), didn't mean that the Christian Church would follow suit. Over time, these various decisions occurred: (1) The Roman Catholic Church still considers the Apocrypha as fully scriptural, i.e., these Books are part of the Roman Catholic Bible; (2) The Reformed (Zurich) Lutherans and Anglican Churches consider the Apocrypha as useful without being scriptural; (3) the Calvinistic and other Protestant Churches completely omit them from their Bibles.

By 90 C.E., the Jewish canon had been set. It is summarized in the following table.

The Torah (or the Law) Fixed circa 400 B.C.E.	The Prophet Fixed circa 200 B.C.E.	Writings Fixed circa 90 C.E.	Apocrypha Fixed circa 90 C.E.
Genesis	Joshua	Psalms	1-2 Esdras
Exodus	Judges	Proverbs	Tobit
Leviticus	1-2 Samuel	Job	Judith
Numbers	1-2 Kings	Ruth	Additions to Esther
Deuteronomy	Isaiah	Lamentations	Wisdom of Solomon
	Jeremiah	Ecclesiastes	Ecclesiasticus – The
	Ezekiel	Esther	Wisdom of
		Daniel	ben Sirah

The Torah (or the Law) Fixed circa 400 B.C.E.	The Prophet Fixed circa 200 B.C.E.	Writings Fixed circa 90 C.E.	Apocrypha Fixed circa 90 C.E.
	The Minor Prophets Hosea Joel Amos Obadiah Jonah Micah Nahum Habakkuk Zephaniah Haggai Zechariah Malachi	Ezra Nehemiah 1-2 Chronicles	Baruch The Letter of Jeremiah Susanna Bel and the Dragon Prayer of Manasseh 1-2 Maccabees

Table 5. *The Jewish Canon.* The canon consists of the Law, the Prophets, and the Writings. The Apocryphal writings are useful as instructive material only.

Summary

Following the breakup (Schism) of the nation, Israel, into the northern kingdom of Israel and the southern kingdom of Judah, as well as the Exile (first of Israel, then of Judah), the first destruction of the temple occurred and the process of assimilation into surrounding nations began—Babylonia, Persia, Greece, and finally the Roman Empire. During the Schism, the role and writings of the early prophets "came of age." During the Exile and the rebuilding of the temple, the priestly class began interpreting history in ways that reinforced the emerging institutions of Judaism, especially the temple ritual and the emerging institution of the synagogue—to the point that the line between religious belief and the institutionalization of the faith was so blurred there was no distinction between belief in YHWH and belief in the rites and rituals themselves. Of course, the preservation of the rites and rituals also preserved the wealth and status of the priestly class. The later prophets noticed this blurring, discerned the lines of distinction, and preached to the true elements of faith.

Following the Maccabean revolt (165 B.C.E.) and the restoration of the damaged temple and its altar, the same blurred distinction between belief in YHWH and the rites and ritual themselves occurred—but this time there were no prophets nor writers who produced books like Ruth or Jonah to admonish the priestly class. This heightened priestly state grew unchecked for over 150 years—from the Maccabean Era until the time of Herod. This was the Israel, with its powerful priesthood, into which Jesus was born.

Chapter 3 Notes

[7] Anderson, *Understanding the Old Testament*, pp 3-4. *Italics are mine.*
[8] Anderson, *Understanding the Old Testament*, p 319

Chapter 4

The Primary Authors of the Old Testament

This chapter examines more closely some of the most influential sources of biblical writings. This discussion does not cover how each and every book of the Old Testament came into being, nor does it cover all of the prophets. Only the major sources mentioned in the previous chapter are covered. The following discussion is basically sequenced chronologically.

The Epic of J (or the Yahwist) [circa 950 B.C.E.]

So named because of the author's use of the Hebrew word *YHWH*—Yahweh—for God (or Jahweh [JHWH] in German, the initial "discoverers" of this literary strand).

The "J" writer was a Judaean who lived in Jerusalem. This was a time when Israel, under the Monarchy, was enjoying great power and prosperity. The outlook for the future was most promising. With the assurance that Yahweh would continue to guide and protect Israel as He had in the past, the Yahwist wrote a superb epic, which magnificently expressed the national pride of Israel and thus kept it alive to the present day. The nationalism depicted in the Epic was unparalleled in ancient times—long before the Greeks and the Romans. It was a nationalism based on a sense of superiority over other people and nations, pride in past achievements under the guidance of Israel's God, Yahweh, and an undying faith in Israel's glorious future.

At the very beginning of the Epic, in the discussion of Yahweh's three promises to Abraham, the Yahwist presents the contents and plan for his work. (Gen. 12:1–4a, 7) "I will make of thee a great nation ... and in thee shall all the families of the earth be blessed ... Unto thy seed will I give this land." In Gen. 12–33 he shows how from Abraham the Twelve Tribes were descended. In Gen. 37–50, how through Joseph all Hebrew tribes were blessed by being saved from starvation. From Exod. 1–Judges 1, he shows how Yahweh gave to the seed of Abraham the land of Canaan. The Yahwist drew his material from the rich oral traditions of the tribes of the northern kingdoms.

The genuine traditions of the Tribes of Israel did not reach back beyond the deliverance from Egypt. However, in Genesis the Yahwist used ancient Canaanite traditions about Abraham, Isaac, and Jacob—the founders of the ancient and holy cultic sanctuaries of Hebron, Beersheba, and Bethel, respectively—and composed the brilliant tale about Joseph to explain how the people of the Hebrew tribes happened to be in Egypt until their deliverance by Yahweh through Moses.

The Epic continues, showing how Israel overcame all obstacles under the guidance of its Lord. His fascinating story is built around the heroic figures of Abraham, Isaac, Jacob, Moses, and Joshua. However, most of his Epic about Joshua and the conquest has been virtually lost or completely woven into E's account of the Conquest.

Additionally, the author appends a prologue to his Epic that is an unbelievable Late-Bronze-Age/Early-Iron-Age statement of faith. In the first eleven chapters of Genesis, the Yahwist takes well-known Babylonian wisdom (represented within the Hammurabi Code), the Gilgamesh Epic (the Great Flood), and Babylonian creation myths/folktales to spin a story of Creation, underlying which is the belief that Yahweh is not only the revered local tribal God of Israel, but the Lord of the Universe. In effect it laid out the monotheism (or perhaps, monolatry)—after the fact— of Israel's patriarchal heritage.

A note on the stories of Creation: Neither the Yahwist nor the later priestly writers designed their Creation stories as a scientific explanation of how God created the world as they knew it. The Yahwist's version (Gen. 2:5–25) emphasizes that Yahweh is the Lord of the universe. The Priestly (P) account (Gen. 1:1–2:4) emphasizes the six days of Creation in order to place the emphasis on keeping the seventh day (the Sabbath) holy. The statement of faith behind both versions simply is that Yahweh created. Whether mankind was created early in the process (J) or late (P) doesn't matter. Whether Yahweh snapped his fingers and—poof—there was a zebra, or whether he created a hydrogen atom that, over time, gravity, heat, and environmental influences, became the life form we recognize as a zebra doesn't really matter. The fact of the statement of faith still remains: In the beginning God created.

The Yahwist's Epic proved to be a controlling factor in the formation of virtually all subsequent literature. Everybody adhered to the Yahwist's framework. For the first time the religion began moving from tribal, oral-based traditions to written literature.

The Court Historian (during the reigns of Saul and David)

Much of 1–2 Sam. and the opening chapters of 1 Kings, specifically: 1 Sam. 4–6, 9–11, 14–16, 20, 26–31; 2 Sam. 1–6, 9–20, 24; and 1 Kings 1–2. Although most believe the historian was Ahimaaz, son of Zadok (2 Sam. 15:27, 36), there are a few, e.g., Burton Mack, who suspect it could have been the Yahwist. This material is considered to be among the oldest recorded eyewitness histories ever. Its style indicates a single author. The account indicates an amazing knowledge of court proceedings, Saul's mood swings, awareness of the plots and plans within Absalom's rebellion, as well as David's subsequent lament at Absalom's death, and overarching portrayals of Saul and David that are less than flattering. Together, all these indications point to remembrances that were reasonably current with the actual events themselves.

There are some, e.g., *Bible Dictionary* contributors, who also attribute to the Court Historian the Book of Jasher (extinct—cf. Josh 10:13) and the Book of "The Wars of the Lord" (extinct—cf. Num. 21:14–18).

The Elohist [circa 750 B.C.E.]

Named because of the author's propensity to use the Hebrew word *Elohim* for God. This is the Epic composed in northern Israel, presumably by a priest in Beth-el, about 750 B.C.E. This would have been not long before the northern kingdom came to an end (722) when Sargon of Assyria took Samaria. Though similar to J in scope and content it is subtly different in its ardent nationalism and in the classic beauty of its style. For example, compare Gen. 31:3 (J) with Gen. 31:11, 13 (E). God (Elohim) no longer appears visibly to men but reveals himself in dreams or through an angel. The patriarchs no longer have to rely on lies, tricks, and questionable actions but achieve their safety and success through divine blessing. The cultic nature of tribal worship, rather disregarded by J, is stressed by E, whose masterpiece is the story of the sacrifice of Isaac (Gen. 22:1–13, 19), which was ignored (or not known) by J.

The Prophet Elijah [circa 9th century B.C.E.]

Known as Elijah, the Tishbite from the northern kingdom. Although we cannot validate the historicity of much of Elijah's life and words, he had the force of personality and was significant enough to elicit numerous tributes throughout the following centuries. He lived during the time when Ahab, King of the northern kingdom (Israel) married Jezebel, a Phoenician and worshipper of Baal. In deference to her, Ahab relaxed many of the tribal customs to allow for the citizenry to engage in those customs, including Baal worship and fertility cults.

Elijah was known throughout his life as a champion of the "little people." In the narrative of Naboth's vineyard (1 Kings 21) we can visualize Elijah standing strongly against Ahab and all the subtle (and not so subtle) messages of the king's wife, Jezebel— shrewd and calculating as the emissary of the Phoenician god Baal. When Ahab comes to take the vineyard, Elijah confronts him with the terrible word of doom from Yahweh. Elijah is supporting this common peasant against a king. His passion for fearless support of the "little man" is deeply rooted in the religion of Yahweh—very similar to Nathan's condemnation of King David over his theft of Uriah's wife, Bathsheba (2 Sam. 11–12).

Secondly, of course, is Elijah's challenge to the prophets of Baal on Mount Carmel. Elijah, with Yahweh on his side, challenged Phoenician priests, with their god Baal on their side, to a "duel of the gods." For Elijah this was a "fall on your sword" issue. Yahweh is the God of Israel. All the highly sophisticated civilization of Phoenicia, under the god Baal, could not withstand the dynamism of Yahweh, the covenant God of Israel—the same

God who thundered on Sinai/Horeb and went to war on behalf of his people. Elijah/Yahweh won the contest.

However, an interesting and touching note: Following this highly dramatic pyrotechnic confrontation, Jezebel, the queen, threatened Elijah. He feared for his life and hid in the mountains looking for the Lord to protect him. He looked in an earthquake, in mighty winds, in fire. He finally heard the "… still, small voice …" of the Lord (1 Kings 19: 9–14).

The Prophet Amos [circa 8th century B.C.E.]

Known as Amos of Tekoa. It is believed the recording of the Book of Amos is relatively contemporary with the prophet himself.

Politically, it had been a bad time for the northern kingdom of Israel. Assyria was warring against Aram and needed all the tribute they could get from their vassal states. Earlier kings, Jehu and Jehohaz, were forced to subsidize Assyrian campaigns. But now the fighting was over. What a welcome relief! After all the fighting, Israel was reviving itself under King Jeroboam III. They were entering a period of great prosperity—their last—and Israel was increasingly sophisticated and urban. Commerce flowed at a flood tide.

In Amos, Yahweh speaks the language of history, naming names, nations, cities, kings, and events. As badly as the nations can behave (including Israel), Yahweh is more powerful. For Amos, *all* nations, not just Israel, are under the sovereignty of the Lord. *He is the first prophet to set the religious faith of Yahweh completely free of the "nationalism" of Israel.* This belief of Amos will become more and more pronounced in later prophets and wisdom writers.

Overall, however, Amos paints the picture of the times: Prosperity of the rich and the grinding poverty of the poor; dishonesty of the merchants and the exploitation of the disadvantaged; corruption of justice; and callousness and intemperance toward women. With a brutal candor he exposes the rottenness of Israel's social, economic, and religious life—at the core of which is the king's sanctuary and the royal palace (Amos 7:10-17). Yahweh will not notice all the various surface "niceties": generous tithes (from abundance); moving music; stupendous festivals; costly sacrifices; pilgrimages to the shrines of Bethel and

Beer-Sheba. These are not the actions that make God notice. What Yahweh wants is righteousness and justice.

Amos is also the first to refer to the "day of Yahweh." On this "day" Yahweh will reveal himself, engage in battle, and will triumph. The focus of Amos is on the outcome of things. This judgment of the northern kingdom dominates his earlier thoughts, while his later judgment holds out little hope for Israel, making it clear that the "end has come." That being said, there is a small hope (e.g., Amos 5:15) that God will be gracious to the remnant of Joseph.

The Prophet Hosea [circa 8th century B.C.E.]

Known as Hosea ben Beeri. Was a younger contemporary of Amos. His book is set in the political environment that followed the death of Jeroboam II and the rise of the Assyrian King Tiglath-Pileser III. The times were ones of disintegration and confusion in the northern kingdom. Scholars believe Hosea was of the Tribe of Benjamin—southern kingdom—and he was in a good position to see the threats that lurked beneath the surface in both Israel and Judah.

His is a beautiful allegory—the story of the infidelity of his wife Gomer, as compared to the relationship of Yahweh to the Hebrews. Gomer's faithlessness and whoredom is like Israel's breaking of the covenant. The repeated purchases by Hosea of Gomer are the revelation of God's reconciling and redeeming love. Yahweh's relationship to Israel is painted in pictures of husband/wife, father/son, and parent/child.

The final message: Yahweh can no more reject Israel than Hosea can reject Gomer. The love of God is triumphant—triumphant over wrath and judgment. What binds Yahweh and Israel is, in the end, stronger than what separates them. In the end there will be a new covenant, a new marriage, grounded in justice, faithfulness, righteousness, mercy, and love.

The Prophet Isaiah of Jerusalem [circa 8th century B.C.E.]

The material of this prophet is found in chapters 1–39 of the Book that bears his name, specifically chapters 1–12 and 28–33. Isaiah lived during the period of the most dynamic phase of the Assyrian imperialistic aggression. The period of the usurper Tiglath-Pileser

III (745–727 B.C.E.), whose principal policy of control was based on shifting conquered populations from one part of the empire to another. This policy was coupled with the death of the king of Judah, Uzziah, and the decline and fall of the northern kingdom (Israel). These were also the events that marked the lives of Elijah, Amos, and Hosea. But their prophetic focus was on the northern kingdom. Isaiah's was on the southern kingdom, Judah.

Isaiah seems to have been from the upper classes. He was a citizen of Jerusalem, he speaks with the grammar of the more urbane, and simply possesses a sense of dignity and sophistication. He's never able to break from the conservatism of Judah, and he has an innate regard for the genealogical House of David. His patriotism and loyalty to Jerusalem and to the Monarchy are never lost, even after the final crisis of Sennacherib's invasion. He was deeply influenced by Amos, although in a more measured, classical sense.

Like Amos, he sees the activity of God's purpose in the history of his own times. Judgment is falling until mankind will have lost every support. Also, like Amos, he denounces the false security, the outward show, of the cult—despising sacrifices, attendance at the sanctuary, new moons, and Sabbaths. Yahweh will not endure them, Isaiah says.

Isaiah's message, like Amos, is one of judgment. He describes the imminent day of Yahweh—a day that is final and decisive. The pride, arrogance, and egoism of mankind has erected lofty structures of security and self-sufficiency but it will all be brought low. In short, Yahweh has abandoned his people. Against the measuring rods of justice and righteousness, Yahweh's verdict will be destruction.

However, he believes a remnant will survive—an inconspicuous minority will become the community who will bear the word of God. Within this framework he penned his hopes for a coming Messiah. Although many of his messianic passages are highly suspect and some have a greater claim to authenticity than others, there is a certain amount of interior consistency with his religious thought, his concern for the Monarchy and, above all, the House of David. The Messiah will not simply overthrow and destroy. Rather, he will fulfill. "For unto us a child is born, to us a Son is given. And the government will be on his shoulder, and his name will be called Wonderful Counselor, Mighty God, Everlasting Father, Prince of Peace ..." (Isa. 9:6–7).

The Prophet Micah [circa 8th century B.C.E.]

Known as Micah of Moresheth-gath. We know very little of Micah. He was a peasant farmer from Shephelah and experienced firsthand the harsh and grinding life of the poor. He speaks in bitter outrage at the injustices done to those who have neither power nor capacity to resist. Equally, he speaks with warmth and compassion for those who suffer at the hands of shrewd, wily, and prosperous men. He condemns the landholders trying to fleece their tenants; the rulers (be they priests, prophets, or political leaders) for demanding cash fees for oracles, prophecies, or rulings; and finally, the temple, which Micah, unlike Isaiah (who declared it to be inviolate), consigns to destruction.

The latter portion of the book of Micah, written long after his death and focused on the evil reign of King Manasseh, is centered on the great controversy of Yahweh with his people. The whole drama of the legal trial between God and the Hebrews is found in verses 1–8 of chapter 6. The conclusion? It isn't sacrifice, not even those of her children, that God demands. What, then, is demanded of Israel by God? The answer given is the Great Commandment: "What does Yahweh require of you? To do justice, and to love righteousness, and to walk humbly with your God." (Mic. 6:8)

The Reformation and the Deuteronomic Code (D) [circa 625 B.C.E.]

Nowhere in the Old Testament is Israel's sensitivity to history better illustrated than in her response to the momentous events between the death of Ashurbanipal (last of the great Assyrian kings (circa 633 B.C.E.) and the destruction of Jerusalem (587 B.C.E.). No period of comparable extent is so rich in biblical writings. These momentous events led to the production of Zephaniah, Jeremiah, the Code of Deuteronomy, the first edition of 1–2 Kings, Nahum, and Habakkuk, Ezekiel, and a number of the Psalms.

In 622 B.C.E., Hilkiah the high priest found a book of the Law of Moses in the collection box at the entrance of the temple in Jerusalem. King Josiah read the book before the Judaeans and they made a covenant to observe Yahweh's commandments written in it (2 Kings 22–23). That book was The Deuteronomic Code. Written by priests shortly before it was found, it is a redaction of what the authors felt had been the final prophetic oracle of Moses. Although it has been revised by P and others, the original D document read by Josiah can be found in chapters 12–26 and 28 of Deuteronomy. It's referred to as the Deuteronomic Code.

The Deuteronomic Code: Times as disturbed as those of the decline and fall of Assyria naturally inspired a great longing for a return to tradition. The writers of Deuteronomy doubtless intended to present a transcription of the Mosaic faith, as they understood it, for their own times.

Dominating all else in the Code is the demand for an exclusive loyalty to Yahweh. Its classical formulation appears in Deuteronomy 6:4–9: "Hear, O Israel, Yahweh our God is one Yahweh. And you shall love Yahweh your God with all your heart [mind] and with all your life [spirit] and with all your strength. ..." The code repeats its assertion of Yahweh's unity over and over and in different ways:

- Historically – applying it to the whole period of the Conquest;

- Practically – demanding an extermination of Baal-worshiping and other alien elements from existing worship;

- Cultically – reorganizing the worship and the centralization of the sanctuary;

- Ethically – insisting on the complete commitment to the will of God.

Jerusalem is now the only place where men can truly worship. This centralization of the sanctuary now required people to travel to Jerusalem, the nation's capital, with all its associations with David, Solomon, Isaiah, and the Davidic dynasty. The cult, with its rigorous practices and defined priesthood, was absolutely controlled.

One main characteristic of Deuteronomy is its strong emphasis on love—Yahweh's love for Israel and Israel's loving response to

Yahweh. This is to be a love that is all encompassing, that requires holiness, that will dominate Israel's life, that will be the heart, soul, and strength of her. Israelites must love each other, but more, must love the resident alien, "... for you were once aliens yourselves in the land of Egypt." (Deut. 10:19)

These laws of love as they were understood by the priests and prophets, who were responsible for the Code, are set forth in great detail. However, the moral sense of these reformers reflects itself in another way. The consequences of good and evil are seen in a perfectly simple way: *The motivation for doing good is reward.* Justice demanded that good should produce good consequences and evil should produce evil. This simple view of divine sovereignty dominates the Book of Deuteronomy and this simple view is its Achilles' heel.

This interpretation of history, in reaction to their current situation "... was one of the chief defects of Deuteronomy. ... A theodicy which saw life in terms of [only] rewards and punishments could not cope with the realities of national tragedy."[9] Although their hearts may have been in the right place, they overreacted to the situation. *They were succumbing to the same Garden of Eden temptation—wanting to be as right and powerful as God by controlling the knowledge of good and evil. They wanted to make a set of codes that, if followed to the letter, would automatically gain Yahweh's favor.*

A second defect of the Book was its emphasis on exclusive nationalism. With Deuteronomy began the movement that was to make Judaism the "people" of the Book. This became most evident in emphasizing the single sanctuary in Jerusalem. "The absolutizing of the cult and its temple ... led to superstitious veneration of the temple, and it needed the terrible castigations of Jeremiah and later Jesus of Nazareth to expose the dangers of exalting even the temple too highly."[10]

The Prophet Jeremiah [circa 600 B.C.E.]

Known as Jeremiah of Anathoth. Called as a prophet during the critical period before the southern kingdom, Judah, was destroyed (587 B.C.E.). He was uniquely qualified for his confessions and utterances: his poetic temperament; his solitariness; his profound sense of communion with Yahweh; and his constant preoccupation with the problem of the meaning of Israel's life and destiny. All this allowed him to offer a distinct interpretation of the religious significance of world-shaking events that were going on.

Although Jeremiah soundly condemns the priests and scribes for being too legalistic and hypocritical, he doesn't call for political reform or for a reformation of the temple-centered religious life. He calls for a deep inward transformation, a circumcision of the heart (Jer. 4:14) in which all people will truly know God as they had known him in a covenant relationship.

Jeremiah's message of an inward revolution was reflected in his attitude toward the principal aspects of Israel's three great institutions: the temple, the Law, and the city of Jerusalem. Agreeing with Micah, and not Isaiah, he believed the temple was not inviolate. The Law had been turned into a lie by the scribes. The city of Jerusalem, with all its hallowed associations with David, the Cult, Isaiah, and the Deuteronomic reformers, would be destroyed and the people sent into exile. "Above all, Yahweh will make a new covenant, not like the old one on tablets of stone, but graven on the hearts of mankind."[11] This knowledge of God will be a new kind of inward relationship in which all men will know the Lord.

The Prophet Habakkuk [circa 600 B.C.E.]

Almost a contemporary of Jeremiah, Habakkuk rebuked the overly simplistic view of divine justice as portrayed in Deuteronomy and practiced by the priestly class. He wonders whether or not history does justify the righteous—or whether it is just raw power that really determines mankind's history. Ruthless invaders (the Chaldeans, a.k.a. Babylonians under Nebuchadnezzar) rule by defining justice in their own terms; they are "guilty men" whose god is might (Hab. 1:7–11). From his brief prophecy, his "watchtower" of faith, Habakkuk states: "Behold he whose soul is not upright in him shall fail, but the righteous shall live by this faith." (Hab. 2:1–4) It is faith in God, not the empty satisfaction of codified ethics, that really matters.

The Prophet Ezekiel [circa 590 B.C.E.]

Almost a contemporary with Jeremiah, and some of Jeremiah's influence can be seen also in Ezekiel. With the destruction of

Jerusalem and its temple, Ezekiel becomes a prophet of hope. His holy people will be vindicated before the eyes of the world. He is commanded to prophesy: "O, ye dry bones, hear the word of the Lord." (Ezek. 37:4) In his vision as the word is spoken, the bones become living flesh. So it will be with Israel. Israel will become a holy people, not by her own work or by performing rituals, but by the gracious act of her holy God.

Together with Jeremiah, Ezekiel forms a mighty witness to the meaning of the decline and fall of the nation Judah in an international world. Their focus was on the individual. What couldn't be explained easily in terms of the community or nation of Israel might be more readily understood in the life of the individual. Personal religion received a new and profound emphasis.

The Prophet Second Isaiah

Known as Second Isaiah (or Deutero Isaiah), this is the prophet behind chapters 40–55. [Chapters 56–66 have been postulated to have been written by another author, often referred to as Third Isaiah.] This unknown poet/prophet (probably during the Exile [587–520]) had his words added to the existing Book of Isaiah. His writings represent one of the highest (literarily) contributions of the Hebrew mind to the religious history of the world.

In general terms the principal ideas of the prophet are of the end of times—known as eschatological writings. The end of Israel's historical "warfare" has come: "The glory of the Lord shall be revealed and all flesh shall see it together." (Isa. 40:5) The poet/prophet is convinced that the meaning of Israel's history—in fact, all of history—is to be seen in the purpose of God. He interprets and elaborates Israel's sacred history in concrete terms to illustrate the purpose of God leading even to the end of days, or to the imminent eschaton.

Yahweh is both universal (Lord of history and nature) and particular (the God of Israel). However, his redemptive acts are not confined to his own people. In chapter 55 he concludes that all nations are to be included in the covenant relationship with God.

Throughout his poems there appears the figure of the "servant of the Lord." Is this a person? The balance of evidence favors that it is a reference to Israel rather than an individual. More important,

90

however, than who the servant is, is the nature of the servant's task or mission. The servant poems need to be read in light of the poet/prophet's whole view of the End Times. Israel was fashioned in the womb to be Yahweh's chosen child. She was called to be a servant. She has been charged with bringing judgment to the nations. She is appointed to be God's witness—that all people will know he is the one God. She is the light of the nations, so God's salvation will reach the ends of the earth. (Isa. 44:6). Through her, all nations will be forgiven and redeemed. Above all, the servant will be a vicarious sufferer for the transgressions of the nations. Yet despite this, the ultimate vindication of the servant nation will be exalted. This is not to assume that God was punishing the servant or taking out on him punishment that was due another, but rather that God identified with or was involved in the servant's voluntary pain and sacrifice. [*As will be seen in Part II, this theme (especially in Isa. 53) was picked up and applied, very quickly after his death, to Jesus of Nazareth.*]

Ezra-Nehemiah [circa 425 B.C.E.]

These are two books in the Old Testament, although they were originally known as 1–2 Esdras. 1 Esdras was Ezra and 2 Esdras was Nehemiah. [Not to be confused, the apocryphal writings Esdras I and II, originally were Esdras III and IV.] Ezra was a Jewish priest during the period of the Babylonian Exile (587–539 B.C.E.). A contemporary of Ezra, Nehemiah was a Jew who had amassed a considerable fortune in Susa and was known to the king of Persia.

In 539, Cyrus, the tolerant Persian (Iranian) king defeated the Babylonians and issued a decree permitting Jews to return to Jerusalem. Many did return but many remained in Babylonia where they had begun to prosper. [*The term Diaspora (from dispersed) originated from this period: Jews that live and have roots other than in or near Jerusalem.*] Nehemiah had heard that the city of Jerusalem was still in wretched condition, without strong city walls and gates. About 450 B.C.E., Nehemiah approached the Persian King Artaxerxes I (465–424 B.C.E.) for help, and became governor of Judaea, with guarantees of safe conduct and letters instructing the Persian authorities in Syria to provide the necessary materials for the city's reconstruction. About the same time, Ezra was allowed to return to Jerusalem with an edict from Artaxerxes to rehabilitate the temple and the religious life of the people of Jerusalem.

Ezra the priest and Nehemiah the layman achieved the reconstruction of Jerusalem's walls and the temple. Their reforms, designed to revitalize Judaism, were very influential from this time until the temple was severely damaged during the Maccabean revolt in 165 B.C.E. and then totally destroyed under Roman rule in 70 C.E. Under Ezra and Nehemiah were found the elements of reform, ritual, and religious education. Together they sought to purify the race by having men divorce non-Jewish wives, return to strict obedience of the Book of the Law (Deuteronomy), revive the Feast of Booths, and reestablish the ecclesiastical art in ritual. All of this furthered the rise of the synagogue, the rise of the rabbinate in Judaism (following the professional scribes), and ultimately the Sanhedrin, with its powerful judicial prerogatives.

The Priestly Writings [circa 400 B.C.E.]

The Priestly Code is a concise, dogmatic history of God's organization of his holy congregation through Moses, and his establishment in Canaan through Joshua. It was written by priests in Jerusalem about 450 B.C.E., perhaps as a part of the reforms of Ezra and Nehemiah. The writings are imbued with an atmosphere of worship—the holiness and majesty of God. There are no dramatic narratives about human affairs, but rather *torah* (or instruction) about how God should be worshipped—a *how* that was truly understood only by the priests of Jerusalem. It was as if the whole life of the nation of Israel was to be a continuous scripted worship service of God.

Ritual legislation is the essential part of P—designed to ensure the Jews could maintain their identity as God's own people, even though they were without a state and country of their own. Many of these codified laws and rituals appear in what is called the Holiness Code (Lev. 17–26). The bulk of Leviticus, Numbers, and edits throughout the Pentateuch comprise the P writings. For example, the P writers added the second account of Creation—the story of the six days of Creation—in order to emphasize the seventh day, the Sabbath, which was crucial for the survival of the synagogue (Gen. 1:1–2:4).

Wisdom Literature

A description of biblical writings that include Proverbs, Job, Ecclesiastes, and sometimes the Song of Songs. Most scholars believe much of this writing occurred during the Post Exilic period.

Although we think of the Greeks when it comes to philosophy (literally: "love of wisdom"), they didn't "own" the emphasis on wisdom. The wisdom movement was international. It was a key in the cultures of the Eastern nations of the Old Testament—the Fertile Crescent and Egypt. "It is no exaggeration to say that wisdom literature was the noblest monument of Egyptian culture."[12] Babylonian wisdom literature was popular, e.g., the Babylonian Book of Proverbs, or the poem of the Righteous Sufferer (commonly referred to as "The Babylonian Job"). Fragments of the Elephantine Papyri, written by Egyptian Jews in the 5th century B.C.E., contained portions of the "Wisdom of Ahikar" of Babylonian origin.

The Wisdom Literature of the Old Testament stands out from the rest of the Books. All the historical narratives as well as the prophets are marked by an unswerving awareness of the unique history of Israel: Yahweh is the God of Israel; Israel is the people of Yahweh. In the Wisdom Literature these distinctive themes are lacking. In fact, during the Council at Jamnia (in 90 C.E.), when the Jewish Scriptures were completely finalized, there were intense arguments that the Books of Ecclesiastes, Song of Songs, and Esther be excluded from the canon.

Wise men had always been a part of Israel's life, but not as distinct as prophets or priests. Sprinkled throughout the historical narratives and the writings of the prophets are references to wise men/women or sages. But in Israel's view, wisdom or insight didn't come as a function of maturity or observance of human behavior. Israel believed that God granted the wise man wisdom, as he did his "word" to the prophet and the Torah to the priest.

Job is the greatest monument to Wisdom Literature in the Old Testament. Job is a god-fearing, good man. He is tested by God because one of God's Heavenly Council suspects his sincerity. The doubter is called The Satan (The Adversary). *The Satan is an angel whose responsibility is to investigate affairs on earth. The term "Satan" is not a proper name, like Donald, for instance.* Job undergoes trial after test after trial but is finally restored by God and lives happily ever after. Scholars cannot really date Job—any time between 600–200 B.C.E. can be defended. The hero, Job, is an Edamite, not an Israelite, and there are peculiarities in the language used. It was an old oral story, to be sure, before it was reduced to written form. Ezekiel mentions Job (Ezek. 28:1–8) and Daniel as legendary wise and righteous men. We know from the Ras Shamra texts (discovered in 1929 and dated to about 1300 B.C.E.) that Daniel was a celebrated Canaanite legend. The Babylonians also had a similar story, The Righteous Sufferer. Like our Job, the hero of the Babylonian poem was very wealthy, was stricken with illness and trouble, complained his prayers were unheard, protested his innocence, and insisted that the will of his God was beyond understanding.

Wisdom Literature became regarded as being in a "class of its own," and that is exactly how the Hebrews treated it. As the canon of the Jewish Scriptures was finalized, the Scriptures were separated into three parts: the Torah, the Prophets, and the Writings. The Writings include the Wisdom Literature. In fact, several books that were argued to be included in the Scriptures at the Council of Jamnia were the "Wisdom of Solomon" and "Ecclesiasticus: The Wisdom of ben Sira." Although not included in the final canon of Jewish Scripture, they remain part of the Apocrypha and are still included as such in the Roman Catholic Old Testament.

The Psalms are also considered part of the Wisdom Literature. Although they are very personal statements, they are poems and hymns that were recited at public events. Like many Christian hymns, they were initially poems that were later set to music. I have always considered them as personal affirmations, meditations, or prayers.

Apocalyptic Literature

This is a group of writings that includes the Old Testament's Book of Daniel (circa 200 B.C.E.) and many of the writings found in the Apocrypha. Embryonic seeds of apocalyptic literature (writings about the end of times) can be found with the prophets themselves. Its growth, following the Exile, represented a deepening of Israel's prophetic consciousness in the light of the destruction of the nation and the bleak years that followed. Most Old Testament apocalyptic writings were influenced by imagery drawn from mythology and from the Babylonian and Persian (Iranian) influences of dualism, demonism, and angelology. Growing Hellenistic or Greek philosophical concepts (immortality of the soul, for example) augmented this Persian imagery. Apocalyptic literature abounds with bizarre visions, strange symbolism, and all sorts of supernatural happenings.

For example, Daniel paints the imminent coming of the Kingdom of God as: He "shatters the great image of the four beasts," which represent the four pagan empires of Babylonia, Media, Persia, and Greece (Dan. 7:17–18). Israel is represented by the "son of man" or by the "saints of the most high." For Daniel, Israel itself is a messianic community performing the function of a messiah for Yahweh.

The central theme of apocalyptic literature is God's revelation concerning the end of times—the time when God's kingdom will come. Yahweh's work is in history and it is purposeful. History is not simply spinning in circles, like the cycle of seasons. Nor is history ruled by blind Fate. Israel understood her life was involved in a great drama, which God would direct to the conclusion of his choice. Beyond the terror from the Day of Judgment there would be the dawning of a new era. In these last days, said the apocalyptic prophets, the schism of the Davidic Monarchy would be mended, blessings of fertility would be poured out abundantly, nations would beat their swords into plows, lions would lie down with lambs, and the wilderness would blossom. *Stirring imagery, such as I remember from Martin Luther King's "I Have a Dream" speech on the steps of the Lincoln Memorial.*

But the prophets didn't speculate on the coming New Age. Their concern was with the future as it influenced the possibilities of the present. The coming Kingdom would work within mankind—a new heart, a new covenant, a new people transformed from the inside out. They did not expect that the course of human affairs would come to an end. Rather they envisioned the course of Israel's rebellious history would be ended. When that occurred, Israel would be in the Kingdom of God—under Yahweh's sovereign rule—as the covenant had envisioned from the beginning.

Donald L. O'Dell

Chapter 4 Notes

[9] Muilenburg, *Interpreter's Bible, Volume 1*, p 326
[10] Ibid.
[11] Ibid., p 329
[12] Anderson, Understanding the Old Testament, p 465

Chapter 5

Old Testament Themes to Remember

We began Part I with a summarized version of the history of Israel from the book by Bernhard W. Anderson, *Understanding the Old Testament*. Now we can witness how that initial tribal and patriarchal clan religion was always rooted in its unfolding history, as recorded in one of the oldest recitations in the Old Testament. It is describing the old cultic ritual of the first fruits. It is found in Deuteronomy 26:5–9:

> "A wandering Aramean [Jacob] was my father; and he went down into Egypt and sojourned there, few in number; and there he became a nation, great, mighty, and populous. And the Egyptians treated us harshly, and afflicted us, and laid upon us hard bondage. Then we cried to the Lord the God of our fathers, and the Lord heard our voice, and saw our affliction, our toil, and our oppression; and the Lord brought us out of Egypt with a mighty hand and an outstretched arm, with great terror, with signs and wonders; and he brought us into this place and gave us this land, a land flowing with milk and honey." (*New English Bible*)

The Role of History in Israel's Faith

The Hebrews could not conceive of their history without thinking of their God. Neither could they conceive of their God without thinking of their history. The history that revealed God *was* the religion of Israel. From this collection of tribal roots came a loose cultic confederation of related tribes. During the Exodus they were forged into an idea of one people under one common God. God's name was YHWH. That is their history. That is their religion.

In that gray area between the reporting of the history and the interpreting of that history the Israelites came to define (and redefine) God, as well as define (and redefine) themselves. The Old Testament account concerns the revelation of God—but it is in the concrete affairs and relationships of people that God makes himself known. God is not an abstract idea, some primeval "first cause" consisting of abstract ideas about him. The faith of the Old Testament is fundamentally historical in nature. Old Testament doctrines are events and historical realities—not abstract values and ideas existing in some sort of timeless realm. God's revelation did not come like a bolt out of the blue. It came through the crises and affairs of human life, interactions with other cultures, and the persons who perceived the divine dimension in those events. For example, no external historical study can demonstrate that the Exodus was an act of God. But to Israel, the "political" event was the medium through which God's presence and purpose were disclosed.

It was wonderful. Then the Monarchy collapsed, the idea of an eternally loved and protected Israel collapsed, and the people of Israel were very confused and bewildered.

The Codification of Sacrifice, Worship, and Identity

We've seen the Hebrews' concept of God evolve from an institutionalized, tribal reward and punishment to a prophetic call for an inward, personal righteousness. We saw how the Hebrews flowed back and forth between these two ideas as their history unfolded. After the shock of the Exile and the loss of the temple, the concept of God retreated back to a (albeit more sophisticated) form of tribal reward and punishment. We saw how, after the fall of the southern kingdom, this retreat was compounded by the growth of a professional priesthood and the beginnings of rabbinic traditions. Now there were institutional reasons to begin resisting change and castigating those that disagreed with the powers that were. The same thing happened again after the Maccabean Revolt.

As we will see in the development of the New Testament, there were institutional or political forces that began to dictate what writings were included or excluded from the canon. In the development of the Old Testament, that was not as apparent. Since the Israelites were so rooted in the connection between their knowledge of Yahweh and their history, they simply edited (or re-edited) existing texts to reflect whatever were their current thoughts. Sometimes they simply rewrote something and let it stand beside the previous account, e.g., the two Books, 1 and 2 Chronicles (circa 350 B.C.E.) constitute a priest-like version of 1 and 2 Kings (circa 750 B.C.E.); the priestly account of Creation (Gen. 1:1-2:3) was simply inserted prior to the Yahwist's account of Creation (Gen. 2:4-25).

The Yahwist wrote about the temptation of mankind—mankind, represented by Adam and Eve, wanted to be as right as they believed God thought he was right. If we can only practice harder and better on our rites of purification and our rituals of sacrifice, then God will smile on us again. After the fall of Judah the same desires to "get it right" were reignited—but this time with a twist: Those desires to know what made God tick, and therefore what would get him back on their side, were wedded with a newly emerging priestly class. The result? A straitlaced legalistic approach to pacifying Yahweh in order to regain his favor. A respite for a while and then the Revolt of the Maccabees, and it started all over again. This influence was still in effect when Jesus castigated the money-changers at the temple some 175 years later.

The schism happened and the idyllic Davidic Monarchy was to be no more. Then the northern kingdom of Israel fell, the southern kingdom of Judah fell, the Exile was endured, and the rebellion of the Maccabees over the forced influence of Hellenism came and went. In these repeating atmospheres of fear, doubt and confusion, two things kept popping up over and over.

- ### *The Danger of Ritualized Righteousness*

  The repeated desire to "go back" to a more familiar, more "cut-and-dried" form of religion—the certainty of a simple reward-and-punishment approach in dealing with Yahweh. But the prophets kept telling us: Righteousness or faithfulness is not a question of saying the correct prayer or offering the correct sacrifice at the correct time while wearing the correct clothes. In twenty-first-century terms: It's not a question of supporting the perceived "correct" things—America, free enterprise, prayer in school, constitutional amendments for the definition of a marriage—in order to defend God's honor. It's not a question of condemning the perceived "correct" things— gays, nudity, abortion, stem cell research, communism, right-to-die advocates. God doesn't care about your causes. He wants your heart and mind and attitude, the prophets told us. All along, the prophets kept telling Israel: God doesn't want ritual. He wants in your heart his sense of justice for the little guy.

But at the time, most of the people didn't listen.

- ### *The Danger of Exclusivity*

The desire to build cultural and spiritual walls around themselves—designed to keep outsiders "out" and to keep the "favored" people "in." That way Yahweh couldn't miss where he was to impart his blessings. He would always know where to find his people: Look for those that are circumcised; look for those that honor me with their tithes and first fruits; look for those that can invoke the Torah; look for those that wouldn't miss a festival at the temple if their lives depended on it. Of course, the prophets were telling the Hebrews that Yahweh wasn't looking for those things. He was looking for those that … do justly, and love mercy, and walk humbly with him.

But that could be anyone! Precisely!

Yahweh is interested in all his creation and he wants to use Israel to touch all of his creation with loving kindness, justice, and mercy. He cannot do that if Israel is cutting herself off from the world by making herself an exclusive club—a gated community— of those loved by God.

But at the time, most of the people didn't listen. We still aren't listening. We're still focusing on the wrong people: him, her, them. We need to focus on ourselves. Look in a mirror. There's your problem. That's what God wants to fix. A church that focuses on the "evil" world "out there" is missing the point. A sermon that deals with the evils of drugs and prostitution, for example, is appropriate if the congregation is full of drug dealers and prostitutes. If that's not who's sitting in the pews, then that's not appropriate. If the sermon is dealing with immoral, power-driven political officials and the horrors of Hollywood movies, then it's appropriate if there are politicians and movie producers in the congregation. If the congregation is full of just "plain old ordinary folks," then the sermon perhaps should be focused on greed, on the habit of making ethical and political decisions based on one's pocketbook, on the hypocrisy of criticizing people who seem not to stand up for their moral beliefs while you hold on to your job because if you really stood up, you fear you'd be fired, on the motive or intention behind an act, or on the inability of most of us to take full responsibility for the consequences of our actions because we are certain that someone else must be at fault.

We must always remember the prophets weren't preaching to the "evil" enemy "out there": the Canaanites or the Philistines. They were preaching most often to the religious leaders and congregations of churchgoers of their day.

A congregation that is trying to grow so that they can create their own little universe—with schools and nurseries, a social environment for everybody (preteens, teens, young adults, singles, 30-plusers), continuing education, counseling—why would any member need to go anywhere else for anything (except maybe the grocery store, auto repair, and a medical facility)—is missing the point. To be the People of God doesn't mean we're to create and live in a "bubble-boy" environment. The world out there isn't evil. God made it and he pronounced it good. To focus on the evil world "out there" and preach about all the sinners "out there" and be really glad we're "in here," feeling as spiritually snug as a bug in a rug, is to miss the point in a terribly big, important way.

In Part II we'll see many of these same issues continuing through the New Testament. The early Church made these same mistakes—with more disturbing results—during the first four hundred years of the first millennium of the Common Era.

I love the Old Testament. Something magical, mystical, long lasting, and divine occurred during all this. The events in Israel's history are the roots of three of the still-existing world religions: Judaism, Christianity, and Islam. That's a fact that you cannot afford to take lightly. There was no Old Testament at the time of Jesus. To Jesus and his followers the Old Testament was known simply as "The Scriptures."

We now understand a little about the Yahwist, the Elohist, the Deuteronomic Reformers, and the Priestly editors (J, E, D, and P). We understand the prophets and their message of rebuke to those priestly elements who wanted to be as powerful as God by controlling the knowledge of good and evil. When it comes to the actual writings of the Old Testament, we understand that God didn't telepathically fax these words to men. However, please do not let that over-influence your opinion about what did happen during the history of the Old Testament. God's spirit did work through the evolution of the history of these wandering Habiru people. Their knowledge of him initially was that he was a small, tribal, cultic god working in the pure arena of reward and punishment. To the early patriarchal Hebrews, like their Bronze-Age neighbors, this made perfectly good sense.

But somehow there was always a "personalness" to these patriarchal clan gods of the wandering Habiru; their sense of history and their sense of the oneness and universal nature of Yahweh cannot be explained nor can it be explained away.

That sense of "personalness" grew and matured as the centuries and collective experiences of the Hebrews continued to unfold. It was always in their history that they knew God, and as they matured as a people, their understanding of God matured and ripened. Until, by the time of the prophets, the idea of a personal sense of righteousness began to surface and challenge the national consciousness of ritual sacrifice and worship and a sense of exclusionism.

If one of these prophets were here today, we could imagine, rather easily, hearing him think out loud:

"Maybe it isn't about having all the right laws, temple festivals, elaborate rituals of sacrifice and food, and wedding customs. It isn't about supporting all the "right" causes or condemning all the "wrong" causes. Maybe it's about having the right heart—wanting people to see the love of God in me while seeing God in them. Not codified national morals, but honest, upright people who'll do the right thing (the God thing) even if nobody's looking. Maybe that's what Yahweh really wants.

"Maybe he wants you to concentrate on a sense of righteousness and justice that you have determined is right for you and your situation. Your "job," then, is to live up to those standards you have established for yourself. Your "religion" is to pray for continued guidance concerning your standards, to pray for forgiveness when you have failed, and to pray for strength when you feel like quitting. Your "job" is not to spend your energy trying to convince others that what you have determined to be right for you is the only way to be right. Your "job" is not to be the judgmental watchdog for Yahweh—condemning those you have determined do not live up to the sense of rightness you have established for yourself. Your "job" is simply to encourage others to discover the right solutions for themselves.

"If people ask you, then tell them: *'I have witnessed the power, mercy, and love of Yahweh in my life and it has made such a difference in me! I no longer do "x." I no longer believe "y." As a result, I find myself condemning less and judging less and praising more. I find that there are fewer and fewer "fall on my sword" issues for me. My anxiety level is down. My impulses are more under control. I am no longer buffeted about by my feelings. You know what I think? You need to find the same kinds of right solutions for yourself as I have for myself. It'll make all the difference in the world. I can attest it has for me.'* "

If we continue to make codified laws and use our norms and causes as proof of our goodness to God, maybe we'd be making the same mistake as wanting to eat of the forbidden tree—wanting to be as good as God, beating God at his own game, wanting to find ways to trap him into pronouncing us good and faithful servants so he'd have to bless us because we went through all the right steps—the steps, when we think about it, we created for ourselves and attributed to him.

Hmmm.

That's the Old Testament. At the time of the prophets, most of the people didn't listen.

Part 2

The Development of the New Testament

Introduction to Part 2

𝔉rom the time I was approaching junior high school (they didn't have middle schools then), I can remember wondering about historical oddities in the New Testament. They were simply little flitting ideas that would pop into my head, spin around a few moments, and then pop out. I paid these small notions no real matter, but they never really left me. They were generally things like:

- If all Jesus' disciples, family, and friends fled the scene after his arrest, then how did the Gospel writers know what was said between Jesus and Pilate, between the High Priest and Pilate, or between Jesus and the High Priest? If this wasn't a newspaper reporter's account of history, then what was it? Who "created" the reported dialogue? Why?

- I could understand and accept little differences between the Gospel accounts of Jesus' activities, miracles, and speeches or sermons. When I raised a discrepancy, it was generally explained to me as being the same as three different people having three slightly different accounts of a two-car accident they all witnessed. Fine. However, that didn't explain big differences like Mark's and John's account of the Last Supper. Mark's account was rather straightforward. John's account had Jesus making very long-winded speeches. To me that was like having the three witnesses describe the same accident as (1) between two cars, (2) between a car and a bus, and (3) between a bus and a train. It just didn't make any sense.

- I wondered where all these other congregations came from. I wondered who thought up the idea of having Deacons (*diakonoi*), Elders (*presbyteroi*), or Bishops (*episkopoi*). They were just—all of a sudden—there in Rome, Antioch, and other places. They weren't, however, in or around Jerusalem. James, the brother of Jesus, Phillip, Timothy, Stephen, Barnabas, and others were sometimes called Evangelists, but they weren't called Deacons, Elders, or Bishops. What was the real story here?

- I never understood why the High Priests, Sadducees, or Pharisees didn't show up at Bethlehem. If the birth of the Messiah in Bethlehem was such a well-known prophecy of Micah—known well enough that shepherds were aware—then why weren't the Jewish scholars there? If the star was so visible that magi (wise men) from Persia (Iran) came to witness it, why weren't the local Jewish scholars and religious community there? It simply didn't make any sense to me then.

After all these years, after seminary, and after reading such scholarly authors as Armstrong, Crossan, Mack, Pagels, and Spong, just to name a few, a general, realistic picture of what happened before and following Jesus' death began to emerge.

Chapter 6

The Time of Jesus (4 B.C.E.–30 C.E.)

𝔚e left the discussion of the Old Testament following the Maccabean Revolt against Antiochus IV, which had begun as a way to assault the "culture creep" Greek influence was having on Judaism. Under Alexander the Great and his following Hellenistic dynasties in Syria, Greece, and Egypt, the influence of Hellenism was a significant cultural gale blowing through the Empire. The Greeks had established a new political form—city-states—throughout the Empire, e.g., Sepphoris and Caesarea in Palestine. The Greeks had literary traditions that went back to Homer (850 B.C.E.). They had drama and poetry. They had the significant philosophical schools of Plato, Socrates, Aristotle, as well as the Stoics and mathematicians. They had the concept of *collegia,* or small gatherings for intellectual or cultural discussions. Over three hundred years these cultural forces had changed the way the Western world worked.

The Romans, however, did bring law and order to the general populace, including Judaea or Palestine. Roads were safer to travel and people were thankful for that. However, the Jews in Palestine still did not like the very visible military presence of the Roman army, which often only reminded them of their additional taxes. The situation could be defined as stable but tense. As Mack put it: "Law and order are never enough to keep a people dancing."[13]

People had been moving to cities, and because of the concept of the Greek city-state (the *polis*), the cultural, political, and economic impact of cities was increasingly important. No longer simply a bigger marketplace or a more defensive position against

107

marauding enemies, they became places with their own culture-in-microcosm that people could relate to and identify with. These city-states were becoming exceedingly multicultural. Ideas between groups flowed as freely as water.

The question on everyone's mind was: "How do I keep my particular culture, my ethnic roots, alive and still function in this cross-cultural world I live in?"

People enjoyed the cultural freedom, but it also posed a threat to their "old" identity. Just as Paul, discussed later, railed against homosexuality, we must understand that he did so because it was a symbol of Greco-Roman encroachment and much of its accompanying hedonism. Prostitution, both female and male, and homosexuality were quite common among the top one percent of the population, the landed gentry, if you will. They were the only segment of the people who had the time and money to indulge themselves. It was a terrible affront to the moral Greco-Roman family man as well as to the pious Jew. It was enjoyment for enjoyment's sake—hedonism—something only available to the "idle rich." Additionally, there certainly was an aspect of the Greek culture that adored the beauty of the human body, both male and female, and the cultural/sexual reverberations that went with that. Just as there are "meat markets" (gay and heterosexual) in our society that are shunned by many in both the gay and straight communities, that form of hedonism existed in the Greek culture as well. Paul railed against that. He was not railing against a gay or lesbian lifestyle, with commitment, nurturing, caring—albeit between same-sex partners. That lifestyle was generally unheard of in the first century. It basically didn't exist. It was simply unaffordable, thus undoable, for 99 percent of the populace.

Homosexuality had been feared by the Israelites—not so much because it was a sin against God, but because it was a threat to their idea of eternal life through the ancestry of their loins. The same kind of "threat" could be said for Greco-Roman laws that governed marriage; divorce; the cultural significance of foods, festivals, and family meals; the public role of women; attire; and attendance at public baths and athletic events. We can see this same kind of threat when we look at the great influx of immigrants to American cities like Boston, New York City, and Philadelphia. Immigrants had "quarters" that were identified with them and they could identify with: Italians, Polish, and Irish. Normally, local ethnic churches maintained the "native" customs—foods, dress, language, piety, honor, social ranking, festivals, and lifestyles in general. It doesn't take much to imagine a nineteenth-century Lutheran minister in New York, when reminiscing about the wonderful "ways" of the rural "old country," railing against the loose, disrespectful, materialistic, sinful ways of this "new world." This was the context of much of Paul's exhortations to his congregations, as he was desperately trying to maintain his authority. Besides, Paul thought the world was going to end quite soon, so sexual abstinence, foregoing marriage, and other "hardships" would be bearable.

Searching for an identity

In Alexandria, Egypt, there were distinct districts for Egyptians, Cyprians, Jews, Syrians, and Greeks. People gravitated to associations as a way to keep their culture alive. These associations created a smaller, more familiar social unit within the larger multicultural society. Associations were organized around varying focuses: ethnic fellowship, common craft guilds, mystery clubs, protecting religious shrines, preserving cultural traditions, and intellectual discussion groups. The Greeks had fellowships (*koinoniai)* or clubs *(collegia).* The Jews had developed associations around a "house of prayer" during the Temple-less Exile. These became known as a "gathering place" *(synagogue)* and buildings were built to serve as educational, religious, and social centers. Eventually, Christians would find these associations a perfect vehicle for themselves as well. They referred to them as assemblies or churches (*ecclesia*).

For many intellectuals, regardless of nationality, the imposition of Roman "order" on the overall Hellenistic culture, especially the city-state, had a very muted effect. It simply took the wind out of the sails of the city-state. The *polis* simply became another multicultural town. It had its multicultural aura and its safety and its marketplace, but it had lost that sense of belonging, that sense of "my hometown." Pervaded with this sterile sense of the Roman presence in the form of law and order (the *pax romana*), people began wanting to see their world as a whole again. Each culture had had this—once: A world-view that integrated their concepts of their universe, their gods, their national government, their communities, their festivals, and their sense of belonging as individuals. The Jews had it, of course, but so did the Egyptians and the Greeks. Where was that now? Certainly they could catch glimpses of their cultural heritage in the local "quarter" of their town. But that wasn't the same.

Plato's myth of the Creation was well known and popular: The world was made by a divine craftsman who was executing construction plans from the most-high god. Plutarch used this myth in an attempt to integrate the stories of Isis and Osiris. Jews referred to this Platonic ideal in trying to determine how the world got to be so bad since it was God's wisdom that had planned it. Using either the schools of Greek philosophy or cultic national epics—like those of Israel—philosophers of all ilks pursued the goal of finding an integrated social-political anthropology. "Three factors immediately came to the surface, and the attempt to understand them exercised the best minds in all of the school traditions struggling to revise their conceptual grasp of the world: (1) how to define law, (2) how to understand political power, and (3) how to describe personal virtue."[14]

Law was fundamental to the Hellenistic *polis*, to the Jewish Temple-state, and to the Roman labyrinth of courts and governance. For the Greeks, law meant an accepted standard of legality and social rightness—determined by debate and consensus. Just because one was legally right, however, didn't mean that one was virtuous. To the Jew the law was divine and was, in essence, a commandment from above. It was not legislated. To live by the law was synonymous with being righteous. The law for Romans was very practical. It came from the emperor, was ratified by the Senate, but was under constant judgment in terms of its effectiveness. If it maintained peace and orderliness, then it was good. If it didn't, then it was changed or scrapped.

Power was eventually described as being exercised by the perfect king. The Jews had images of Yahweh and specific references in the Scriptures referring to David and Solomon. Basically, no one really wanted the perfect king nor expected one. They believed that a universal description of such a ruler would be helpful in determining who might be a "good" king or a "bad" king. Additionally, "good" kings would allow themselves to be chastised against this image of the perfect king. "Bad" kings wouldn't allow themselves to be chastised. They would be tyrants.

As for personal virtue, real cultural differences arose. Many cultures, including the Greeks, had no problem with a concept of personal virtue. Personal virtue was the result of right living and was an individual responsibility. For Semitic peoples, like the Jews, the concept of individual virtue was foreign. An individual "sense" of virtue was simply a reflection of the "sense" of belonging to a people. It was the tribe/the clan/the people that was an important social unit and their social anthropology reflected that. A call for virtuous living would have been a call to a new kingdom or a call for a renewal within an old kingdom, rather than a call simply for some form of renewed personal piety.

Jewish scholars were able to revisit the old Jewish Epics—of Adam, Noah, and Abraham—and see universal inclusion there of all mankind. For example: "Adam" literally meant humankind in Hebrew, Noah's sign of the rainbow was for all of humanity, Abraham's covenant was long before there were any "specifically Jewish" laws given to Moses. This kind of approach allowed Jews to maintain their sense of exclusiveness, but at the same time recognize certain inclusiveness in their new multicultural world. Philo Judaeus (30 B.C.E.–45 C.E..), a Jewish philosopher from Alexandria, made a major effort to interpret Mosaic Law in ways Gentiles could understand. He hoped they would comprehend, appreciate, and personally adopt the Law for themselves.

Gentiles fascinated with Judaism

As a result of all these thoughts and movements, non-Jews (sometimes referred to as Greeks, sometimes as Gentiles) in the Diaspora became fascinated with the Jewish Epics and did study, discuss, honor the one God, Yahweh, and begin to adopt the high ethical standards of Judaism. Often a Gentile would attend the synagogue, go home with a Jewish friend, eat, and talk. The question of whether Gentiles could actually become "full-fledged" Jews was a great topic of debate. They would have to be circumcised, maintain the strict kosher diets, pay a Temple tax, and participate in feasts and festivals. Some Jewish leaders said yes; others said no.

These kinds of debates were not occurring just at the great centers of the Greco-Roman world. They were occurring all over the empire. Galilee was no exception. It was a crossroads territory situated to the west of the sea that bore its name, and otherwise

111

surrounded by mountains. They had always been "an adjacent" people—almost an inland island people. They had never been a nation. No capital had ever been there. Invading kings, including Jewish ones, had come and gone. Empires had come and gone. Their cultural survivability, however, had remained. They would pay the proper "lip service" to the ruling monarch, mind their own business, and find ways to protect themselves from the "long arm" of the ruling/taxing authority. They had plenty of annual rainfall and had developed an agricultural economy that allowed them to be self-sufficient. The Sea of Galilee (a.k.a. Lake of Genneseret) maintained a rather tropical climate which, along with hot springs around Tiberias, made it an attractive health resort and vacation destination. It was a "nice place to visit." It was an easy place to visit. Two main north-south highways, one near the Mediterranean and the other near the Sea of Galilee, traversed the territory. It was a cultural and commercial crossroad.

During the three hundred plus years of the Hellenistic period, Galilee was introduced to Greek philosophy, language, education, and art. Greek city-states were founded there. Along with the cities came Greek schools, forums, gymnasia, theatres, and political institutions. In fact there were twelve Greek cities (among them Sepphoris, Tiberias, Caesarea, Bethsaida, and Caesarea Philippi) within a twenty-five-mile radius of Nazareth.

This was the Galilee of Jesus.

The Maccabees ruled (165–63 B.C.E.) through an inherited line of high priest/kings known as the Hasmonean Dynasty. These Hasmonean leaders had moved into Hellenistic palaces, the high priests ruled like tyrants, and the Hasmonean armies of liberation became soldiers of conquest as far as Judah's neighbors were concerned. Trying to recapture the "look and feel" of the times of David and Solomon, the "anointed ones" governed a Temple-state, and it did not go well for these Maccabean leaders.

The Hasmonean Dynasty

Besides the flagrant behavior of the priests, one of the problems was that Judaea wasn't simply Jewish anymore. There were Samaritans, Galileans, and Idumeans, all of which had their local shrines and traditions. Finally, the Jewish Hasmoneans had reclaimed (i.e., conquered) most of the lands held by the Solomon

Empire—the lands only, however, not the loyalty of the people. For example, the Idumeans, who lived immediately south of Judaea, were forced to be circumcised. Temple taxes were imposed, in many ways more harshly than they had been under the Alexandrian Seleucids of Syria.

It has been usual to think of the Maccabean, or Hasmonean, Dynasty as "Camelot revisited" in terms of the Second Temple revival in the face of the Hellenistic threat to Jewish religion and culture. But continued internal squabbles, corruption, and the unrest of the population led, finally, to capitulation. Pompey, taking advantage of the general civil unrest, marched his Roman army to Syria. The Seleucids immediately handed over Jerusalem. Syria-Palestine became a Roman province.

The Romans separated the rule of high priest/king. Following Herod the Great (ruled 37-4 B.C.E.), Palestine was carved into provinces ruled by tetrarchs, with Judaea becoming a Roman procuratorship. The priests, appointed by Roman rule, were supposed to keep the Temple system going and keep the unrest under control. Rome was already beginning to feel a bit stretched. The prevailing attitude of the Roman rulers was to keep the Temple system functioning in Jerusalem for the Jews. They were very conscious of the high ethical standards of the Jews and respected them for it. Consequently, they allowed the Jews to remain autonomous in their religious beliefs within the Roman Empire. The only small requirement was that the Jews must begin Temple ceremonies with a small prayer for their temporal Roman leaders. The Sadducees allowed for that with little problem. The Romans understood that Judaism kept the basic structure for economic and political stability in Palestine. The Romans, however, were always the ones in control. The Hasmoneans were only puppets. But the general population could see through that and the priests were losing the respect of the people.

General unrest and the fall of Jerusalem

By the time of Jesus, the high priest's council—the Sanhedrin—no longer presided over a true Temple/state but over a network of scribal stations concerned only with cultic matters. Sects were beginning to form again in Jerusalem, enforcing some form of the "sense" of Judaism and national pride. Quite a few of the priestly families in and around Jerusalem left to establish the

Essene Community at Qumran, the site where the Dead Sea scrolls were discovered in 1947. The Pharisees (the *Separatists*) became more politically active and developed their own "more pure" schools of thought on matters of ethics and piety based on the Law of Moses and their growing collection of oral interpretations. This movement was based in part on the priestly reforms of the Ezra-Nehemiah era some four hundred years earlier. This was in direct opposition to the Hasmonean tendency to continue to accommodate Hellenistic practices and Roman rule and thought that was such an affront to the devout Jew.

Though disappointed and frustrated at their priestly leaders, the general populace thoroughly detested Roman rule. About a decade after Jesus' death a widespread famine engulfed the region (circa 40s C.E.). Frustrations and anger were fueled among the populace. Banditry ensued, as did small rebellions. Some rebellions erupted that were aimed at the Temple itself. The wealthy were plundered and the high priest was driven out of town.

These kinds of events were disturbing to the Roman protectorate. Judaism had long been considered a "favored" religion since the time of the Greek's dominance. Both they and the Romans honored the Jewish concept of justice for the "little guy" as well as the Jewish code of personal ethics. The poor, diseased, and unfortunate were accounted for by the Temple-state system of Judaism. This Jewish system of governance was in place for Judaea and it was left pretty much alone. *This became especially important in the decades of the fifties and sixties. The early Christian sect was considered to be simply a "branch" of Judaism and, as such, enjoyed the status afforded the Jews. As the Christian sect became distinctly different from Judaism, they lost their "favored" status with the Roman government. Subsequent trials and persecutions over issues of loyalty and treason came to the fore. Individuals in the small Christian sect were constantly suspected of treason—of being disloyal to the throne of Rome. Leaders of the embryonic Christian sect were sometimes persecuted as a result. For example, this attitude of loyalty led Nero to "blame" the small Christian sect for the fire in Rome (64 C.E.), which he, himself, had started as an attempt at "urban renewal." Rumored stories of the deaths of Paul and Peter occurred during this time. Several years earlier the Hasmoneans, in collaboration with the priestly class, were able to eliminate*

James, the brother of Jesus and head of the Jerusalem Christians, referred to by Paul as the "pillar of Jerusalem."

Anyone in the country at the time would have been aware of the influence of Rome, even though power was formally exercised via the servile Hasmoneans. As mentioned earlier, grating on the sense of Jewish nationalism was the system of collecting the imperial Roman taxes and the limitations of judicial rights and privileges. There always seemed to be a simmering head of steam or revolutionary spirit that lay just beneath the surface. Small sects of dedicated Jewish patriots—known collectively as Zealots—were attracted to Jesus from time to time. In Luke 6:15-16 there is a reference to Simon the Zealot. These Zealots, like members of a Jewish Nationalist Party that hearkened back to the days of the Maccabees, took every opportunity to disrupt and harass Rome any way they could.

Bands of Zealots and "Dagger-Men" formed in protest against this misrule. They vowed to kill any disloyal Jew. The Dagger-Men, for example, would mingle in street crowds, spot their "prey," stab them from behind, and then melt into the crowd. Well-to-do Hebrews counseled patience with Rome's misrule and plundering. The young and poorer elements of Judaism accused the well-to-do of connivance. These two factions divided the city and attacked each other. After a heated battle in 68 C.E. the wealthy faction was virtually destroyed. The winning side began marauding Greek towns outside Jerusalem, who in turn attacked other Jews. The general rebellion had become a full-fledged revolt.

Eventually, with the Roman army approaching to quell the rebellion, the rebels gathered in Jerusalem. In the pitched battle, tens of thousands of people were killed—many committing suicide by mercy killing each other rather than being captured. In 70 C.E. the Temple was burned to the ground and plundered for valuables.

The Jerusalem Council was gone. The Temple was gone, which meant the temple tax and treasury were gone, as well. The temple would never be rebuilt. Judaism became what we know of it today: a religion without a central shrine, without a dominant priesthood, and without a sacrificial service. However, the Diaspora synagogues were still thriving away from Jerusalem.

The Jewish Christians in Palestine, especially those around Jerusalem, had begun to flee. This was not their war. The

Jerusalem Christians, under a group referred to as the "pillars" that had been headed by James, the brother of Jesus (until his death), fled to the Transjordan. Many other groups fled to Pella and to Egypt. What influence they had had over the emerging collective groups of Christians throughout Hellenized Syria and Asia Minor was forfeited by reason of their flight. Even though this was not their fight, the loss of the Temple in Jerusalem affected them greatly. Many believed the end of the world was near. Many formed their own small but reclusive communities. The Johannine Community was one of these, as was the community in which Mark taught. The Matthean Community was attempting to revitalize their community through the marriage of Jesus' words and the Torah. The destruction of the Second Temple revival of the Hasmoneans gave birth to an unmistakable apocalyptic tone to the emerging literature of the reorganizing Jews as well as of the struggling new Jewish Christians.

It is imperative we remember the forty years from 30–70 C.E. were the last forty years of the Second Temple revival as well as the first forty years of fledgling Jewish Christians. It was a very turbulent time. Judaism thrashed about redefining itself, eventually settling into a reformed synagogue system, which had married the successful Diaspora synagogue with a revised Temple cultic ritual and theology. Most important, for our discussion, the Jewish Christian movement was forming itself out of these same Jewish people at the same time.

This was the state of the world into which Jesus was born.

Jesus of Nazareth

As the millennium changed, Jesus of Nazareth had been introduced to the world. The older time frames ended (B.C.E.) and the Common Era (C.E.) began. The biography of Jesus of Nazareth, as told in the four Gospels of the New Testament, is exceedingly sparse. He was born about 7–4 B.C.E. during the reign of Herod the Great. More than likely he was born in Nazareth, in Galilee, which was considered his hometown. Our knowledge of the typical Jewish family's social, educational, economic, and religious customs of the times allows us to make certain assumptions. He was of normal Mediterranean Jewish peasant stock, probably classified as an artisan since his father, Joseph, was a carpenter. Of his childhood, boyhood, youth, and early manhood, we know nothing. We have no knowledge how he came to know his moral and spiritual insight. From the time of his baptism until his death, only about two years (maybe even fewer) elapsed.

According to the Gospels of Mark and John, the earliest and one of the latest, accordingly, Jesus appears on the scene of human history at his baptism at the hands of John the Baptist, who was a typical "man of the desert" eating wild honey and locusts—a combination of prophet, wandering preacher, Zealot, and/or mystic. He would not have been an uncommon sight in the Jewish countryside.

The following description is from Flavius Josephus, *Jewish Antiquities*, 18.116–119, (circa 93 C.E.) as referenced by Crossan.[15] Herod Antipas had stolen his half-brother's wife, Herodias, and was subsequently defeated in battle by his father-in-law, Aretas.

"But to some of the Jews the destruction of Herod's army seemed to be divine vengeance, and certainly a just vengeance, for his treatment of John, surnamed the Baptist. For Herod had put him to death, though he was a good man and had exhorted the Jews to lead righteous lives, to practice justice towards their fellows and piety towards God, and so doing to join him in baptism. In his view this was a necessary preliminary if baptism was to be acceptable to God. They must not employ it to gain pardon for whatever sins they committed, but as a consecration of the body implying that the soul was already thoroughly cleansed by right behavior. When others, too, joined the crowds about him, because they were aroused to the highest degree by his sermons, Herod became alarmed. Eloquence that had so great an effect on mankind might lead to some form of sedition, for it looked as if they would be guided by John in everything they did. Herod decided therefore that it would be much better to strike first and be rid of him before his work led to an uprising, than to await for an upheaval, get involved in a difficult situation and see his mistake. Though John, because of Herod's suspicions was brought in chains to Machaerus ... and there put to death, yet the verdict of the Jews was that the destruction visited upon Herod's army was a vindication of John, since God saw fit to inflict such a blow on Herod."

Donald L. O'Dell

At this time the only place where Jews could offer sacrifices was in the Temple in Jerusalem. Adding up the travel, lost work time, and the sacrificial preparation, it was an expensive proposition for a typical peasant family. John's greatest legacy, perhaps, was that he offered a new, inexpensive, authorized rite—baptism—that was effective for the remission of all sins and consecrating their lives from that time forward. This was something the average person could do to get ready for the coming kingdom that John preached. Jesus' coming to John the Baptist and agreeing to be baptized enhanced both men and marked the beginning of Jesus' ministry.

Jesus gathered personal followers and several seemed closer than others—principally, two pairs of brothers: Peter and Andrew; and James and John. What may be regarded as a "standard" day's activity is described in Mark 1:21–38. There was some public speaking, friendly conversation, works of mercy, some private instruction, and personal prayer time. The constant theme of his message—sometimes in sayings, sometimes in parables, sometimes in works of healing and attending remarks—was to proclaim the "good news": *The Kingdom of God is at hand. Repent. Quit looking at the world 'out there' as the source of your problems or the source of your solutions. Look inside you. The Kingdom is already there and has always been there. The Kingdom is now, and now is always eternal. Just as leaven is invisible, yet changes the nature of dough, the Kingdom of God in your heart will change your perception of reality. This will change your world. What was important now isn't, and what wasn't now is. The first will become last and the last first. The exalted will be humbled and the humbled exalted. Your world will turn upside down. You need to recognize it, acknowledge it, and grow with it. I, myself, am involved with this Kingdom.*

Most of his sayings were short, punchy, almost cynical, and dealt mostly with the nature, laws, and possession of this Kingdom. It was almost as if he were challenging his listeners to a form of "counterculture" movement—a way individuals could maintain some sense of personal ethics in their very mixed-up, mixed-cultural world. He, as well as his message, was all about being transformed. His message was not about convincing people to believe in particular ideas about him in order to avoid the legal wrath of God the Father. His Kingdom analogies are about change and transformation, not about salvation.

Jesus and the Cynics

Many of his sayings bear similarity to those philosophical mainstays in the Greco-Roman world: the roving Cynic and/or Stoic. Known for his wit, quick thinking, and social commentary, the Greek Cynic (a noble philosophical profession) was able to engage in conversation with the learned, draw a crowd, and then— verbally—"bring blood." The crowds thought it very entertaining and, yet, they learned lessons about life or, for example, the weaknesses of some "official" political or religious position.

The following examples are from Burton Mack's discussion of Pronouncement Stories:[16]

- When asked why he ate with tax collectors and sinners, Jesus replied, "Those who are well have no need of a physician." (Mark 2:17)

- When censured for keeping bad company, Antisthenes [a Cynic] replied, "Well, physicians attend their patients without catching the fever."

- When asked why they ate with unclean hands, Jesus replied, "It is not what goes into a person, but what comes out that makes unclean." (Mark 7:15)

- When someone reproached him for frequenting unclean places, Diogenes [a Cynic] replied that the sun also enters the privies without becoming defiled.

Cynics were loosely connected to the Socratic tradition and were well known for their profession of social critique and honor, of a life lived well, simply, and naturally. To the Cynic all forms of conventional authority and social existence were under constant scrutiny. Their general ideal was to live simply, endure hardship, and, above all, don't do things simply because you believed that was what was expected. Jesus' use of parables, one-liners, and other clever responses is very similar to the Cynic's way with words.

Jesus' theme was of the Kingdom of God and his style often similar to the philosophical school of the Cynics. His message, however, was not an apocalyptic one—an end-of-the-world divine encounter. It was calling for an ideal society that was a viable alternative to living in the current Greco-Roman society. It was a reference to a way of life that God wanted and that could be undertaken at any time. It called for a people to recognize that God lived within them just as God lived within him. It called for people to change their behavior and change it now. It was a dare to live life differently and to live differently now. To live in this new Kingdom was to live with purpose in the midst of these complex social circumstances. The words attributed to Jesus, which allow us to see him as a prophet—or an apocalyptic prophet—came from writers some fifty years later, as we'll see in the following sections.

Appendix B contains a compelling list of sayings and parables that come as close as we can determine to be actual words Jesus said. This remarkable achievement contains what Dr. John Dominic Crossan has concluded through a rigorous and disciplined scientific methodology. Perfect? No. Complete? Probably not. As close as we can get? Pretty close.

Jesus, consorting with the most socially undesirable elements, often was friendly with the Jewish tax collectors (viewed by the populace as agents of the oppressors) and was thus associated with civil unrest and political enemies of the State. Zealots sought him out, as well, believing he might be of support to them. Additionally, any claims about another king or kingdom was bound to raise both eyebrows and suspicions—both among the Roman political and Hasmonean religious leaders.

The features of Jesus' message

Three undeniable features, however, of his personhood and his message were:

- The Kingdom is here! Eternally now! Just look! God is within you just as he is within me. You can be transformed and do and accomplish the same things I do.

- He walked the talk. How he lived and acted, personally, were consistent with his verbal message.

- His followers (core, peripheral, and hangers-on) would eat together.

"Eat together—big deal," you might say. It was a very big deal! Jesus associated with all types of people from all walks of life:

Roman soldiers, prostitutes, tax collectors, the socially estranged, and diseased (lepers, congenitally blind, beggars). They would all go to a house, usually witness a healing or some teachings or both, and eat. The underlying importance of the meal together was common in virtually every fragment of early literature from the period. The common meal was a big symbol of the "now-ness" of God's new Kingdom. Of course people were poor and hungry and the prospect of a sit-down meal was mouth watering, to say the least. But it was almost revolutionary for most of these Palestinians to eat with a homeowner, with guests of all social classes, without some form of ritual washing/cleansing, without some sense of proper dress or decorum. This was still a society of a pretty fixed social caste system—not from the heritage of Judaism, but from the Hellenistic and Roman cultural influences of the previous three hundred years. Crossan, in his book *The Historical Jesus,* outlines a complete hierarchy of an agrarian social system, applicable to Judaea-Palestine in the time of Jesus.[17] I have summarized this information in the following table.

Class	% Nat'l Income	% of Population	Comments
Ruler & Family	25%	-	
Governing Class	25%	1%	Political & appointed leaders
Retainer's Class	10–15%*	5%	Scribes & bureaucrats to soldiers & generals. Absolutely indispensable as a group while totally expendable as individuals.
Merchant's Class	10–15%*	5%*	Confronted the governing class—but in the marketplace rather than in terms of authority.
Priestly Class	15%	2–4%*	Preserved cultic/religious symbols and traditions and administered the redistribution ethic, if available.
Subtotal – The Privileged Classes	90%	15%	

Class	% Nat'l Income	% of Population	Comments
Peasant Class		60%	Vast majority of population—mostly farming or husbandry. Normally could feed themselves regularly.
Artisan Class		5%	From the ranks of dispossessed peasantry & non-inheriting sons.
Unclean or De-Graded Class		5–10%*	Origins or occupations separated these from agrarian peasantry or artisans, e.g., porters, miners, prostitutes.
Expendable Class		5–10%*	Those forced to "live by their wits": petty criminals or outlaws, beggars, underemployed migrant workers.
Subtotal – The Peasant Classes	**10%**	**85%**	
			NOTE: *Alluded to, but are my estimates

Table 6. *The Nine Social Strata in Agrarian Societies. The disproportionate gulf between the five upper classes and the lower four is overwhelming, exceeding those found in today's most stratified horticultural societies of Africa and other Third World countries.*

All these people would go to a house, be taught, be healed, and eat. No admittance fees. *All* came. This was the Kingdom of God! The exalted are humbled. The humbled exalted. We all ate together. Healings occurred. *The healing of the sick was especially vibrant. For four hundred years, since the Persian influence of demonology and angelology had entered Hebrew culture, demons had become the way illness was described. Healings were exceptional, not because they represented a "physical" miracle, but because first-century people believed disease to be the equivalent of being possessed by an evil spirit(s).*

This message of the Kingdom, coupled with the actions of healings and the eating together in homes or on hillsides where sharing with strangers became the norm (for example, the Feeding of the five thousand—Mark 6:30–44), became visible demonstrations of the eternal now-ness of the Kingdom of God—here at hand.

When you look at the conduct portrayed in many of Jesus' discourses, sayings, or parables, it "fits" quite nicely with what we know of Galilee. As you read these stories a picture emerges of how large estates were run; the duties of servants, especially with absentee landlords; and the great gulf between the wealthy and the poor. We learn about the daily grind of the poorer classes, of which he was familiar. The smallest things could make such a big difference: late night requests from the landowner; a lost coin; gifts or loans from friends; hassles over wages; what to do about salt, bread, and wine; social and ethnic mistrust and/or outright animosity—for example, the Samaritans or the tax collectors.

"He did not take the Romans to task, nor inveigh against the Temple establishment. He did not suggest withdrawal from strife and ungodliness to form a convent. He did not propose to do battle with Pharisees or synagogue leaders for the control or cleansing of a religious institution. He did not philosophize about the *polis*, how to legislate a better law, what to do about tyranny, or the chances of finding a perfect king. He did not suggest a people's revolt to storm the palace [of the Roman tetrarch] in Tiberias, or raise a guerilla band to march on Jerusalem. He proposed no political program. He did not organize a church."[18]

The incident at the Temple

Then, as tradition has it, Jesus came from preaching in Galilee to celebrate the Passover in Jerusalem, probably for the first and only time. That he had been heard of would not be surprising. However, when he became enraged at the money changers in the Temple (Mark 11:15–19), he was no longer a Galilean rumor. He had become the incarnation of the earlier, powerful Old Testament prophets. All this flew in the face of the priestly upper classes of the time. The Sadducees had controlled the Temple ritual, which had grown even more elaborate, costly, and ritualized in the 300–400 years since the reforms of Ezra and Nehemiah. When Jesus threw out the money changers from the Temple, it was these

Sadducees, from whose ranks came the high priests, who were deeply angered knowing he had called them a "... den of thieves."

Crossan believes that the incident at the Temple appears to be at the historical core of Jesus' troubles with the Jerusalem authorities.

> "I am not sure that poor Galilean peasants went up and down regularly to [*Jerusalem*] to the Temple feasts. I think it quite possible that Jesus went to Jerusalem only once [*agreeing with Mark's Gospel, not John's, which has him making several trips*] and that the spiritual and economic egalitarianism he preached in Galilee exploded in indignation at the Temple as the seat and symbol of all that was non-egalitarian, patronal, and even oppressive in both the religious and political level. His symbolic destruction [*of the Temple*] simply actualized what he had already said in his teachings, effectuated in his healings, and realized in his mission of open commensality.

> "But the confined and tinder-box atmosphere of the Temple at Passover, especially under Pilate, was not the same as that in the rural reaches of Galilee, even under Herod Antipas, and the soldiers would have moved immediately at any disturbance. None of this [*can be grounded in the methodology Crossan set out to follow in his book*], so it must be taken very carefully. ... Therefore, I think the symbolic destruction was but the logical extension of the miracle and table conjunction, of open healing and open eating; I think that it actually happened and *if* it happened at Passover, *could* easily have led to arrest and execution."[19]

In short, although the circumstances were quite different, the tension between Jesus and the Sadducees was a repeat performance of the tension between the prophets and Deuteronomic Reformers and again with the priestly reforms under Ezra and Nehemiah.

Initially, following Jesus' death, his followers knew nothing more about "The Passion" than that of his crucifixion. Jesus' closest followers had fled. They were scared. They were concerned as to what would happen now. Would his untimely death negate all that Jesus had said and done? Would it negate all they had accepted and believed? If the Gospel accounts are not historically accurate about his passion, arrest, and trial, then do we know for sure he was killed? Yes. We have two independent accounts to attest to that. Josephus, a Jewish historian, wrote about it in his *Jewish Antiquities* about 93 C.E. Additionally, Cornelius Tacitus in his *Annals* (circa 120 C.E.), while writing about a rumor that had blamed Nero for burning Rome in 64 C.E., wrote:

> "Therefore to scotch the rumour, Nero substituted as culprits, and punished with the utmost refinements of cruelty, a class of men, loathed for their vices, whom the crowd styled Christians. Christus, the founder of the name, had undergone the death penalty in the reign of Tiberius, by sentence of the procurator Pontius Pilatus, and the pernicious superstition was checked for the moment, only to break out once more, not merely in Judaea, the home of the disease, but in the capital itself, where all things horrible or shameful in the world collect and find a vogue."[20]

After the death of Jesus

Now what? What happened after Jesus died?

We know Paul began preaching about 50 C.E., maybe earlier. His letters,[21] to various congregations, were written in the decade between 50–60 C.E. and are the oldest documents in the New Testament. He got the blessing of the "pillars" of Jerusalem so he could preach to the Gentiles. We know that the leader of the "pillars" wasn't Peter, who is supposed to be the first "head of the Church." It wasn't even one of the original disciples. It was James, the brother of Jesus (Gal. 1:18f; Acts 15:13–34; 21:18f). How did he get to be the leader? We don't know for sure.

We also know, after his conversion, Paul was "ushered" to and stayed with a Jewish Christian congregation in or around Damascus and, later, near his hometown of Tarsus. It was fourteen years before he began preaching. That date would place his conversion somewhere around 37 C.E., perhaps eight to nine years after Jesus died. But the congregation in Damascus was already there when Paul came. How did it get there? How long had it been there? What did it do? How was it organized? What did they preach?

We know that during the time when Paul was still studying in Damascus and Tarsus, there were other successful preachers. For example, Philip (Acts 6:1–5) was one of the seven chosen by the

Jerusalem Twelve (apostles? pillars?) to do benevolent work among the needy—widows and orphans. He went to Samaria, preaching Christ in the desert, as well as the coastal cities between Azotus and Caesarea, with the result that joyous believers in Jesus were baptized. Perhaps Philip's most famous convert was the treasurer of the Ethiopian queen. Didn't any of these chosen people, including Philip, write letters or epistles? I'm sure they did. Where are the letters? What did they say? I can understand that the letters are lost. However, the thoughts, ideas, and concepts that would have been common to Philip and the other six evangelists (which is what they were called) would have been familiar to the Jewish Christians in the region. The twelve would have instructed the six, just as they did Paul, on what to say when preaching. Additionally, we know Peter was entrusted to preach the gospel to the Jews (the circumcised), just as Paul was entrusted to preach the gospel to the gentiles. What was Peter's Gospel?

This kind of information is virtually absent from the New Testament. Even if the writings were honestly lost, you would think there'd be some attempt by the early Church Fathers to want to include something about the Jerusalem Church—the role of the twelve, the subsequent "pillars," and their immediate thoughts.

Why isn't there anything in the New Testament to explain why Jerusalem is the center of the fledgling Jewish sect called Christianity, from Christ's death until about 50 C.E.? Then, it's all Paul and his ministry to the Gentiles of Asia Minor, Greece, and Rome. Yes, there are a few obscure references to the deaths of Stephen and James and Peter. But that's about all. When it comes to the growth of the congregations in Samaria, Judaea, and possibly Egypt, where many fled after the Romans squashed the revolt in 70 C.E., there is just nothing.

Apparently little, if any, of that "flavor" of preaching (of sermon content) was revered enough by the early Church to repeat it, honor it, or incorporate it into documents. Perhaps the Jerusalem Jewish community lost its influence when it fled to Pella and Egypt during the civil unrest during the 60s? Perhaps the form—specific, isolated communities, rather than a network of common believers—of the Jewish Christian movement contributed to its lack of influence? Perhaps Paul—with his ability to speak both as a Jew and as a Roman and who was educated with the whole of Hellenistic import—was just more palatable. Or maybe, to emphasize the Pillars of Jerusalem, per se, would minimize the growing importance of the Hellenistic centers of influence around Antioch and Smyrna, where they were organizing congregations around *presbyters*, elders or bishops.

Probably it was a combination of all of that.

We'll begin addressing these questions as we begin our journey as to how the New Testament developed.

- Chapters 7 and 8 will cover the early, "missing" years, and the earliest sources, approximately 30–70 C.E.: Early Q, the Gospel of Thomas, and Paul.

- Using my own personal experience as a backdrop, Chapter 9 will discuss the critical issue of how hard it is to "find the right words" to discuss a spiritual experience.

- Chapters 10 and 11 cover the period from 70–400 C.E. Chapter 10 will cover the New Testament writings as the focus shifted from the Christ of Faith to the Christ of Theological Doctrine, and the influence of that focus on subsequent sources: the Gospels, Acts, the later writings, and early church fathers. Chapter 11 continues the discussion of the previous chapter, leading to the finalization of the New Testament in support of Church orthodoxy.

- Chapter 12 will present some conclusions that will reinforce the observation that the early, emerging church did the same kinds of things, albeit in differing ways, as the priestly reformers. This is a very important issue because I believe some of the ideas and concepts that didn't make it into the New Testament should have. What we can learn about Jesus from the early Jewish Christians of the Jesus Movements, *who were pretty much "out of the loop" in the formation of the early Church and its "founding" documents*, is of utmost relevance today.

Chapter 6 Notes

[13] Mack, *Who Wrote the New Testament*, p 26

[14] Ibid., p 32. For an excellent discussion see Chapter 1, "Clashing Cultures"

[15] Crossan, *The Historical Jesus*, p 230, 231

[16] Mack, *Who Wrote the New Testament*, pp 54–56

[17] Crossan, *The Historical Jesus*, pp 45, 46

[18] Mack, *A Myth of Innocence*, p 64

[19] Crossan, *The Historical Jesus*, p 360

[20] Tacitus, *Annals*, 15.44, as reported in Crossan, *The Historical Jesus*, p 374, 375

[21] 1, 2 Thessalonians, Galatians, 1, 2 Corinthians, Romans, Philemon, and Philippians

Chapter 7

Part 1: From Jesus of Nazareth to the Christ of Faith – The "Missing Years" (30-70 C.E.)

𝔇uring the forty years following Jesus' execution, a variety of small Jewish-Christian associations or groups formed throughout Palestine and the Hellenized city-states of Syria. By the time their oral traditions began to be written down, the excitement of Jesus' Kingdom of God had resulted in a wonderful mix of associations.

> "One line can be traced from the earliest Jesus movement through Matthew's Gospel, to later communities that understood themselves as Jewish Christians. These people emphasized lifestyle and found a way to bring the behavior of the Jesus movement into line with more traditional Jewish codes of ethics. This approach produced communities that lasted for centuries, such as the Ebionites and the Nazareans. But they were not the ones that gave birth to the Christianity of the Bible. Another line takes off from the Sayings Gospel Q, runs through the Gospel of Thomas where Jesus' teachings were understood to bring enlightenment about one's true self, and end up in Gnostic circles. These people cultivated an invitation to personal virtue and thought of the Kingdom of God as an otherworldly dimension of spiritual existence where the true human being had its origin and end. This approach may have been the most attractive form of Christianity during the second to fourth centuries. But it was finally squelched by the institutional form of Christian tradition that called itself the Church. The Church's trajectory had worked its way through northern Syria and Asia Minor where the Christ cult formed to

justify the inclusion of both Gentiles and Jews in the Kingdom of God. It was this trajectory that converged on Rome, developed the notion of the universal church (from *catholicus*, meaning 'general') and created the Bible as its charter."[22]

These various groups or associations can be broadly separated into two types: Jesus movements and Christ congregations. These movements, their interplay, and their discord with Judaism proper will be discussed in this and the following chapters. During these forty years, called the "missing years," the development of these movements spawned the sources of the New Testament: The original written "collections" of Jesus sayings, his pronouncements, his miracles; the Sayings Gospel Q; the Gospel of Thomas; and Paul's letters.

Who Was Jesus and Why Did He Die?

Suffice to say here that Jesus was many things, depending on your circumstance. He was a prophet/cynic. He was a healer. He was a teacher or rabbi. He was a roving itinerant preacher. Was he something else? Was he more than a "real" man? Was he divine?

He was a man more full of God-love than anyone we've known. As a result, we believe he was the Incarnation (the "enfleshment") of the love of God. Based on stories about him, his faith was so strong and focused that it made him appear exceptional and divine. Yet he said we could do what he was doing, if we would but open our eyes and see. We also could "move mountains," or heal the sick, or forgive. If he was divine, then according to him, the kind of divinity he "had" is available to us.

Within a decade of his death, people were aware of the continued spirit of love he had embodied. That spirit hadn't been killed. How can that be explained? Maybe he hadn't died after all. Maybe. ... They tried to explain. Since all of this began within the Jewish community, it was logical that vibrant Jewish images played the most significant roles. The roles of the prophet and of purification and sacrifice were real, and early explanations abounded around those images. Explanations dealing with sacrifice, especially those images of the Suffering Servant (Isa. 53) eventually seemed to win out.

I believe the love of God expressed through Jesus was confronted by the egoistic desire of mankind to be in control—or in the Yahwist's terminology: to possess the knowledge of good and evil and be as the gods. This was coupled with the fear people felt at the thought of losing the control and predictability of God's desires. When one considered Jesus, one had to let go of any preconceptions of God. People in his day had to choose between their concept of God, their concept of religion, and how they believed God wanted to be pleased, or accept the reality of the love of God and the immediacy of his new Kingdom expressed in Jesus, who gave us, not specific formulas, but rather vague "commands": Love the Lord your God; love your neighbor as yourself; love each other.

We don't like vagueness. We want predictable, concrete, repetitious, black-and-white rules and regulations. We want to know that what we're doing is right, is pleasing to God, and is something for which we'll eventually be rewarded. All of this is egoistic and controlling, which is often why it's comforting.

In that confrontation between mankind and the love of God for his creation, mankind's egoism, coupled with the fear of loss of control and power, killed Jesus. But the love of God won. I am greatly influenced here by my professor of Systematic Theology at Princeton, Dr. George S. Hendry, and his remarkable little book, *The Gospel of the Incarnation.*

The same spirit of love that Jesus embodied continued in dozens of small groups throughout Palestine and the Diaspora. Initially that spirit was enough. Shortly, however, the need to be able to verbalize and explain the phenomenon became paramount. Over the next five or six decades the spirit got left behind as efforts to develop a rational theology became more the focus. The emphasis shifted from faith because of the experience of the spirit to faith as intellectual assent or faith in the theology of rational doctrines about that spirit.

Jesus Movements

During the years immediately following Jesus' death, oral remembrances were all that held together the small band of people who had personal memories of being with Jesus. These were all Jewish people. They were mostly Palestinian. Most were poor and uneducated. They were a collection of lower class and "blue-collar" Jewish Palestinians. They continued to observe Jewish laws and traditions, they observed the Sabbath, they participated in temple rituals and rites in Jerusalem, and they went to their synagogue services. These Jewish groups spawned the Q writings, as well as the Gospel of Thomas and other Gnostic writings and groups.

From critical textual evidence we can surmise these oral traditions were remembered or grouped into his teachings, his healings and miracles, and his cynical one-liners, generally referred to as pronouncements. For example, scholars believe there was an early collection of miracle stories. Both Mark and John refer to it. The context of this collection is similar in that they allude to epic themes and figures. This is indicative of their use in giving people in the Jesus movements a sense of identity—claiming for their founder a combination of mysterious and miraculous powers, which is common in groups where the members have undergone a personal transformation of some kind. Comparing the similarity between the sequence and content of the miracle stories in Mark's Gospel (there are two similar "sets") and those of John's Gospel, scholars conclude that both writers were referring to a common collection of miracle traditions.

In addition to these oral sets of material, we know that there were preachers or prophets that roamed the countryside of Palestine during this time. They would visit small groups of Jewish Christians who were meeting in homes after synagogue services or during the week to eat a common meal and discuss issues concerning them. Both early and later writings that appeared in the Didache[23]—a very influential document in earliest Christianity that was designed for the newly baptized or for those preparing for Christianity—dealt with, among other things, the "proper" protocol on handling these itinerant preachers. For example, the Didache instructed families to welcome them into their homes, feed them, invite friends to listen—but only for one or two days. If the person needed to stay longer than that, he was a "false prophet." If these visitors were simply travelers, they should begin working for their keep after a day or two. Although this advice was written initially toward the end of our current time period (70 C.E.), it indicates there were issues early on with these itinerant preachers. It would seem that these "false prophets" came, stayed, took advantage of guests, and exhibited behavior that wasn't in keeping with their message.

Following Jesus' death, perhaps within a year or two, these remembrances began being written down in "collections." We have Sayings (or Wisdom) Collections, Miracle Collections, and Collections of Jesus' Pronouncements. These collections more than likely were both used by itinerant preachers/prophets as well as enlarged by them. For instance, I can imagine a situation where a roving preacher referred to wisdom sayings A and B from a written collection, only to have a hearer later (probably around the dinner table) tell a story of personally hearing Jesus also discuss C and D. The preacher later would add C and D to the collection he was carrying. At his next stop he would talk about A, B, C, and D.

Jewish Jesus Groups

In addition to roaming preachers and group discussions in local households, there were discussions of Jesus' life and works within the confines of the normal synagogue. The normal routine of a typical synagogue follows an annual liturgical calendar just like our churches do today. Most of us recognize our annual (or liturgical) Christian calendar: Advent, Christmas, the Epiphany, Lent and Easter, Pentecost, then various themes on the life of the Church as well as the Christian life, which brings the liturgical calendar back to Advent. As the synagogue would progress through their annual liturgical calendar, the rabbi would read from the Torah, the Prophets, and sometimes from the Wisdom scrolls. Following the readings from Scripture, the rabbi might have made comments and invited comments from the attending males. As they would celebrate the Feast of the Paschal Lamb, for example, it's not hard to imagine these Jewish Christians commenting, "Jesus was like that." The same kinds of things occurred during readings of the Prophets concerning the suffering servant, the sacrificial lamb, the Messiah, the Logos (the Word), or the Light (Hanukkah) of the World. "I'd like to make a comment," someone would say. "Jesus of Nazareth was like that. He (did or said) …"[24] This scriptural imagery was familiar and helped them verbalize and, perhaps, visualize what they'd personally experienced. It also helped give credence to those experiences when talking to someone who had not known Jesus personally.

Some of the sayings of Jesus that had an "apocalyptic" tone to them—for example, his Son of Man sayings—were not interpreted as end-of-the-world predictions by these early groups. The term "Son of Man" was a term that would be more correctly interpreted as "human being" or "one of mankind." More recent

English translations of the Bible reflect this better translation. To these early groups, and to Jesus, the pronouncements about "the end" would have been understood as meaning a coming dramatic change in Israel's history or perhaps a radical change in an individual—speaking of the "old" world coming to an end for that individual. Theologians have long coined the term "realized" eschatology—namely that Jesus sensed the actual presence of God in his ministry, especially in his healings (for example, Matt. 12:28). The purpose of God to establish his Kingdom was here at hand. Now. In your heart. Not at some future time.

From the literature we do have, refined (but based) on these early "missing years," we can conclude that the focus of the discussions of the Jesus Movement centered on: Just who was Jesus, and how did he "fit" within traditional Judaism? The death of Jesus, however, was not their eminent concern. They had known of wandering prophets (like John the Baptist) as well as devout Pharisees who had been executed under the Romans and Herod Antipas. This is evident in our reconstruction of Q and clear in the text of the Gospel of Thomas.

Early Q

During the nineteenth century, German scholars had surmised the Gospel of Mark to be the first account written because, among other things, both Matthew and Luke used Mark's Gospel. They noticed something else as well. There were significant sections of text that were very similar in Matthew and Luke, that were absent from Mark. These German scholars concluded that this mysterious missing source (German: Quelle) was a written collection of Jesus' sayings that was unknown or unavailable to Mark. It has never surfaced as a stand-alone manuscript. Its existence, though, cannot be denied. Over decades of scholarship it has become known as the "Sayings Gospel Q," or "The Lost Gospel," or "The Gospel of Q."[25]

It is probably the earliest written record we have from these Jesus movements. It documents the history of one of these Jewish Jesus groups from the time of Jesus until the end of the Jewish-Roman war in the 70s. According to Burton Mack, at least three "layers" of text have been isolated in Q. The first and earliest layer (Q1) consists of the least embellished sayings (just as Mark's Gospel is the least embellished when compared to Matthew, Luke, and John) and represents as close as we can get to actual words of

Jesus. The second layer (Q2) comes from the timeframe of the decade preceding the war (50–60 C.E.), as Jewish tensions are building, but the war hasn't erupted and the temple in Jerusalem still stands. The last layer (Q3) is after the war (and the temple!) is over.

Layer	Comments
Q1: 30–50 C.E.	Jesus is primarily a wisdom teacher. Consists largely of sayings about the wisdom of being a true follower of Jesus. **IMPACT:** Themes of a thoroughgoing critique of conventional culture: riches, misuse of authority and power, hypocrisies and pretensions, social and economic inequities, injustices, and even the normal reasons for family loyalties are all under suspicion. The Kingdom ideal is being set over against traditional mores by directing followers to practice voluntary poverty, severance of family ties, renunciation of needs, fearlessness in speaking out, nonretaliation and, in general, living as children of God, even though he makes his sun rise on the evil and the good. The focus was not just on a list of codes for defining a true disciple, but on setting standards for recognition and authentic relationships within the community of fellow followers.
Q2: 50–60 C.E.	Introduces prophetic and apocalyptic pronouncements of judgment on those who have refused to listen to the Q-Group's message. **IMPACT:** The process of Q1 had taken its toll: families were torn apart; true Jews were ostracizing them for not being pure in observance of Jewish codes; they were expelled from certain towns; many had abandoned the Q-Group. Loyalty was now the key issue. They were beginning to be more judgmental of those outside the group. Threatening apocalyptic messages of doom were directed to those who didn't agree with their interpretation of the Kingdom. Jesus is now becoming thought of as an apocalyptic prophet.
Q3: after 70 C.E.	Registers a retreat from the fray of public encounter. [*The group probably fled Palestine as the war began and established some form of isolated "community."*] This layer entertains thoughts of patience and piety for the enlightened ones while they wait for their moment in glory [*some time soon*] at the end of human history. **IMPACT:** With the war over, the rhetoric is "toned" down in terms of other Jesus groups. The predominant issue is over Jesus' ultimate authority. Textual additions include the Lament over Jerusalem, the story of Jesus' temptation by Satan, statements about the importance of Mosaic Law, and more promises about the future reward of the faithful.

Table 7. *Summary of the Sayings Gospel Q.* *Understanding the layers within Q helps us understand the history of this Jesus group.*[26]

Donald L. O'Dell

Gospel of Thomas

Among collections of materials found at Nag Hammadi in the later 1940s was the Coptic manuscript ending with the words "The gospel according to Thomas." Scholars were ecstatic! Thomas is about the same length as Q, consists of similar material—sayings, instructions, analogies, parables—explaining the Kingdom of God, and is a Coptic translation of a Greek original that has been dated to the early 60s C.E. Almost one-third of the sayings in Thomas have parallels in early Q. The discovery of Thomas confirmed the reality of Q and other missing Q-like documents. Indeed, there were written documents—sayings, collections, gospels—that were associated with certain groups before those writings that we know in the New Testament were composed. Some of these writings—Q, Thomas, the Miracle Stories Collection, and others—influenced those that wrote the four Gospels.

The overall tone of Thomas is a Gnostic interpretation of the Jesus events: The true interpretation of his teachings has become enlightened just as he is the Enlightened One. "When you know (*gnosis*) yourself, then you will be known, and will understand that you are the children of the living Father" (Gospel of Thomas 3).

The turn to Gnosticism on the part of the Thomas people would indicate they took a turn the Q people didn't. Perhaps these Gnostic Thomas people interpreted many of Jesus' sayings about the Kingdom of God—its reality of "here-ness" and "now-ness" if you will but open your eyes and really begin to see—as a call to understand your true Self. Perhaps, as many subsequent philosophers had, they discovered that the journey to totally "see" will lead eventually to a "seeing" of one's true Self. There, sitting beside your Self, will be God.

From many of the sayings in Thomas, scholars have concluded the Thomas group was distancing themselves from apocalyptic communities (like Q), as well as from those Jesus groups that still thought of themselves as being simply a subsect of Judaism. The Thomas group did follow some rituals, namely baptism and table fellowship traditions. Overall, however, they developed a style of Jesus movement by investing the sayings of Jesus with esoteric, Gnostic significance.

What Is Gnosticism?

The appeal of Gnostic-type thinking, especially as practiced within the Johannine community, was rather widespread. It took the "official" emerging Church almost three hundred more years to eliminate it. Its appeal today is still present in many New Thought religious movements. The following is from the book *The Gnostic Gospels*, by Elaine Pagels. It's as good a brief explanation as I've read. Speaking about the early first- and second-century Gnostic Christians who had been declared heretics by orthodox church leaders, she writes:

"But those who wrote and circulated [Gnostic] texts did not regard themselves as 'heretics.' Most of the writings use Christian terminology, unmistakably related to a Jewish heritage. Many claim to offer traditions about Jesus that are secret, hidden from the 'many' who constitute what, in the second century, came to be called the 'catholic church.' These Christians are now called Gnostics, from the Greek word *gnosis*, usually translated as knowledge. For as those who claim to know nothing about ultimate reality are called agnostic (literally, 'not-knowing'), the person who does claim to know such things is called Gnostic ('knowing'). But *gnosis* is not primarily rational knowledge. The Greek language distinguishes between scientific or reflective knowledge ('He knows mathematics') and knowing through observation or experience ('He knows me'), which is *gnosis*. As the Gnostics use the term, we could translate it as 'insight,' for *gnosis* involves an intuitive process of knowing oneself. And to know oneself, they claimed, is to know human nature and human destiny. According to the Gnostic teacher Theodotus, writing in Asia Minor (circa 140–160), the Gnostic is one who has come to understand 'Who we were, and what we have become; where we were ... whither we are hastening; from what we are being released; what birth is, and what is rebirth.'

"Yet to know oneself, at the deepest level, is simultaneously to know God; this is the secret of *gnosis*. Another Gnostic teacher, Monoimus, says: 'Abandon the search for God and the creation and other matters of a similar sort. Look for him by taking yourself as the starting point. Learn who it is within you who makes everything his own and says, 'My God, my mind, my thoughts, my soul, my body.' Learn the sources of sorrow, joy, love, hate. ... If you carefully investigate these matters you will find him in yourself.'"[27]

Regardless of the variety of Jesus movement groups, it is clear that these people did not view themselves as some form of Jewish reform movement. They were not after a revitalized Judaism. These groups—the Q Community, the Thomas Community, synagogue-based Jesus groups—had found an altogether new sense of identity.

In the earliest years following Jesus' death, he was remembered as a teacher who challenged people to think of themselves as belonging to a new kingdom—the Kingdom of God. The groups grew rapidly as they attracted others. The different groups developed their own social practices and group identities. For each of them, in the beginning, they attributed their wisdom to Jesus of Nazareth—often putting this wisdom in the form of "instruction" with subsequent revisions piled onto revisions, as both time and circumstance passed by.

The key was the need for Jesus to be recognized as the authority for what the group had evolved to. They used his teachings. They found models in the history of Israel. They associated him with images from their common past. As this progressed, little by little, their understanding of their past changed and, as a consequence, their images and descriptions changed.

As Mack explains, the Q Community began with images of Jesus as a cynic-like sage, which evolved to an image of prophet, then to an image that would account for all the knowledge attributed to him. At the end, the community had envisioned him as an envoy of divine wisdom and the Son of God. The teachings of Jesus were now a revelation of cosmic arrangements.[28]

The Jewish Christians, who produced the Pronouncement Collections, didn't appear to be as audacious as the Q Community. They never doubted they belonged to Israel until they clashed with the Pharisees over external purity codes. They tried to compare Jesus to David. They tried to construct their pronouncements in the form of arguments between Jesus and the Pharisees. They did not develop some form of mythic role for Jesus as an attempt to give them some sense of legitimacy.

The Thomas Group—the True Believers—tried more to reconstruct the nature of the cosmos rather that try to reinvent the history of Israel. They too, however, took stands against the Pharisees and their purity codes as well as the temple and its sacrificial system.

The Miracle-Stories Group picked up on the Moses story and delighted in thinking of themselves in a similar fashion: the Jesus Movement to them was what the formation of Israel was to Moses.

Christ Congregations

Simultaneously, and very quickly, similar groups of Jewish Christians began appearing in cities and towns in the Diaspora (outside Jerusalem's immediate influence) in Sepphoris, Caesarea, Damascus, Antioch, and eastern Syria. In these areas there already was a tradition of including Gentiles in the synagogue and, more than likely, including them in follow-on discussions around meals in homes after the service. After the meal they would discuss, argue, and present ideas about this Jesus. They were familiar with the Greek idea of social clubs, where dining and discussions followed a small tribute to the patron deity of the club. This pattern of meeting had been adapted very nicely to these small, Hellenized groups of Jews and Gentiles.

Although the Scriptures would be referenced, these Hellenistic groups would be inclined to include the logic of Hellenistic literature. After all, whether Jew or Gentile, they were primarily cosmopolitan Hellenistic people. Like the Jewish groups of Palestine, they too focused on the question: Who was Jesus? But their more pressing question was: Why did he die? These Greco-Roman Jews and non-Jewish "friends-of-the-synagogue," or "god fearers," as Paul called them, were much less tied to the temple and much more familiar and comfortable with thinking about "the divine" in terms of the overall cosmos. Gods and deities—the divine—helped explain the universe. While Jesus movements took on various forms, depending on the predominant form of Judaism of the group—Hasidic to Gnostic to Essene—these groups in the Diaspora began almost immediately to see Jesus as a divine being. They began using the term "Christ," as opposed to the Jesus-as-sage-or-prophet image of the Jesus Movement. For the Hellenistic Jews, Christ was synonymous with the "anointed one," or Messiah. Based on some of the problems that arose in Corinth, it implied that other Hellenistic congregations simply found these new associations exciting as a new religion in the model of other Hellenistic cults. Although Jews probably introduced the term "the Christ"—meaning Messiah—the Gentiles simply absorbed it as Jesus' last name.

In these congregations "the Christ" had become a symbol or agent of the Jewish God Yahweh in a Greco-Roman world. Scholars generally refer to these Hellenistic Jewish/Gentile groups as Christ congregations. These concepts of Jesus date from the earliest beginnings in these towns of the Diaspora and had become relatively formalized by the time Paul came to an area around Damascus. This was only eight to nine years after Jesus' death.

These concepts were essentially spin-offs of available Greek myths—though they had been used as well by Hellenistic Jews to restate their Jewish ideals of justice, caring for the needy, watching out for the "little guy." This mingling of Hellenism with Judaism was common in northern and eastern Syria. The Hellenistic Jews could talk about Jesus' death in terms, perhaps, of the sacrificial substitute so prevalent in Old Testament imagery and emphasized during the last four hundred years of Jewish history—since the reforms of Ezra/Nehemiah. The sacrificial substitute also would fit nicely within the framework of the Gentile Greeks' longstanding tradition of storytelling. Since Homer, the Hellenistic culture was infused with stories of the hero/martyr, and his noble causes and death. It doesn't take much to merge these two traditions. Jesus was the supreme sacrifice. He died for his cause. What cause? Why, these budding Jewish/Gentile Christian associations, of course. His death was a noble sacrifice that imputed righteousness and pleased God, just as did the "scapegoat" in the Old Testament, where the goat was imparted with the sins of the people and sent into the desert to please Azazel, demon of the desert.

As we have seen, the Palestinian-based Jesus movements were focused on finding "images" that were familiar within the context of Jewish literature, namely their Scriptures. It is important to notice that these hero/martyr images of Jesus were developed in the Hellenistic groups of the Diaspora only. These images were eventually summarized in brief statements of faith called kerygma (seed or kernel of the message) by scholars. The earliest kerygma would probably have been "Jesus died for our sins." After many initial meetings the Jewish half of these Jewish-Gentile groups, who would be literate in their Scriptures, would have found parallels there, e.g., the suffering servant, the Paschal Lamb. Then the *kerygma* expanded to include "He died as the Messiah (the Christ)." These kinds of kerygmatic statements were in place in Damascus, for example, by the time Paul was taken there following his conversion event. 1 Cor. 15:3–5 and Rom. 3:21–26 represent some of these earliest statements of faith that Paul inherited.

The martyrdom theme Paul referenced in Rom. 3:21–26 was that it was Jesus' death that was the saving event. He doesn't mention the Resurrection. We can also see the language of this Hellenistic/Jewish martyrology in 4 Macc. (contained in the Apocrypha). This is the language that both Hellenistic Jew and Gentile could latch onto and believe explained what was happening to them. However, the martyr myth of Greeks and Hellenistic Jews (such as represented in 4 Macc.) indicated that not only did the sufferer of the noble death become vindicated, but so did his "cause." What was Jesus' cause? He didn't try to start a church. So what was it? Perhaps a new concept of Israel? One that included Gentiles? A movement from a Jewish Israel to a Jewish-Gentile Israel? Again the whole imagery of the sacrificial substitute would be attributed to the Christ, the Messiah. Then the Hellenistic influence would come to bear in order to explain the "spirit" of the group—the transformation of individual people that was occurring. It is but a short leap from the "living spirit" very much present in the group, coupled with a more literal rendering of Jesus' Movement groups' surviving songs of lament over Jesus' death, and the foundation of the resurrection is born. In any event the Spirit of Jesus was still alive transforming both the group and the individuals in it.

A Current Example of a Living Spirit

This sentiment of a "living spirit" and its verbalization is still alive in the Middle East today. Although it is a sentiment we understand, we (in the West) verbalize it differently than those of the Middle East. A relevant example illustrates this. Yasser Arafat, leader of the Palestinian Liberation Organization (PLO) died in Paris of an undisclosed illness. His body was returned from Paris for burial in the PLO Headquarters compound in the West Bank town of Ramallah.

"The scenes were a vivid reflection of the grief of a people, many of them young and angry, who had lost the only leader most of them could remember. ... One of them, Nisrin Dabaka, 25, said, 'I love the rais,' using the Arabic word for president. 'He is like a father to me, and to me he did not die. He is in my heart, and I will never forget this day in all of my life.' " [29]

Notice the present tense of Ms. Dabaka's sentences. "He is like a father. He did not die. He is in my heart..." Ms. Dabaka's children will grow up hearing about Yasser Arafat from their mother, an eye-witness to the events of the funeral, who repeatedly will say, "... He did not die. He lives on." Later, Ms. Dabaka's grandchildren will also hear of these events, both from their parents as well as from their grandmother, who will ever forcefully remind them, "I was there! He lives on! He did not die! I was there!"

It doesn't take much intellectual capital to imagine this same kind of scenario in the Middle East in days of yore. As discussed by Crossan, the role of women's laments in establishing and influencing cultural and oral tradition was quite significant. Women's laments often became the core of poetic recitals of emotive reactions to events. Over time these laments became songs or recitations that were passed from generation to generation.[30] The forty years between Jesus' Crucifixion and the penning of the initial Gospel account would be a timeframe equivalent to the time period between Ms. Dabaka's initial comments (above) and subsequent, hypothetical, future discussions with her grown grandchildren.

We in the West understand the sentiment, even though we may not appreciate the feats or infamy of Mr. Arafat himself. However, we would have expressed the sentiment differently. For example, at Rev. Martin Luther King's death, we would have said, "I know his murderers thought they killed him, but his spirit will continue to live. His movement will press forward. They killed the man but not the dream he stood for."

But Arabic or Mideastern peoples express themselves differently. "He did not die. He lives on. He is in my heart." Could not Ms. Dabaka's emotive response at Yasser Arafat's funeral *become the seed, the* kerygma, *of a poetic lament? Her response is typical of her culture. It would have been typical also of the several persons called Mary who were close to Jesus—Mary his mother, Mary Magdalene, and Mary the sister of Lazarus. As close female family/friends, they would have tended his body or his burial place. Wouldn't they have developed a spontaneous lament—one that could be recited or sung—very similar to "He did not die. He lives on. He is in my heart"? Might this be the powerful sentiment first expressed by Jerusalem-based Jewish Christians—a sentiment misunderstood and taken literally within several generations by Hellenistic Christ congregations? I found it fascinating to read and understand that this sentiment, described very well by Crossan, of first-century Jewish Christians, is still very much alive in the twenty-first century.*

However, in Greek circles, what good is a martyr's death without some form of eventual vindication? The Resurrection stories provided that. He was raised, he overcame, he was vindicated, granted divine reward, status and destiny in spite of death. This was a "flavor" of the Hellenistic Christian groups or associations that was simply not found in the Jesus movements in Palestine. To reiterate, scholars refer to these groups or associations as Christ congregations, as opposed to the Jesus movements within Palestinian communities.

Regardless of the specific Hellenized town or *polis* that congregation was in, these new Christians thought of themselves as an alternative society. They looked for ways to show the Greco-Roman world that their vision of the human community, and how it needed to interact, was much better. Their model for this alternative society was one of a new kingdom. They were thinking of themselves as congregations that belonged to a kingdom, one that was independent from and superior to all other kingdoms of the world. "… With a lord more exalted than the Roman emperor? Yes. With a lord exalted by the God of Israel? Yes."[31]

For all the dislocated peoples in the Diaspora—Jew and Gentile alike—this was an attractive option. Sensitive souls had experienced spiritual transformations when encountered by the spirit of love. These congregations provided a place for excited debates about this new, cosmic Kingdom. Hymns, doxologies, acclamations, poetic blessings, invocations, and prayers abounded. Doxologies or poetic hymns are scattered throughout Paul's letters. The realities of the spirit of the Lord's presence, felt in terms of the "spirit" of the congregation, were attributed to the Lord's continued presence. Indeed, his spirit lived despite his execution. As Paul stated: "Now the Lord is the Spirit, and where the Spirit of the Lord is, there is freedom" (2 Cor. 3:17).

Exhibit 1, The Early Growth of the Christian Movement (below), will help visualize much of what we have discussed.

Commonality Between Groups

Regardless of the variety of the Jesus Movement groups within Palestine and the Jewish-Gentile Christ congregations of the Hellenistic Diaspora, there were some unmistakable common denominators:[32]

- All groups recognized Jesus as their founder.

- All groups seemed to have formed around gatherings for meals, followed by a discussion.

- Most groups seemed to acknowledge baptism.

- All groups shared in a belief in the "Kingdom of God," although different groups defined in different terms what the social notion of "Kingdom" meant—usually, though, some form of personal piety was emphasized.

- All groups were probably synagogue-based, initially with probable meals and discussions in homes afterward. Small, home-based "congregations" sprang up, if synagogues were not nearby.

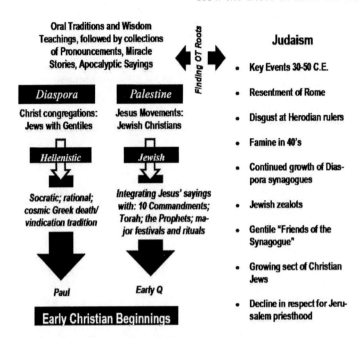

Exhibit 1. *Early Growth of the Christian Movement.* The early Christians were comprised of a variety of Palestinian-based Jesus movements and Diaspora-based (Hellenistic) Christ congregations.

The Ritual of the "Meal"

Regardless of the group, we know that meals were critically important as well. There was something happening in these groups that was transforming. They sensed it. It was changing them. It was changing their outlook. It may have changed the way they looked at the Scriptures. That change, that "spirit," was new and it was real.

These home-based groups would gather for meals together, a small ritual around the meal (which would later become the Lord's Supper), and discussion. Within Palestine some of these home-based groups would be purely Jewish—strict in their keeping of the Jewish law with regard to rites of purification, kosher foods selected, and traditional cooking and serving methods. These stricter groups still attempted to maintain their separateness from the Gentiles or *goyim*. Other Jewish-Christian groups would be less strict in these areas, and perhaps more politically "zealous." They would have been less focused on the "externals" of Jewish religious identity and more focused on rebuilding a true Jewish sense of nationalism—a return to a true Israel under just and true "anointed" priest-kings like David and Solomon. Some groups were more Gnostic, following traditions of the Essenes, focusing on the individual's inner spirit and wisdom.

If a "strict" Jew went for dinner in a "less strict" Jewish home, there would be arguments about appropriateness, identity, tradition, or truth of the Scriptures. If a less zealous Jew went to dinner among more zealous friends, there would be heated discussions and thinly-veiled comments about patriotism. Maybe the less strict would become stricter. Maybe those who were more strict would become less so. Many would have felt exasperated and would have left to find a more compatible group, or start their own.

From the kinds of material we have been able to glean, all these groups focused on Jesus from within their traditions of Judaism. For some Jewish Christians, Jesus was a teacher or rabbi. For others he was a prophet. Others might have thought of him as a healer. For some his pronouncements of a new Kingdom would have contained the "ring" of political revolution. Others would have found in Jesus' message elements of being more free from the external food, dress, and diet restrictions that they believed were superfluous. Still others would see him as a revelation of the divine. Regardless of their focus, these small groups celebrated a meal and discussed the new reality of the Kingdom of God in their midst.

Jesus' use of the term "Kingdom of God" was a new phrase. It does not appear in the Old Testament. It was used some in the writings of the Apocrypha—in the Books of the Maccabees, and Ezra. The term was understood in these early Jesus movements not as an apocalyptic vision of some future theocracy headed by Jesus himself, or God. These words of Jesus would have been interpreted simply as "I am my own man. I follow my heart according to the 'spirit' of the law and the prophets. I understand that God is my father, but God is within you as well. I pay little attention to Greco-Roman or ritualistic Jewish views. You can do this, too."

Jesus would have been thought of in a similar ilk as John the Baptist. But he was more than that. How was he more? To find an answer, they struggled with Scripture. They used patterns of Greek literature. They struggled with themselves. They argued with each other. They got angry. They condemned each other. They railed and ranted and got frustrated with each other.

Baptism

Throughout the ministry of Jesus was the shadow of John the Baptist. Baptism had become a replacement for blood sacrifice, as well as being a sign of cleansing after repentance. There had been a growing tendency in Judaism to increase its number of ritual washings, and baptism was being practiced as a form of proselyte "washing" for Gentiles converted to the Jewish faith. John's use of baptism for established Jews was rather novel, however. It provided an alternative to the (sometimes) expensive process of securing repentance via temple rituals.

Since John's message of "repent and be baptized" was accompanied by sermons requiring strong ethical behavior, scholars have assumed that John did not visualize baptism as being something sacred in its own right. In short, the rite of baptism didn't guarantee purification. The act of baptism was to be followed by active compassion and justice. After John baptized Jesus, the acts of compassion and justice that Jesus performed were contained in his ministry.

Difference Between a Jesus Movement and a Christ Congregation

Jesus movements rarely discussed or theorized as to why Jesus died, focusing on the activities and teachings—the life—of Jesus. The Christ congregations rarely discussed any of Jesus' teachings or sayings, focusing only on explaining and interpreting his death. This difference is evident in Paul's letters. He almost never mentions anything about Jesus' sermons, healings, or his life in general. It is all about Jesus' death. Even the Gospels reflect this. Virtually one-third of each Gospel is devoted to the last week of Jesus' life—all leading to his death.

We are able to see this difference between the Jesus movements and the Christ congregations in a comparison between another tradition and statement of faith that came from these "missing years." This is the story of the meal that eventually became "the Lord's Supper."

The following table compares the tradition of the Eucharist (the Lord's Supper), that had already been in existence in Damascus and Antioch when Paul was converted, with the Eucharist as is recorded in the Didache from the Jesus movements.

Notice that the Didache makes no reference to Jesus' death but links him to David. That this difference came to be gives us a real clue as to how events probably unfolded in these "missing years."

Since we are more familiar with the words from 1 Corinthians—after all, it is in the New Testament—it would mean that the Christ congregations and their traditions, rather than the Jesus movements, began exercising more and more influence over the developing course that Christianity took. That is exactly what occurred. But why?

1Corinthians 11 (circa 55 C.E.)	The Didache IX (circa 75 C.E.)
For I received from the Lord what I also delivered to you, that the Lord Jesus on the night when he was betrayed, took bread, and when he had given thanks, he broke it, and said, "This is my body which is for you. Do this in remembrance of me." In the same way also the cup, after supper, saying, "This cup is the new covenant in my blood. Do this, as often as you drink it, in remembrance of me." For as often as you eat this bread and drink this cup, you proclaim the Lord's death until he comes.	And concerning the Eucharist, hold Eucharist thus: First concerning the cup, "We give thanks to thee, our Father, for the Holy Vine of David thy child, which thou didst make known to us through Jesus thy child; to thee be glory forever."
	And concerning the broken bread: "We give thee thanks, our Father, for the life and knowledge which thou didst make known to us through Jesus thy child. To thee be glory forever."
Whoever, therefore, eats the bread or drinks the cup of the Lord in an unworthy manner will be guilty of profaning the body and the blood of the Lord. Let a man examine himself, and so eat of the bread and drink of the cup. For anyone who eats and drinks without discerning the body eats and drinks judgment upon himself. (vs. 23–29)	As this broken bread was scattered upon the mountains, but was brought together and became one, so let thy Church be gathered together from the ends of the earth in thy kingdom, for thine is the glory and the power through Jesus Christ for ever."
	But let none eat or drink of your Eucharist except those who have been baptized in the Lord's name. For concerning this also did the Lord say: "Give not that which is holy to the dogs." (vs. 1–5)

Table 8. *Comparison of the Eucharist. The Christ congregations, represented by the Corinthian statement, emphasize the death of Christ. The Jesus movements, represented by the Didache, emphasize Jesus' life.*

Why don't we know any more about these early Jesus Movement congregations? Why do we only seem to know about the Gentile (Diaspora) congregations from Paul's letters and Luke's Acts? Some of the answer may lie in the fact that many of the members of Jesus movements were perhaps poor, nonreading peasants. Being poor, when they wrote they would use a lower-grade papyrus that would not endure long. Except for the scrolls in the temple, perhaps they simply weren't from a culture of respecting or appreciating the written word. The fact that many of them fled Palestine during the Jewish uprising in the years leading up to the destruction of the temple in 70 C.E. would account for loss of documents. Perhaps documents and members of Jesus movements were intentionally destroyed.

To answer that question of why Christ congregations exercised the preponderant influence of the development of the New Testament and the early Church:

- We need to understand Paul;

- We need to understand what was happening between the various "Christian" groups;

- We need to understand what was happening between Judaism and all Jewish-Christian groups—Jesus Movement groups as well as Christ congregation groups;

- We need to understand the inherent difficulty in finding the "right words" to talk about this man Jesus and how individual lives were being transformed.

Discussions of these topics constitute the contents of Chapters 9 and 10.

Summary

The following exhibit graphically depicts the various simultaneous movements that were occurring during "the missing years."

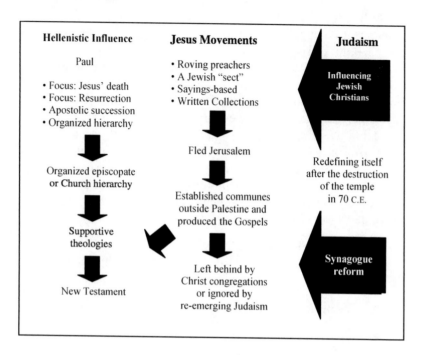

Exhibit 2. *Overview of the Development of New Testament.* The eventual emergence of the Christ congregations and their theology does not mean that the Hellenistic evolution of the Gospel is the "right" theology—only the primary surviving one.

Chapter 7 Notes

[22] Mack, *Who Wrote the New Testament*, p 41

[23] One of the oldest documents of Christian antiquity, dated between 75–90 C.E. Author unknown. It was designed for the newly baptized or for those preparing for Christianity. Highly esteemed by Jewish Christians in Palestine, Syria, and Egypt.

[24] Spong's writings, especially "Liberating the Gospels from Fundamentalism," covers this very well.

[25] Mack, *The Lost Gospel: The Book of Q*. Chapter 5 has an English translation of the reconstructed text.

[26] Data for this table is from Mack, *Who Wrote the New Testament*, pp 49-53

[27] Pagels, *The Gnostic Gospels*, pp xix-xx

[28] Mack, *Who Wrote the New Testament*, p. 71.

[29] Source: *The Tampa Tribune*, November 13, 2004, p. 1, "Chaos Engulfs Arafat Burial," byline: Steven Erlanger, *New York Times*.

[30] Crossan, *The Birth of Christianity*, Chapter 26: "Exegesis, Lament, and Biography," pp 527ff

[31] Mack, *Who Wrote the New Testament* p 95

[32] For further reading on these "missing years": John Dominic Crossan: *The Historical Jesus; The Birth of Christianity;* Burton Mack: *The Lost Gospel–The Book of Q; Who Wrote the New Testament; A Myth of Innocence;* Elaine Pagels: *The Gnostic Gospels;* John Shelby Spong: *Liberating the Gospels; Rescuing the Bible from Fundamentalism.*

Chapter 8

Part 2: From Jesus of Nazareth to the Christ of Faith – The "Missing Years" (30-70 C.E.)

𝔉ollowing his Crucifixion, the spirit of love embodied in the man Jesus continued to radically change the lives of people. But that commonality, felt by Jewish Christians or members of a Hellenistic Christ congregation, was complicated because, as real as it is, it is extremely difficult to verbalize. As we have seen in the previous chapter, each of these different groups was distinct primarily in how they communicated the reality of this indwelling spirit of love or of Jesus. All these groups were searching for a voice. There were voices of the Q Community, the Thomas group, the Miracle Stories groups, synagogue-based Jewish Christians who produced the Pronouncement Collections, and Hellenistic Christ congregations.

There were other voices as well. In this chapter we'll discuss the voice of Paul. In Chapter Ten we will discuss the voices of the Gospel writers. There is not a "correct" voice, nor a "right" one. *That's difficult to understand until you ask yourself the question: Is there a "correct" way for children to express their love for their grandparents?* All the voices are simply voices of people who have been transformed and who have found their distinct way of communicating that reality. Unfortunately, they did not understand that at the time. How their transformations were verbalized became more important than the transformations they had all experienced and had in common. So they fought and argued and splintered.

The Voice of Paul

What we know about Paul, known originally as the tentmaker Saul of Tarsus, we glean from his letters. His letters, not all of which are original to Paul, are the earliest surviving accounts, written in the decade of the 50s, of the years following Jesus' death. He tells us that he was a Pharisaic Jew. He was proud of his lineage. He was devout in the observance of the purity codes (of cleanliness and Jewish separateness) as the primary prescription for Jewish piety and righteousness (Phil. 3:5–6). All of this was typical for a Pharisee in the Diaspora, who would be zealous about being Jewish and obsessive about the role of Judaism in the larger world of peoples and cultures. From the tone of his letters, his knowledge of Greek, his vocabulary, and his ability to use the Greek forms of rhetoric, we know his education went beyond just understanding the Scriptures. In addition to being "very Jewish," he was also a Roman citizen. He was a well-known figure in Syria among the Diaspora synagogues, involved in their intellectual life as a proponent of Pharisaic standards of behavior.

The Pharisees had been known since about 300 B.C.E. as a group that championed Jewish exclusiveness—over and against the heathen and the *goyim*—and were generally quite liberal in their interpretation of Torah Law. They kept oral interpretations of the Law, and those collections, known first as the Mishnah, then as the Talmud, were used as legitimate guides for the living of a good Jewish life. However, by the time of Paul their views became more and more dogmatic and inflexible. Their view of the essence of Judaism was an endless round of man-derived external rituals: proper fasting, proper diet (e.g., kosher foods), strict adherence to the Sabbath, and proper preparation for evening prayers.

According to Gal. (1:14 and 5:11), Paul was well educated in Jewish Scriptures, zealous for the traditions, and preached circumcision. In effect he was a first-century Billy Graham, a "Jewish" missionary among Diaspora synagogues actively involved in discussions of practicalities and policies regarding Gentiles joining Hellenistic synagogues.

Being Jewish was both a way of life as well as an ethnic heritage. Circumcision was the mark of a Jew. So, obviously, gentiles had to be circumcised. But did that make them truly Jewish? Also, there were the promises to Abraham, prior to the

Mosaic Law and subsequent Torah, that through Abraham's descendents, all the nations will be blessed (Gen. 22:18).

Paul knew of the Christ congregations and was angry with them. To understand why the appearance of these Hellenistic Jewish-Christian groups upset him explains what happened to him. These Hellenistic Jewish-Christian groups had solved this "Gentile" problem simply by accepting gentiles into their Christ congregations. The mission of Israel, as a vehicle by which all nations were blessed, was now a reality for them. They were the new Kingdom and the new Kingdom included gentiles. This was a position absolutely opposite to all Paul stood for. It would destroy the Diaspora synagogue. It would destroy the Pharisaic sense of Jewish uniqueness.

Then something happened and Paul changed.

Paul knew of the *kerygma* of the Christ congregations and somewhere he came to the realization that it was true. Luke, writing some seventy years later, romanticizes Paul's change—calling it a conversion while on the road to Damascus. However, Paul doesn't call it a conversion. Sometimes Paul describes this new realization as a "call" and sometimes as a "revelation." Sometimes he says he received the Gospel (the *kerygma*) from these congregations, while at others he claims he received it straight from Jesus Christ through the Holy Spirit. It doesn't matter. I understand what he's trying to say.

Paul came to some sort of personal "seeing" that the Christ congregations were right. Circumcision will not make a gentile a true Jew, but it doesn't really matter. They can be part of God's new Kingdom anyway. Judaism's role in God's plan is not just for the Jews. God is using Judaism to reach all nations and it's working. Here are congregations of Gentiles and Jews together already. The external rites of the Jews don't really matter. What a breath of fresh air! What freedom! Paul uses different words at different times to say the same thing over and over again because these life-changing revelations are difficult to verbalize. For fourteen years, first in and around Damascus and then near his hometown of Tarsus, Paul studied and continued discussions about the inclusion of gentiles and what that might mean to his sense of Jewishness as an heir of the promises to Israel. Paul needed time to work out all the implications of his revelation in terms of his knowledge of the Scriptures and his background in Pharisaic practices.

Paul began to develop his thoughts from the primitive *kerygma* he had inherited. Then he expanded on the rationale to explain it—essentially to himself—to answer his own burning questions: What about the Law (the Torah)? I can't just toss that overboard. What about the rituals of purification that mark me as being Jewish? If these go away, what am I? He would espouse an answer after dinner in the home of one of these Christ congregations. He would refine it. Rethink it. Espouse it again. After developing answers to these questions—his questions—he began to build the framework that transformed his answers to a full-blown proclamation. Once again it was practice, revision, more practice, and more refinement. His construction followed the traditional Hellenistic style of debate and argument. This proclamation was something he could orate in public, Greek marketplaces, or *agoras.* He did this. He began to develop converts. It was working. It took him fourteen years.

I absolutely relate to this. After all, I waited seventeen years before I started to write this. Revelations take their time. For me, the difficulty was the verbalizing of real spiritual events. How are you supposed to do that? This issue is discussed in greater depth in the following chapter. Paul experienced something on the road to Damascus. Then he grew in the reality of that experience for fourteen years as he began preaching and before he began writing his letters. I feel a commonality with what Paul must have felt. He tried to integrate his new experience of grace and freedom within these Jewish-Gentile congregations with the reality of the Law (the Torah) as he knew it as a Pharisaic Jew. I am integrating my experience of the reality of a sense of spirituality in sobriety with the "proper" orthodox religious teaching I learned as a child and later as a graduate student in seminary.

Following his fourteen-year "sabbatical," Paul visited the "pillars" in Jerusalem—James, Peter, and John—to get their blessing on what he had termed his Gospel to the Gentiles. They apparently agreed to disagree. Yes, Paul could preach his Gospel to the Gentiles, but, no, that wasn't the "only" Gospel. Yes, gentiles didn't need to follow Jewish ritual practices, but no, Jews still needed to. Peter would be entrusted with the Gospel for the circumcised, and Paul would be entrusted with the Gospel for the uncircumcised (Gal. 2:3–14). It would appear that the "pillars" envisioned Christian congregations of practicing Jews—perhaps a Jewish sect within the umbrella of Judaism?—as well as Christian congregations of gentiles. There was no discussion about how (or if) they would interrelate.

Luke's account (Acts 9:1–31) written some seventy years later, really glamorized this "conversion" event. According to Luke, Paul began preaching immediately, even in Jerusalem. Paul's own words paint a more realistic picture—it took him a long, tedious time to develop his Gospel.

Paul found his initial converts among the "god fearers," otherwise known as gentiles who were already associated with Diaspora synagogues. He founded some congregations while others, namely Damascus, Corinth, Ephesus, and Rome, had been founded by other anonymous leaders. Up until this time these Hellenistic Christ congregations were not truly worshipping communities with an articulated, orthodox creed. Their gatherings were a social arena for those who were creating a brand new Kingdom—Jew and Gentile alike—built around some elemental beliefs and common, real experiences.

An example of the reality of these transformed lives—the new freedom in the love of Jesus the Christ—that was occurring in these small congregations can be found in Paul's tiny letter to Philemon. He is asking Philemon to take back his runaway slave Onesimus. Paul urges Philemon to take back Onesimus, not as a slave but as a brother. A transforming reality indeed! Here is a concrete example of the difference between the "renewing" behavior of these societies within Christian congregations and the Greco-Roman society of the "real" world.

Paul's Greatest Contribution

Paul's unique contribution was to turn the primitive *kerygma* of these embryonic Christ congregations into a full-blown proclamation. He had worked out his explanation that God's plan all along had been a divine invitation, through Israel's divine history, to all the nations to join the House of Israel and share her special Covenant. The same "fire in his belly" that had given him so much energy in proclaiming the Pharisaic system among

157

Hellenized synagogues, now propelled him to become a missionary to the gentiles.

The touchstone of his Gospel was "freedom from the Law." Gentiles could become Christians, join the House of Israel, and not keep Jewish law, i.e., the Pharisaic codes of Jewish identity: purity codes of diet and foods, circumcision, and reliance on genealogy. Paul did not intend to imply that gentiles could forsake the high ethical standards of Judaism, based on Mosaic Law, and for which all Jews were known and respected throughout the Greco-Roman world. Paul's Gospel, however, created some problems. If it took God this long to offer all the nations the invitation to join Israel, then what of those that had died before this invitation was issued? In virtually all of his letters he tries to deal with this issue. His explanations and imagery vary as he works through it, as does his understanding of the apocalyptic. At times his Jewish belief in the resurrection comes through, at times it sounds more like the Greek concept of immortality. Sometimes his discussions have an apocalyptic ring to them, sometimes not.

There were two other significant issues Paul raised in the elaboration of his Gospel that became critical for the spread of the brand of budding Christianity espoused by Christ congregations. One was his revision of Israel's history. The other was his claim for authority as an apostle.

Revising Israel's History

In short, Paul was trying to force-fit the spiritual freedom of grace and unconditional love he had experienced (the round peg) into the theological framework of purification and sacrifice (the square hole) that was so integral to his Jewishness. He began by attempting to revise Israel's history. That process was convoluted, torturous, and based on the primitive beliefs of the earliest Christ congregations. This revision focused on Abraham. The elements of Mosaic Law (Torah), the temple ritual, and the monarchy under revitalized anointed priest-kings were all but disappeared. The argument went like this: Abraham was promised a great nation (Israel) and through him all nations would be blessed. This promised blessing was because of Abraham's faith and righteousness, because he believed Yahweh. Since the Law came much later in Israel's history, the Law was obviously "added" to the original promise. Why? The Law helped serve the people of

Israel by keeping them on the right track. Without the Law, they would have floundered. But the Law didn't "save" anyone. All it could do was condemn a wrongdoer. The promise made to Abraham before the Law was finally fulfilled in Jesus of Nazareth who was faithful and righteous, like Abraham, even to death on a cross. By believing in Jesus as the Christ, the blessing of God in Abraham was now available to all nations, Jew and Gentile alike.

This all makes sense because, to us, it is quite familiar. This is what we have come to understand about the relationship of the Old Testament to the Gospel. It all makes sense until we begin to look at what Paul had to omit from the Scriptures:

> "The early history of the covenants is missing. The covenant with Moses is negated. The Leviticus charter for the system of feasts, festivals, and sacrifices is completely overlooked. David and Solomon do not appear. The Kingdom ideal and history are not mentioned. The proclamations of the prophets do not play a role. Messianic ideology is not the bridge. And there is only the slightest mention of an apocalyptic end of history—the ending of the epic that played such a large role in Paul's letter to the Thessalonians. Everything hinges on the Abraham-Christ connection. ... Christ was no longer being thought of as a historical person, a martyr, or a god, but as a spiritual field of force and divine agency. Christ in this conception combines the notions of personal deity, tribal patriarch, genealogical agent, ethnic principle, cultural spirit, and cosmic power"[33]

By ignoring (or being ignorant of) the life and teachings of Jesus—the message of the reality—NOW—of God's new Kingdom—Paul moved his Gospel into the arena of theory and abstraction. In so doing, Paul took the first steps in transforming the Christ of Faith to the Christ of Theology. In Paul one finds virtually no mention of the teachings, preaching, sayings or healings of Jesus. That's because Paul was overwhelmed by two events: (1) the focus of the Christ congregations in the Diaspora—an approach of Hellenistic philosophy coupled with Roman sense of orderliness; and (2) how to resolve this cosmic Christ's death and atonement of sins with Paul's own understanding of the role of the Torah Law and the temple rites and rituals of sacrifice and worship that satisfied Yahweh. In wrestling with these, and developing "arguments" that he could proclaim in Greek agoras,

Paul found little reason to discuss the life and teachings of Jesus of Nazareth.

Paul's letters, although most were written in response to specific issues or questions, contain all that we know of him. They don't present a coherent, systematic picture of his "theology." Paul struggled to find the words, the language, to express what he had experienced. It was not a series of "logical" arguments in the vein of Greek rationalism. In fact he described "logical" (hence, Greek) rationalism as "foolishness" (1 Cor. 1:22-25). What "logic" is in his writings is in the vein of the rabbinic use of proof texts from Jewish Scripture, for example, as he tried to recast Israel's history to illustrate how it had accounted for the inclusion of gentiles all along. Paul was communicating from a sense of a subjective and mystical experience "... that made him describe Jesus as a sort of atmosphere in which 'we live and move and have our being.' "[34]

Did Paul believe Jesus was God?

Neither Paul nor other New Testament writers attempted to articulate a precise, definitive explanation of the personal transformations they had experienced. Instead they painted verbal portraits using phrases such as "new creation," "new life," "in Christ," and "baptized into his death." Jesus was the first example of a new kind of humanity—consistent with Jesus' own words that his "powers" from God were not simply for him but for all who had the Kingdom of God inside them. In this sense Jesus was the new Adam—new humanity—in which Jews and gentiles could fully participate. Was Jesus God to Paul and other early Christians? No. Paul must be understood within his Jewish contexts.

From Phil. 2:6–11 (*New English Bible*):

"Let your bearing towards one another arise out of your life in Christ Jesus. For the divine nature was his from the first; yet he did not think to snatch at equality with God, but made himself nothing, assuming the nature of a slave. Bearing the human likeness, revealed in human shape, he humbled himself, and in obedience accepted even death—death on a cross. Therefore God raised him to the heights and bestowed on him the name above all names, that at the name of Jesus every knee should bow—in heaven, on earth, and in the depths—and every tongue confess, 'Jesus Christ is Lord,' to the glory of God the Father."

When I look at this early Christian hymn, Paul is reflecting on the fact that to be a follower of Jesus means to be self-sacrificing as was Jesus. In no way is Paul, still a good Jew (although a Christian one), assuming that Jesus was somehow a divine god second only to YHWH. Yes, Jesus was exalted and had the title "Lord" conferred on him by God. But Jesus was a man who, in Jewish context, had become the Messiah. He was still distinct and inferior to YHWH. When John wrote his almost-Gnostic Gospel almost a half-century later, his use of the "Word" as a preexistent form is used within Jewish context as well—the same context he used for words like glory, spirit, divine wisdom, and others. "When Paul and John spoke about Jesus as though he had some kind of preexistent life, they were not suggesting that he was a second divine 'person' in the later Trinitarian sense. They were indicating that Jesus had transcended temporal and individual modes of existence. Because the 'power' and 'wisdom' that he represented were activities that derived from God, he had in some way expressed 'what there was from the beginning.' "[35]

The Jews were absolute monotheists. So was Paul. The Jewish Messiah is not a divine figure. The Messiah would be an ordinary human being that would do privileged "God-things." The Son of God was a simple way to express the closeness of the Messiah's actions to the will and power of God. Only the gods of the pagans had "sons" or offspring. "It should be noted that Paul never called Jesus 'God.' He called him the 'Son of God' in its Jewish sense. He certainly did not believe that Jesus had been the incarnation of God himself; he had simply possessed God's 'powers' and 'spirit,' which manifested God's activity on earth and were not to be identified with the inaccessible divine essence."[36]

Also it needs to be kept in mind, although I mentioned it earlier, Jesus never claimed that his divine powers were his alone or special to him. On many occasions he promised his followers that if they had faith they could exercise these same powers. "By faith, of course, he did not mean adopting the correct theology but cultivating an inner attitude of surrender and openness to God."[37] This inner attitude is the Kingdom of God that Jesus proclaimed: An infusion of God consciousness in the here and now. This was a consciousness or oneness with God that was not only attainable but expected. That's why Jesus could say repeatedly, *"Greater things than I do will you do."* His earliest commands to his followers probably were: *"Go! Visit in a home. Eat what they serve you. Heal their sick. Teach them. Then go on your way after instructing them to become healers themselves."* We are in this Kingdom now. It is an eternal now. This Kingdom is not something to come in some future time.

Who was Jesus according to Paul? Paul proclaimed a Lord who would judge the entire world in righteousness by the man Jesus, whom God had ordained and whose authority God had certified by resurrecting him from the dead (Acts 17:30–31). But this understanding by Paul was clearly all within a Jewish context. He, and all who first heard him, would have understood about the Messiah, the use of Adam as a synonym for humanity, the nature of a spiritual resurrection in the Pharisaic sense, the use of the terms Son of Man, Son of God, or Lord. Unfortunately, later Church Fathers, as well as those of some form of Pauline "school" who penned letters[38] in his name after his death, were thoroughly Hellenistic and didn't fully understand these Jewish nuances.

Paul knew the risen Lord from the Spirit of God who had touched him. As a Pharisee, he believed in both the resurrection of the dead as well as in angels and spirits. [Note: The Sadducees believed in neither.] It is unclear whether Paul believed in the "physical" Resurrection of Jesus. He clearly believed, however, that the Holy Spirit of God touched him and let him know that the spirit of Jesus had not been defeated by physical death. That's all Paul needed to know. I believe he would have thought serious discussions about whether or not there was a physical resurrection would have been moot. He "knew" the spirit of the Lord was alive and that was all that mattered. I also think he would have been appalled at the arguments and near schisms that took place over the next several hundred years as scholars and Church leaders tried to establish the Doctrine of the Trinity, splitting such linguistic hairs (and almost the Church!) over whether the Greek word *homoousion* (meaning: the same) or *homoiousion* (meaning: similar) best described the nature of Jesus in relation to the nature of God.

The Theology of the Atonement or Why Did Jesus Die?

The focus of Christ congregations was on the question: Why did Jesus die? Their answer: His death gave us salvation; his death atoned for our sins. Thus, in theological terms we are dealing with the theology of the Atonement: What did Jesus do to accomplish our salvation?[39] As a Pharisaic Jew trying to verbalize the reality of the freedom he sensed in Jesus, yet wanting not to discard the importance of the Law or Torah, Paul spells out the importance of the death of Jesus. Jesus died for our sins. The work of Christ was, by and large, the work of Jesus' death. Jesus satisfied the Law. Little attention was paid to Jesus' life and teachings. With the predominance of Paul's understanding of the Atonement, it is difficult to comprehend why the Church Fathers agreed to incorporate the Synoptic Gospels and their emphasis on Jesus' life. Perhaps they didn't understand that there was an inherent conflict between the Gospels and their emphasis on the importance of Jesus' life and the primitive *kerygma* of Paul, which paid no attention to his life. Was the additional emphasis of Jesus' life just a sidetrack from the main message or was it an attempt to supply integral elements that are missing from the primitive *kerygma*?

A variety of answers tried to answer the question, What did Christ do to accomplish our salvation? According to my Systematic Theology professor, George Hendry: "If we ask, 'To whom did Christ do what he did, and toward whom was it directed,' we find that the answers which have been given fall into three groups."[40] There is the Classical Theory, the Transactional Theory, and the Subjective Theory.

- The *Classical Theory* postulates that the work of Christ was directed to the powers of evil. Stated briefly: Christ, the God-Man, came to act upon the enemy of God and man, that is the devil. Jesus won that battle.

- The *Transactional Theory* states that the subject of Christ's atoning work is God. In short: Christ did something to God. Sometimes it's stated that he paid a penalty, or discharged a debt, or performed an act of obedience, or made a confession, or offered a sacrifice— something by which he procured forgiveness for mankind. Forgiveness of mankind by God is the byproduct or outcome of a transaction of some sort between God and Christ.

- The *Subjective Theory* is focused on mankind. The atoning work of Christ is really the love of God working through Christ, whose actions evoke a responsive love in the hearts of mankind—a love that cannot die. Christ saves us by the moral influence he exerts on us by being our example.

Of these three theories, the Transactional Theory has held the most sway from Paul to later theologians—both Catholic and Protestant—throughout the centuries. For the Transactional Theory to work, Jesus must have absolutely fulfilled the requirements of the Law (the Torah). That meant he must have been perfect, which meant in turn he must have been sinless. Since sinlessness is impossible for a "normal" human, Jesus must have been "other-than-normal" or divine. But he had to be human, too. Hence a God-Man kind of idea was articulated. So later stories were written about his miracles and about his temptations. If he were divine and sinless, then he could not have been born normally, via a sinful man and a sinful woman. Therefore he must have been born differently. Hence we have the later stories of the Virgin birth. Things begin to fall into place.

But what is the significance of Jesus' life? Well, according to the Transactional Theory, it isn't very significant, nor is it very necessary, except, as Paul puts it: Jesus needed to be born of woman and born under the Law (Gal. 4:4). Paul's letters indicate that lack of importance. He devotes virtually no space discussing the life or teachings of Jesus. Some will say he didn't need to cover the subject. He probably covered it in other letters. But Paul was not shy. He had no problem going over "old" material time and time again. He didn't stress the life and teachings of Jesus because it wasn't germane.

Hendry offers a unique alternative, which does take the life of Jesus seriously.

"Why did Christ die? The answer of the transactional type of theory has been that he died in order that forgiveness might be made possible. But if we view his death in the context of his life and seek the clue to its meaning there, the answer we must give is that he died because forgiveness was actual, because it was present in him, in the personal relations of his incarnate life with men at the human level. [Yes, there was suffering.] But the suffering was not imposed on him by God in order to satisfy the inexorable requirements of the divine justice. Its necessity is grounded in the nature of the divine forgiveness and the human reaction to it.

"The simplest answer to the question why Christ died is that men put him to death. They rejected him and killed him because they hated him. Such behavior might be considered strange toward one who came among them as the bearer of the gift of forgiveness, and indeed, the welcome accorded him in the early days of his public ministry shows that men were not indisposed to receive the gospel of forgiveness. But the gospel was [not separated from] the law, and the forgiveness of God, which Christ brought, was also the judgment of God; and this was his undoing. Those who were ready to welcome the gospel were alienated by the law ["Stop doing what you're doing and change your ways," he said] that went with it, and those who were willing to receive the law were antagonized by the accompanying gospel; and thus Jesus was rejected by both sections of the people, both by the righteous [obedient Jews, Sadducees, and Pharisees] who needed no repentance and by the sinners whom he called to repentance. ...

"The encounter of divine grace and human sin has the nature of a collision, and as such it necessarily involves suffering. ... *The suffering of Christ is not the suffering of our sin as it encounters the judgment of God; it is the suffering of the love of God as it encounters sin.* ... In other words, the necessity of his suffering is a necessity of grace, not satisfaction; for the grace of God in forgiveness is exercised by incarnation, i.e., by his condescension to enter into personal relations with men at their level and thus, in consequence, to place himself in their power."[41]

The conflict evidenced in Jesus' life and crucifixion is the conflict between the love of God and the shortsightedness, selfishness, fear, desire to control, and egoism of mankind. In short, the love of God met mankind's desire to be in control. Mankind's desire to stay in control killed him, but the love of God won. His spirit of love remained alive in these little groups that continued to meet, to eat, to destroy all social barriers, and to simply accept one another. The spirit of those groups was real. His spirit was among them. The personal transformations they were experiencing were real. For them it was as if Jesus wasn't dead after all, and they would have said so, just as the Palestinian mourner at Yasser Arafat's funeral said so.

Paul's Authority as an Apostle

Clearly, there were other preachers of the Gospel besides Paul. Some, like Paul, were in Hellenized Syria and Asia Minor. Some were of the Jewish Jesus Movement thinking, namely that Christianity was a sect of Judaism—some would be circumcised members, others would be uncircumcised. Regardless, Paul railed against those that challenged his view of the Gospel. With Paul came not only a full proclamation of the early primitive *kerygma* but almost simultaneously a focus on governance issues within these embryonic congregations. This focus on governance led him to protect himself with the breastplate of "apostolic" authority and then use that protection as he defended his flock (and his proclamation) against "false prophets." His understandable concern for how a congregation functioned became inexorably entwined with his efforts to articulate a sacred history that blended his Old Testament roots with the experience of freedom he discovered in these Christ congregations.

In Chapter 10 we will discuss how early Church Fathers were impressed with Paul's success at bolstering his credentials by referring to his perceived relationship to the Apostles and "pillars." They used this same logic to bolster their position. Eventually this self-serving, supportive argument led to the rational theology of Apostolic Succession, the cornerstone of papal authority and, incidentally, of biblical literalism.

After reading Paul's earliest letters to the congregations at Thessalonica and Galatia, one can notice that his message begins to shift. When we read Corinthians, it is obvious the congregation there is "overdoing" it. They were exhibiting rather bizarre spiritual behavior: sexual practices, mystical experiences of all sorts, including ecstatic speaking, and ritual powers including baptisms of the dead. This shift in Paul's writing is from the proclamation of his Gospel and mission to the gentiles to the sober governance of these new congregations. His writings change somewhat—depending on the situation in the particular congregation, depending on his emerging theology, depending on his sense of Jewish morality, and depending on his belief that the world was to be ending within the next decade, at most.

By the time of Paul's death (66–69 C.E.), his letters were being widely circulated in Asia Minor. Peter was dead. James, the brother of Jesus and head of the "pillars" in Jerusalem, was dead. The war with Rome was imminent. The Jesus Movement groups were beginning to leave Palestine and with their departure to safer environs went whatever influence these sayings-based groups had over this emerging Hellenistic church of many congregations.

The Hellenized Christian sect was pulling away from their Jewish Jesus Movement brethren. As they did, their protective status as a part of Roman-sanctioned Judaism faded away as well. On their own they were subject to the Roman Empire—and it was awfully jealous of any religious movement—especially one that proclaimed another kingdom with another king. Tests of loyalty to Caesar became the norm, just as it had been with every other religious group. For example, the "love feast"—as early congregations referred to the Eucharist—was misunderstood for sexual or cannibalistic rites. The groups were suspected of political treason by way of their worship of another king. They began being turned in to authorities. They were imprisoned, punished, fined, tortured, executed. They were scared and fearful. Understandably so. Questions, also understandable, arose, whose thrust was more along the lines of church orderliness, governance, and specific instructions for personal behavior, collective actions, and proper belief.

Couched within an emerging fear-based faith that demanded "control" of the situation, emerging Church Fathers began picking up on Paul's themes and the logic of his arguments. They took his Gospel of freedom and his descriptions of accepted behavior (for proper governance of a congregation) and began "converting" these lists into an almost Pharisaic Law of Christian behavior. If you're a Christian, you'll do x and y. If you don't do x and y, then you're not a "real" Christian. If Paul could have heard them, he would have cringed.

The same process we have seen with the Deuteronomic Code was beginning all over again. There were some situations where it was important, in a clandestine way, to be able to identify another Christian. The use of the fish symbol was one of these. The Greek word *ichthus* means fish. The individual letters, however, were used as an acronym for Jesus Christ, Son of God, Savior. But beyond these rather practical intentions, people began latching onto these lists of do's and don'ts as an indisputable litmus test of authentic Christian faith. This process continued, even though the original intention was lost, in the same manner as did the growing "rules" of the Deuteronomic Reformers—almost creating a straitjacket for God. These lists of accepted/approved Christian behaviors created a "neat" box of instructions that eventually allowed the confidence with which one could predict how God would dispense his rewards and punishments. These early Church Fathers were understandably concerned about personal behavior, as well as congregational order and standards of conduct. But to inadvertently twist Paul's Gospel of Freedom into a rigid, dogmatic, pharisaical set of personal ethics violated all that Paul preached.

Emerging Church leaders, shepherding whole districts of congregations, were appearing on the scene: Ignatius of Antioch, Clement I of Rome, and Polycarp. Who were these men? How did they come to call themselves bishops or presbyters? We don't know. How did they decide to organize themselves in this particular way—where a bishop oversaw several congregations? We don't know. Perhaps it was an offshoot of their Roman culture of orderliness and efficient administration. Perhaps it was a natural outgrowth of their desire to help smaller, newer, struggling congregations. Perhaps it was all of that. But we really don't know.

Picking up on Paul's idea of apostolic succession, these early Church Fathers, as they are now called, began writing to each other as well as writing to their own congregations. They circulated their correspondence, along with Paul's letters, among the Christ Congregations of Asia Minor and Greece. The focus of these letters? How to provide assistance, how to act, and what to believe. Later, as other Church leaders disagreed with them, these Church Fathers cited their own "accepted" letters as they defended their positions or condemned their adversaries. What constituted an "accepted" letter or an "accepted" Church Father? Being one whose correspondence was widely circulated. By accepting and circulating only correspondence they agreed with, these early Fathers were able to construct an effective circular argument that built in a certain amount of self-fulfilling, orthodox acceptance of their positions.

Intra-Christian Group Conflict

Since there was no book similar to *Robert's Rules of Order*, there was no specific guide to illuminate how Jesus groups were to operate. Each group followed their own heart. Yes, they agreed Jesus was the founder. Yes, the tradition of a common meal was observed. Yes, most seemed to view the Scripture as some form of authority. But they had to settle in to an organizational model, assign certain common activities, and agree to certain authorities. There were no formal leadership roles. All the evidence we have from this early period indicates the leaders were the "prophets" (from early Q literature), the "pillars" in Jerusalem, and/or James, the brother of Jesus. We do know, as well, of other functions—household patrons or hosts, deacons, teachers, and the like—but are unclear about what leadership, if any, they provided.

Real problems arose, however, as to how to use the Jewish ritual codes that had served for centuries as a common authority for social behavior and identity. Perhaps this was most evident in the arena of ritual purity: "Who came to dinner, who served it, and what was served were truly decisive questions. Those movements that decided in favor of keeping the Jewish codes became Jewish sectarians; those who decided against them eventually had to construct a whole new system of authority.[42]

Paul's letters underscore the intensity with which leaders of the various movements—including Paul himself—competed for authority. Different groups had different roles (or different rankings) to account for the practical maintenance of a group. This could degenerate into open hostility when one group was confronted with different roles or ranking from another group. Paul sought to clarify the rankings (1 Cor. 12:28): Apostles, prophets, teachers, miracle-workers, healers, helpers, administrators, and those who could speak in tongues. When Paul was challenged by other "contending" apostles, he would beat his own drum, praise his own accomplishments, resort to his own "commissioning" by the twelve "pillars" (which made him an "equal" Apostle in his own mind), and finally blast the opposition by calling them "false apostles." Indeed, the conflict over an established authority was intense.

The failure to resolve these conflicts within the Jesus movements, coupled with the historical realities of the impending Roman invasion to put down the growing Jewish revolt (66–70 C.E.), produced a series of withdrawals from the scene. Some of the sayings-based groups were domesticated within Judaism. Others became more gnosticized over time. The "pillars" fled Jerusalem for Pella. The family of Jesus fled to the Transjordan. The Johannine Community withdrew, formed some type of communal retreat that reflected Gnostic themes. The Matthean Community had concluded Jesus' essential message was a call to a personal piety that was consistent with the Law of Moses. They saw themselves as being true to Jesus' message and true to the spirit of the Torah. The community that spawned Mark also seems to have been some sort of communal retreat. Mark's group had severed ties with Judaism and apparently with other competitive forms of early Christianity—both Jesus groups and Christ congregations. As he constructed his Gospel he used the dominate thematic myths of the Christ congregations, wove in many of the themes of the Sayings-Based Collections of the Jesus movements (pronouncements, parables, miracles, and the like), and created a framework for a narrative that would explain why Jesus died and what it meant.

Conflicts with Judaism

As these varieties of "Christian" groups and associations were coming into existence, conflicts with "formal" Judaism were normal and could have been predicted. These new associations threatened Jewish symbols and social markers that had been in place for centuries. Competition arose early on as Jewish Christians urged fellow "traditional" Jews to join their group, movement, association, or congregation. Fifty years later, as many of the Gospels were being written, memories of this competition and Judaism's negative reactions were described in terms of "persecution."

It is likely that the Galilean itinerant preachers/prophets had little conflict with standard Judaism. These itinerants were simply "out there doing their own thing." They were preaching upon expanded themes of Jesus—both borrowing from existing embryonic collections of sayings and probably adding to them as well. The genealogically-based "pillars" of Jerusalem were also not much in conflict with standard Judaism either. They were in Jerusalem, infused with the temple ritual and Pharisaic external practices (diet, codes for clean and unclean, circumcision, basic meal rituals). This would not have caused much consternation with the Sadducees or Pharisees but visibility and popularity would have threatened the high priests and scribes. Whatever sense of conflict there may have been with formal Judaism probably disappeared after James was executed and the remaining "pillars" fled Jerusalem in the mid-60s with the impending Roman legions ready to squelch the Jewish independence rebellion.

The remaining Jesus movements in the Diaspora that were not part of the Christ congregations had a difficult time with formal Judaism and the synagogue. They had tried to remain within these traditional structures. They had tried—and failed—to convince Jews who wanted to keep the temple and Pharisaic signs of identity. They ran afoul of the Pharisees as they tried to discuss new Jewish-Christian ideas that were alterations in the nuance of the Law and were based simply on the authority of Jesus. The Pharisees would counter with reams of Scriptural precedents. If these Christian (but Jewish) groups in the Diaspora were not some form of alternative to formal Judaism, then what were they? They didn't know. By the 60s, with the escalation of tensions with the Romans, these groups too were beginning to fade away. The influence these Jewish-Christian groups in the Diaspora did have was in the creation of the Gospels. We'll discuss that in Chapter 10. However, there were two Jewish-Christian groups who didn't fade away: the Ebionites and the Nazareans. Both of these Jesus Movement groups continued well into the third century, but with little influence on the budding Christian Church.

Summary

As the middle of the first century passed, the Jesus movements were becoming less influential in spite of the reputation of the "pillars" in Jerusalem. This was due to conflicts among themselves, conflicts with Judaism, and fleeing the growing Jewish restlessness, revolt, and impending Roman police action.

The Christ congregations, on the other hand, had achieved a remarkable and distinct identity—and very quickly! They had also gotten organized quickly to help each other, including the congregation in Jerusalem. Their Roman sense of orderliness came into play as well, built around the hierarchy of bishops, councils of bishops, elders, deacons, and other church workers. They had borrowed Hellenized conceptions of Israel and, by the 60s, pretty much left the synagogue altogether. These Hellenized Christ congregations were the groups that had so irritated Paul—in his words: "So, I persecuted them." Paul had no legal authority to persecute anybody but he did, I'm sure, harass them, argue against them, and did all he could to disrupt their rapid rise in Hellenized northern Syria. Now these same congregations were flourishing because of Paul.

Chapter 8 Notes

[33] Mack, *Who Wrote the New Testament*, pp 117-119.

[34] Armstrong, *History of God*, pp 87, 88.

[35] Ibid., p. 89.

[36] Ibid., p. 83.

[37] Ibid., p. 82.

[38] Ephesians, Colossians, 1 & 2 Timothy, Titus, and Hebrews.

[39] In the following discussion I am indebted to my professor of Systematic Theology at Princeton Theological Seminary, George Hendry, and his wonderful book, *The Gospel of the Incarnation*.

[40] Ibid., p 115.

[41] Ibid., pp 141-143. Italics mine.

[42] Mack, *A Myth of Innocence*, p. 129.

Chapter 9

The Difficulty in "Finding the Right Words"

Throughout the previous two chapters, the issue of communicating deep spiritual realities has been raised. If we cannot begin to see these biblical persons as we see ourselves, then they truly will be different from us. They will be from another age, another era. For them, God will be more a part of their lives than he will be a part of our lives today. If that is the case, then the Bible truly will be of another age as well, to be enjoyed or worshipped for its mystique and magic. But if the biblical writers are as we, then we can begin seeing ourselves in them and seeing them in us. In this way the spirit of God allows the many centuries and different cultural trappings to dissolve, resulting in the spiritual realities, not biblical literalsim, of biblical times becoming true for us today.

In order to put a human face on the issue of communicating deep spiritual realities, I want to tell you about my journey to sobriety and a subsequent incident that occurred in an Alcoholics Anonymous meeting five or six years later. Although it's a tiny example, it's real, current, and relevant to what was happening in Palestine and Syria during these "missing" years, 30–70 C.E.

My journey into sobriety was an exceptionally spiritual experience to me. How do I discuss this spiritual experience without sounding "hokey"? How do I find the words to verbalize things I "knew" but didn't understand and didn't know how to verbalize? If I had been in one of these initial groups or associations (either a Jesus Movement group or a Christ

Congregation), would I have driven people out of the group? Been driven out? The issues I talk about below are very real to me and explain a "sense" of connection I feel to these early pioneers during the "missing years."

My Story

Good Friday fell on April 17 in 1987, and I saw a doctor about my sickness. I will never forget that day because it was the day my Self died. Of course my Self didn't decide to die. It had been beaten to a pulp by my abuse of alcohol and all the things that went with it: borderline malnutrition, every kind of deficiency imaginable, and resolute abstinence of exercise.

That weekend my attending physician told me that had she seen my blood workup without seeing me, she would have assumed I had recently arrived from Biafra, Bangladesh, or some other ravaged Third World country. "I cannot recall seeing potassium levels this low. Have you had a problem with muscle cramps—especially in your legs?"

Involuntarily, I winced remembering what I could of the last six months. Three or four nights a week I would be forced awake by pain. I would down a jigger of vodka and in a cold sweat I would beat furiously on my calf muscle. But no matter what I did, I would watch it grow to the size of a softball while my foot twisted and contorted until it looked like a preserved bird's claw. Lordy! Did that hurt!

"Yes," I replied, "I've had some problems with muscle cramps."

I am a miracle. At this writing, I haven't had a drink in almost nineteen years.

I still relish, most mornings, the simple fact of waking up, rather than coming to. I still feel overjoyed sipping my first cup of coffee and remembering last night's conversation, rather than staring into a black void in my memory, forcing down some coffee laced with vodka, and hoping I wouldn't gag.

It's hell to be dead inside and thinking all the while, "This is life!" It's hell trying to time your drunk so that you can just make it to bed before you pass out or fall over comatose on the couch and embarrassing your daughter and her friends. It's hell to dread answering the phone because it'll be another bill collector. Or to let mail stack up, unopened, for weeks because it's bills you can't pay, or 'deadbeat' letters, or some other form of bad news.

Bad news. ... Bad news. ... For me, plain and simple, that's what reality had become—bad news. So I drank my vodka to avoid it, and I avoided it well. I avoided people. I avoided my children. I avoided bad news. I avoided all news. I avoided life. I avoided reality. I avoided everything except my vodka.

During the last year, I was drinking about a fifth a day and a half-gallon over the weekend. I had to have alcohol in my blood at all times, twenty-four hours a day, just to feel normal. That meant I had to have a drink every four hours or so—even in the middle of the night. And during that whole time it never dawned on me that this was abnormal.

Eight or nine months before April 17, 1987, I awoke one morning at three with severe indigestion and had my son take me to an emergency care facility. My diagnosis: critical, acute pancreatitis. "An ambulance is being arranged to take you to the hospital. Oh! By the way, your blood alcohol level is 2.8!" I had gone to bed (a.k.a. passed out) at 10:30 P.M. that summer night. If I had a blood alcohol level of 2.8 five hours later, just how drunk was I when I "went" to bed? In the mid-to-upper-threes? That's well into the range of toxic, fatal alcohol poisoning.

I had done that night after night after night!

That was my life and that's what I thought I had to do in order to "cope." I thought I was relatively normal under the circumstances. After all, if you had my life, wouldn't you drink, too?

I was relatively normal. I was a relatively normal alcoholic—a maintenance drinker who had lived for thirteen or fourteen years drinking a pint of booze every evening between 6 and 11 P.M. Then, all at once, I needed more. My sense of control left. Sometimes I could drink almost a fifth and appear outwardly sober. Other times I could have only several drinks and I'd black out. This loss of control terrified me because it threatened my ability to maintain my pretense—my front—to the world: that I was successful; that I had an important, pressure-packed job; that I was a good father; that ... well, you get the picture. Anything that would crack that shell and let the world see the awful mess and hollowness inside me was to be avoided at all costs.

The last year or so of heavy drinking began with intermittent shots of vodka during the night. I'd wake up at 4 A.M. in a cold sweat with the shakes. Later, leg cramps would come as well. I'd go to the bathroom and then "snitch" a swig of vodka. Soon, that 4 A.M. pattern became a 1 A.M. and 5 A.M. pattern. I didn't understand that I was experiencing alcohol withdrawal. It seemed that three or four hours was about as long as I could go without a drink—day or night, asleep or at work—day after day. I began carrying a flask with me to work because I couldn't last all the way to the two double-vodka gimlets I had for lunch. I kept a bottle in my car so I could make it home after work (as well as one in the trunk—for emergencies! Unless you've been there, it's hard to imagine the nightmarish, stark terror of being stalled in traffic gridlock—alone—with the thought of no vodka.).

Within the blink of an eye I was having mid-morning and mid-afternoon grapefruit cocktails at my desk. I now believe that those two small cans of grapefruit juice were providing me all the nourishment I'd get some days. Co-workers and clients began to complain of alcohol on my breath. I would explain I had a prescription throat spray for my sinuses. I bought a pair of self-darkening prescription glasses to help hide my red, puffy eyes.

Rule number one: Keep up the pretense. Rule number two: There are no other rules.

I was a mess, and it all crashed that fateful Good Friday. For several weeks my guts had been hurting again, and I was fearful that my pancreatitis was returning. In reality it was my liver. That Friday I left work early to go home, drink some buttermilk, and nap. Often, that had helped. This time it didn't.

I got up about five in the afternoon and walked to a corner supermarket to get some food for my cats, a frozen dinner, and some beer. I had thought that maybe beer wouldn't be as hard on my stomach as vodka. Right there—in the middle of a store filled with Easter weekend shoppers, in front of God and everybody—I had an uncontrollable "panic attack" (code words for severe, acute withdrawal). I was flushed, sweaty, and shook like a quaking aspen. I couldn't write out my check. After I told the cashier that I had fallen on a tennis court and cracked my elbow, he filled out my check—all but the signature. I scribbled something on the signature block and left. The check bounced. I still have it, and to this day I cannot read what I scrawled as my name.

At home I fed the cats, tried to drink a beer, vomited, and called the after-hours emergency number of my medical care facility. I still had the shakes but they weren't quite as severe. The advice nurse calmly, quickly, gently, and firmly urged and encouraged me to come in ... immediately—*right now*—if not sooner. "Yes," she had answered, "it does sound like a problem that needs immediate attention." If I didn't believe I could drive, she would help me arrange for a cab.

I remained at the emergency facility for about five hours, until almost midnight. I sat in the waiting room, then I sat in an examination room. A technician came to take some blood and I returned to the waiting room. This whole process was repeated, only this time the doctor waited for me at the end of a long hallway, so she could escort me to the examination room. More blood. Back to the waiting room. Back down the hallway to the examination room. Finally I was told to go get something to eat, asked to come back the following morning, and received a prescription for one 25mg Librium capsule. One lousy pill, and I had to go to an all-night pharmacy to get it filled. I got home about 1 A.M. and ate my frozen dinner.

The next morning was Saturday. More blood. That's when my doctor told me about my potassium level—or lack thereof. "Go home and eat some more. Anything." A prescription for *one* more pill. Back again on Easter Sunday morning. More blood. One more pill. She was showing me the computerized results of the chemical analysis of the blood work. The chemical levels in my blood were changing each day. So was my attitude.

I had set goals before about stopping drinking. I would stop for nineteen hours and then celebrate by having some drinks! Maybe I'd stop for twenty-four hours—or twelve. Whenever I'd achieve my goal, I'd drink in celebration. Most times, however, I didn't achieve my goal. What I was seeing in these blood test results wasn't the result of will power. I was seeing chemical changes, at a cellular level, that were simply the results of no alcohol and some decent food. My addiction to alcohol was at the cellular level, too, and had been for a long time. I hadn't been able to control that addiction by will power alone. [*Next time you have the flu with attending diarrhea, try controlling your loose bowel with will power! That urge, also, is occurring at the cellular level.*]

I found out later from the nurse who ran the eight-week outpatient substance abuse program, that the doctor on duty that Easter weekend was, in her opinion, the most knowledgeable physician in the system in terms of alcoholism and alcohol-related diseases. When she was watching me walk down the hallway and then coming out to visit me in the waiting room, she was evaluating whether or not I could detoxify at home. The alternative was a three-day inpatient stay.

Was her being on duty a coincidence? I don't think so. I don't believe in coincidences anymore. The stage had been set for my getting better, and that stage had been in the making for over thirty years.

Although sometimes I wish events in my life had taken a different course, I know in my heart that it took all that happened to me to get me to where I was—that clinic on that Easter weekend. Just about midway between my bout with pancreatitis in the summer of 1986 and this Easter weekend of 1987, I had my first real experience with helplessness and surrender. My daughter was a freshman and my son was a senior in college. I had taken a loan to finance my daughter's expenses. Money was tight and I was alone. I couldn't live on my budget, and I wouldn't pay my bills—they just stacked up. It was too depressing to pay bills, anyway.

I had gone to work with all my bills bundled nicely in my briefcase and was going to pay them before the workday got started. Something happened at work that demanded my attention and I never got around to paying them. On the train after work I vowed I would do it as soon as I got home. I walked into the door, got my obligatory vodka, opened my briefcase, and out fell two bundles of bills. I had never paid last month's!

I literally died. I couldn't go on like this. If I didn't pay my bills, then my world would collapse—namely my daughter would walk in to register for the spring semester and be turned away. The pretense would be over! That thought was beyond terrifying, worse than death.

Out of the blue I remembered a conversation at a picnic, early in the summer of 1986, where I had met a young woman who kept books for small companies and a few friends. She was a good friend of my girlfriend at the time. I remembered my girlfriend giving me Maureen's number and telling me that if she wasn't home and it was urgent, to try Maureen. Here I was, unable in the morning to remember last night's conversation or television shows, remembering an obscure conversation—and names—six months later. And I knew where I had written her number. Where did that memory come from?

I picked up the phone and called Maureen and explained, not that I needed help with this or that, but that I could no longer do this by myself. To my recollection I had never said that before to anyone—ever. I had asked for help before, but I would always add, in my head, to the request, "... but if you don't help, I'll do it myself." There was no silent addition this time. Where did that thought come from? Why did that thought come at all?

Maureen remembered me and told me she would help. Several days later I arrived with all my bills, unopened bank statements, and threatening letters in a brown paper grocery bag. At her direction I literally dumped my life all over her dining room table; remembering that pile of mess on Maureen's table is as vivid a picture of an unmanageable life as I can imagine.

Six months later, shortly after beginning my outpatient program, I was introduced to Alcoholics Anonymous (AA for short). Even though I absolutely could not imagine a life without drinking, as I listened to men share about themselves, I felt for the first time in my life like I really, truly belonged. The first meeting I attended in my own community was on the Sunday after Easter. It was probably the third or fourth meeting I had attended. (I had been to some meetings, during the week, downtown where I worked.) It was a men-only group that had been in existence almost forty-five years, some ten years after AA began. In short, it was older than dirt.

Whatever the topic had been was quietly dropped, and very gently they began focusing their comments toward me—the newcomer. These fifteen grizzled old men were as tender as lambs and very grateful to their Higher Power. I heard little bits and pieces of my life story in everyone who spoke. For the first time I was hearing people speak words that described how I felt, even though I hadn't known that was how I felt until I heard the words. But when I heard the words, I knew. And I knew I knew.

One man summed up his autobiography by saying, "All my life I've wanted to be someone else, somewhere else, doing something else." My heart leapt: "That's me!" A younger man talked about how rotten he'd always felt because, in the final analysis, he'd "... always compared his insides to everyone else's outsides." That's all he needed to say. I knew exactly what he was talking about. In the course of telling his story another man talked of how he had lived on buttermilk and honey during his last days of drinking and his first week or so of sobriety. I had craved buttermilk, too. Wow! He went on to talk about how marvelous the human body is, if we'll just learn how to listen to it. I went away feeling almost mystical and proud of my body, yet simultaneously feeling genuinely remorseful for all the abuse I had given to the poor little thing.

After the meeting, one man commented to me that he was an alcoholic, "... which meant, of course, that I was an egomaniac with an inferiority complex." I laughed so hard that it made my throat hurt. Yet, even while laughing, I saw myself: An egomaniac; always wanting attention but uncomfortable when I got it; operating out of compulsion to maintain my pretense, which compounded a feeling of inferiority—or, as I had just heard—comparing my insides to someone else's outsides. How did they know so much about me? How did they know I was new to the Program?

On the way back to my condo an hour and a half later, I was so filled with emotion that I pulled my car to the shoulder, rolled down my window, and hollered, grinning ear to ear, "I have hope!" to all the cars that passed. Then the thought crept back into my head: "You've gotten through several days without a drink. How are you supposed to go through a three-day holiday weekend without one?" That thought was absolutely petrifying!

I knew intuitively (that way-down-deep-instinctive-gnosis-type-of-knowing) that I was in the right place, that alcohol was my problem, and that I belonged. That was such a wonderful sense of relief. The tiniest spark of hope—that little remnant of the Divine, crouched deep within me beside my creative Self I call "Little

Donnie," that had all but been beaten to death but that hadn't quite died—that littlest of sparks began to warm and grow and burn again.

Whether it was at this first meeting or not, I cannot recall, but one guy with more than a decade of recovery told me very early on, "Your way of thinking and controlling your life is what got you here. So always remember: If you think of it, don't trust it till you check it out with someone else." I remembered the incident of recalling Maureen's name "out of the blue," and I just knew that I didn't have anything to do with what was happening to me. In light of what I had just heard, that thought made me feel so comfortable and relaxed and confident. For some reason I cannot explain—other than God, as I understand him, taking control of my life—I was willing to be honest, willing to be open, and willing to be willing. That was so unlike the "me" of the past. I had honestly believed I was truly unique. So unique, in fact, that rules and regulations were always for the rest of the world, but not for me. It was such a calming feeling for me to think of myself as just being a "run-of-the-mill" alcoholic, just one of the recovering herd.

Three or four months later, while at a meeting, someone shared that she was praying for the day when she wouldn't think about taking a drink. "When," she asked, "will my desire to have a drink finally pass?" I suddenly realized that I was no longer having those thoughts. When had it stopped? I couldn't remember. There had been no lightning flashes. No cracks of thunder. The daily out-of-nowhere thoughts about my booze had simply ceased.

Six months into my sobriety, Maureen told me that just several days before I had first called her, she and her husband had discussed that she would not take on any new clients. She couldn't understand why she agreed. With a little sobriety and faith under my belt I just smiled and said, "Maureen, we didn't have anything to do with it. It was meant to be."

I was able to intellectually understand what The Program was all about, but I didn't comprehend the magnitude of the changes in store for me. I wanted to get through the Twelve Steps in a month. Why not? The old-timers would nod and smile that little knowing smile and say, "Stick around. Let us love you until you learn how to love yourself." "Sure," I'd reply, without having a clue as to what they were saying. But I stayed around and for some strange reason continued doing what I was told.

For over forty years I had fought against the notion of being "normal," and instead of swimming upstream with leaden arms, I was now allowing myself to float on my back and be carried along by the current. I had hope again. I had life again. I had a tomorrow again. It was absolutely wonderful!

I immersed myself in AA for the next nineteen months, going to about five meetings a week. I read the Big Book.[43] I listened. I talked. I made coffee at meetings. I helped with picnics. I stacked chairs. I helped people move. I did whatever it was suggested I do, because I was deathly afraid of NOT changing.

In the Big Book are words to the effect that the same person will drink again. I didn't want that happening to me. If I didn't undergo some fundamental changes in my makeup, if I remained the same person, then my sobriety wouldn't last. I began to understand how to say, "I'm sorry." I began to understand that it's okay to say, "I don't know" or "How'd you do that?" or "How'd you know that?" I began to understand that it's really a relief not to feel that I had to either baffle with bullshit or dazzle with brilliance.

Before I had gotten sober I would get an unmistakable knot in my stomach every afternoon around four o'clock. I know now it was an early withdrawal symptom. By the time I'd get home the knot would've turned into a real pain. A shot of vodka would make it disappear—just melt it away. After I stopped drinking the knot continued to appear every afternoon, right on schedule. But I was going to AA after work, not home for a vodka. I began noticing, however, that when I simply touched the doorknob to the church basement where the AA meeting was held, my knot began dissolving. This was a physiological phenomenon that I could not ignore but could not explain. As I talked about it, old-timers just smiled.

It also was stated in the Big Book that the only thing that could prevent one's recovery was an inability to be honest—with others and with yourself. I became so honest it was ridiculous. I made Abe Lincoln look like a con artist. If I found a quarter on the sidewalk, I'd give it to a homeless person rather than put it in my pocket, because it wasn't mine. If a lane was closed one mile ahead (according to the roadwork sign), I'd merge to the appropriate lane as soon as I saw the sign. No more trying to sneak past the honest schmucks who were slowing down. I'd put money in the tollbooth even if no one was on duty.

AA's Serenity Prayer (attributed to one of the Niebuhr brothers—theologian Reinhold or church historian Richard) goes like this: "God, grant me the serenity to accept the things I cannot change; the courage to change the things I can; and the wisdom to know the difference." I learned I couldn't control people, places, or things. All I could control (sometimes) was my attitude. When I changed my attitude and became truly centered—knowing that my purpose in life was to help another alcoholic—my whole physical world changed. Problems with my car got "better." Bosses seemed to actually listen. Illnesses began to clear up. Relationship problems seemed to take care of themselves. Financial problems were not the end of the world—they simply came, had to be dealt with, and then went. To me, it's always been a miracle. Change what I can—my attitude and outlook—and my world changes. I don't know how to manipulate it. I cannot predict it. All I can do is accept it, thoroughly relish it when it occurs, and thank God (as I understand God) for it.

This sense of reality and miracle is what I imagine was occurring in these small Jesus Movement groups and Christ Congregations. If I find it difficult and frustrating to communicate to you what happens when I change my attitude, then I can surely imagine the frustration and difficulty that occurred in the decades after Jesus died.

Yes, I had hope again. I had life again. I had a tomorrow again. It was absolutely wonderful! I became a member of the human race again—an actual fallible, frail, feeling, forgetful, forgiving, fearful, frenzied, frolicking human being. It became clear as well, very quickly, that I didn't know how to be that. I'm still learning, but that's another story.

The difficulty of verbalizing spiritual events

However, even as I've read what I just wrote, I'm unsatisfied with how the "spiritual" just isn't coming through. What I really meant to communicate isn't coming through. It sounds just so "blah." It's another alcoholic's "drunk-a-log."

Perhaps I need to tell my story using appropriate "religious" language. Perhaps I need to put the "spiritual gloss" on my story like Luke did with Paul's story. I could have said that God "touched" me in my kitchen when the bundle of bills fell out. I could have talked about how God "revealed" himself, or how I "heard" God through the voices of recovering alcoholics in church basements. Perhaps I could have talked about how silently my urge to drink had vanished, reminding me of the prophet Elijah's comment: "Be quiet. Hear the still, small voice of God." (1 Kings 19: 9–14.) Yes, I guess I could have talked about how God talked to me. Perhaps I could have talked about how "blessed" I was to have God put Maureen in my life at just the right time. *Praise the Lord!* I could have painted excited verbal portraits of the ecstatic rush of redemption I felt as I stood along the side of the road and cried, "I have hope!" or as I touched the church doorknob and felt the knot in my stomach melt away. *Thank you, God. Praise Jesus!* I could have gone on and talked about how that weekend was, for me, what the road to Damascus experience was for Paul. I could have said that all that has happened to me since was a preparation for the publication of this book. I could have described how the mantle of sin and death fell from me—*Amen and Amen! Praise the Lord!*—as I found myself willing to be open and honest, and willing to change. I did change. I was changed. My old Self died and I was born anew into the redeeming life of Christ. *Praise God!*

I could have said that and all of it would have been intellectually true. My Higher Power did (and does) touch me through AA members. I did (and do) feel redeemed. I have witnessed physiological changes as my sobriety matured. But to tell the story that way would have been dishonest—would have created a dishonest image of what occurred—because that's simply not the way it happened. Besides, I didn't perceive it happening that way while it was happening.

Something similar to the following has happened to all of us: We are on our way to the grocery store and suddenly think of Suzy: "I wonder what she's been up to?" We park our car, walk across the parking lot, get our grocery cart, look up, and there's Suzy. She runs over, saying, "I was just wondering about you." You reply, "I just thought of you as I was driving here." We've all had experiences like that. Yet if we read in the Bible about someone who was tending his flock or was on the road somewhere, and then "... I heard the voice of the Lord God speak to me: 'Arise. Go to the store and there you will see Suzy.' And so I gathered my belongings and I arose and went to the store. There I saw Suzy and we talked of the wonders of the Lord." That is so impressive. The faith. The obedience. The reality of the Lord speaking. That is really deep. Yet, we've all had this same experience.

However, when we read it in "biblical" language—WOW! It just sounds different and much more impressive because it's in the Bible—that book of extraordinary events. Why don't things like that happen to me? They do. We just don't recognize it. But it's really no different. The people in the Bible were just like we are. Paul was just like I am. I have trouble communicating the spiritual reality that changed my life—saved my life. Some of what I said—never trusting what you think, for example—is not to be taken literally. Later writers of some of the letters in the New Testament, just like some current ministers, misunderstood some of Paul's message. As we'll see in the next chapter, Mark, Matthew, John, and Luke all had a distinct "spin" they wanted to communicate as they constructed their Gospel accounts. Yet, in spite of all the misunderstandings and human biases, God's loving spirit keeps coming through, touching lives, and changing lives. Just like he did mine.

Searching for familiar images

Trying to tell my AA story raises the truth concerning how difficult it is to verbalize real life-changing spiritual events. Because what happened to me changed me, I want to put words to this experience. I want to be able to tell someone. How do you communicate this kind of thing effectively? How do you tell someone you've changed—really changed deep inside? You're not the same but you cannot explain it. It's frustrating. Yes, maybe I could have used more "religious" language. After all, I was a former minister. Perhaps that would have been a logical step to take. I think that's the logical step the first-century Jewish Christian took. They looked for familiar images from their past—from their history and Scriptures—to find the communicating words: Light of the World, Lamb of God, Logos (the Word), the "new" Adam, Suffering Servant, Prophet, Sacrificial Substitute, Messiah, Son of God.

An incident that occurred in AA some five or six years later dramatically illuminated this difficulty of communicating, as well as the search for familiar images. I believe the same kinds of issues that surfaced at this AA meeting happened among these embryonic Christian gatherings of followers.

I was at an AA Eleventh Step Meeting at the Unity Club in Arlington, Virginia. Eleventh Step meetings focus on one's spiritual growth and daily consciousness of God. AA's Eleventh Step states: "We sought through prayer and meditation to improve our conscious contact with God, as we understood God, praying only for knowledge of His will for us and the power to carry it out." There was a young man attending who shared with the group that he was there at the suggestion of his sponsor, because he was having real problems with the idea of a Higher Power or God or Whatever. He deplored "the religious" and simply couldn't separate out God from all that. We all nodded. His problem was not unusual.

Four of us shared our stories as a way of responding to his concerns. Actually, it was really more like 3 1/2.

As is so common in AA, each of us told essentially the same story, although every detail and event was different. One of the early ones to share was an Indian person. She referred several times to her Higher Power, whom she chose to call "HP." I shared, telling essentially the story you just read, referring to my Higher Power, whom I choose to call "God." A mixed-Asian shared referring to his Higher Power as "Ultimate Love." The last person began to share and then got off the subject by claiming—teeth clenched and neck veins bulging—that the only *true* Higher Power was Jesus Christ. The young man was adamant. If we didn't, or couldn't, acknowledge Jesus as our Lord and Savior, then our sobriety was a "sham" and our spiritual program would succumb to the work of Satan. Jesus, on his throne in Heaven, would be mortified knowing that people were referring to him as "HP" or "Ultimate Love." This last person was so angry and frustrated he stopped sharing, gathered his things, and stomped out of the meeting.

In fact the organization of Alcoholics Anonymous went through this same debate early in its history. Many of the early "fathers" of AA had been loosely associated with the Oxford

Movement, an evangelical method of sobriety via a religious experience with Jesus Christ. They had known of the occurrence of long-lasting sobriety. It had always been tied to some form of spiritual insight and conversion. As AA began developing and refining its suggested 12 Steps of Recovery, there was an effort to "define" God in terms of Jesus Christ. In meetings where that definition was present, discussions of spiritual insight as the reality that had become someone's "key" to sobriety, quickly deteriorated into theological discourses on the nature of Jesus. AA backed off and let stand their simple definition: "... God, as we understand God ..."

The recovering alcoholic who was chairing the meeting that night smiled and closed the meeting by saying that there was a big difference between being "religious" and being "spiritual." Referring to what had just happened, he reinforced that separating your experience of God from the "religious" trappings of God is very difficult. He reiterated the AA description that most of us had heard many times before: "Religion and religious beliefs are very important to those who are trying desperately NOT to go to Hell. Spirituality is critically important to those of us who have already been to hell and don't want to go back." We all laughed.

This last person was a young man who, when faced with the choice between communicating his life-saving reality that was common to all of us or obsessing with the words and phrases used to communicate that saving event, made the choice that the most important thing was to use the proper-to-him language. Without the familiar-to-him language, the reality of the event being described was nullified and denigrated. I agree with Karen Armstrong that fundamentalists are incapable of conceiving that I may experience and think about God differently than they. Similarly, they cannot understand that Abraham as a Middle Bronze Age nomad, or Paul as a first-century Jewish-Roman citizen, could possibly have thought differently.

The age-old tension

Upstairs in the Unity Club that night I believe we experienced the same, age-old tension that existed between the Old Testament prophets and the priestly class: "God doesn't want your perfect rituals and sacrifices (*or "proper" words*). God wants you to do justly and walk humbly with Him." It was the same tension that existed between Jesus and the blatant crassness of the "business" of the Temple in Jerusalem, when he called the Temple ritual-keepers a "den of thieves." The same tension—God doesn't care what words you use, he wants you to experience him. He cares that you have been reclaimed as a member of the human race and are now aware of the reality of his spiritual dimension. To paraphrase Jesus: *"I have come to proclaim a new Kingdom of God—one that lives in your heart in the eternal now. Change your ways. Open your eyes. God is all around you, in you already, even in the hearts of this strange collection of people with whom I eat, and talk, and laugh, and cry. I don't want you to believe in me. I want you to experience my Kingdom. The Kingdom is right here in the eternal now. It's mine. It's yours. Now. Come. Enjoy. It will heal you. I promise you – it'll change your life."*

This true example underscores my point here: Trying to verbally communicate spiritual realities—that have changed your behavior, your relationships, your outlook, your priorities—is difficult. It is hard work, as well, to truly listen—to tune your hearing to the message behind the words rather than to the words themselves.

These were the kinds of issues that were swirling around in the forty years following Jesus' death. These forty years were all about people trying to "put into words" how this man, this Jesus of history, had "touched" them through these newly formed communities—how he had become for them a living spirit of the new Kingdom of God. Within the realities of their new associations—with people of all walks of life, eating common meals, listening to recitations of Jesus' teaching, experiencing true acceptance, and real human bonding—their lives were changing before their very eyes. Things that used to be important weren't anymore. Things that weren't important now were. These changes weren't a passing fancy; they were for real.

I can imagine with no difficulty where someone began to speak, in one of these early first-century meetings, of Jesus being like the prophets of old. Others nodded in assent while several got frustrated, insisting he was not just a prophet, that to speak of him just as a prophet was belittling. I can hear them: "He was like the Paschal Lamb. He gives the Passover a new personal meaning for us. Can't you see that? Harrumph!" Then, like our young man in AA, they might stomp out. Maybe they would go on and start their own group or join another "more familiar" one. Maybe they would go back and start poring over other Jewish Scriptures to try to find more references that would bolster their case. Many toyed with the idea, especially in light of the growing tension between the Roman authorities and Judaism, of withdrawing completely and setting up some sort of self-sustaining community. Apparently, Mark, Matthew, and John all came from these kinds of communities.

Others, like Paul, would search the Scriptures and find totally new ways to "find the right words" or make the overarching points that needed to be made. Some groups would begin to develop traditions or practices that, in others' minds, put the wrong emphasis on the wrong things. So, they argued. They debated. They got angry and fearful of each other. Just like we do.

In the forty years following Jesus' death, people found their lives were changing. Just like mine did. Just like the Indian woman's did. Just like the Asian man's did. Just like the evangelical person's did—only if you didn't talk about it in *his* way he couldn't hear you. He castigated you. He condemned you. This has happened to me. Maybe it's happened to you. I believe it happened, as well, to early, first-century Christians.

Donald L. O'Dell

Chapter 9 Notes

[43] The Big Book refers to *Alcoholics Anonymous*, 3rd Edition, 1976, Alcoholics Anonymous World Services, Inc., New York, NY

Chapter 10

From the Christ of Faith to the Christ of Theological Doctrine (70–400 C.E.)

The Roman-Jewish War (circa 66–70 C.E.) destroyed much more than Jerusalem and her temple. It destroyed a way of life. For devout Jews the destruction of the temple in Jerusalem brought an end to Judaism as they had known it. For hundreds of years, since the end of the Exile and the time of Ezra and Nehemiah, the totality of Jewishness had been wrapped up in the history of this rebuilt, second temple. *It had been almost four hundred years. That's about as long as the New World, settled by the early Pilgrims, has been in existence. The loss of the temple was to Jews what losing our sense of patriotism, as symbolized by our Declaration of Independence and Constitution, would be to us today. In short, it was something unimaginable.*

The temple-state had been the symbol of God's design for the Jews. It had been the cornerstone of the cultural and genealogical identity of the Jews. It was what had defined who they were. Now there were no more temple sacrifices. How would God know how repentant and obedient they were? Now there were no more priests, scribes, and temple courts. How would their social, judicial, and charity programs work? Communities that had distanced themselves from the tainted priesthood in Jerusalem, like the community at Qumran, no longer had a reason to exist. They had wanted a reformed Jerusalem priestly community, not the end of the temple-state. Many former inhabitants, including leaders of the early Jesus movements, had fled Jerusalem. Many others, less fortunate, had been sold into slavery. The city itself was in shambles. Judaism, their hopes, and their understanding of their place in God's universe were in shambles.

This uncertainty had its effect in the Diaspora synagogues as well. Jewish Christians were viewed within the synagogue with a growing distrust and disdain, as were Christ congregations that were in close proximity. Discussions, debates, or arguments between Pharisees and Jewish Christians over teachings of Jesus took on a much more threatening, ominous tone. These debates were no longer merely intellectual exercises. Reading the polemics that were exchanged, they were getting personal and nasty. In an attempt to discourage Christians from continuing their association with synagogues or from continuing their Christianity, oaths to the Torah were developed to be used within synagogues that Jewish Christians would be unable to recite.

During the first century, Christians continued to think about God and pray to him like Jews. They construed arguments and argued like rabbis. Their "churches" were very much like synagogues. Many non-Jew Roman citizens were attracted to the Jewish concept of history, antiquity, culture, and the concept of monotheism. These non-Jew "friends of the synagogue" were often referred to as God-fearers or God-fearing Gentiles. During the latter part of the first century and after the fall of Jerusalem, rather vicious arguments erupted in the synagogues, and Christians as well as many God-fearers were ejected from their membership because they refused to "correctly" observe the Torah—especially the purity codes. This open hostility, when coupled with the trouble Judaism was having with the Roman Empire, made the attractiveness of Jewish life wane in the eyes of these God-fearers. Simultaneously, trying to preserve their identity, the Jews themselves no longer actively proselytized the non-Jewish Roman citizens. Also at the same time, Christian congregations were trying to find their own sense of identity apart from Judaism. It was a tumultuous time and it had some significant consequences for the emerging Church and its subsequent literature.

During the next fifty years or so, while the Christian Church as we know it was emerging, the Jewish community was moving to redefine itself as well. With the temple destroyed and Jerusalem transformed into a Roman city now called Aelia Capitolina, Jews began finding other ways to maintain their sense of identity. All that was left of their culture were the Pharisees and the institution of the synagogue. Building on the importance of oral tradition so critical to the Pharisees, the formal development of this collection of tradition continued—eventually becoming the Mishnah. This would in turn become the Talmud. The significance of the rabbinic traditions in the synagogue increased. temple rites and sacrifices now were redefined and transformed into household customs and rituals. The emphasis to formalize the Hebrew Scriptures found new impetus as a mechanism to clarify the distinction between these Jewish Scriptures and the Christian version of the *Septuagint*. At a city called Jamnia on the Mediterranean coast, a Jewish council debated and finalized their Holy Scriptures circa 90 C.E. By the middle to the end of the second century Judaism had become pretty much what we now recognize. Historians have noted that Jewish diatribes against the Christians had all but ceased by this time, indicating that they no longer found the Christians to be an identity threat.

Yes, it was a tumultuous time, but also a time of growth within the communities of Christ congregations. Why did the Hellenistic Christ congregations begin to exercise more influence so quickly and completely than the Jesus Movement groups? Intra-Christian conflicts of authority had begun but, because of the growing tension between Judaism and Rome, many of the Jesus Movement groups fled the Palestinian area or were caught up in synagogue-based struggles. The competition from Judaism, which affected the Jesus movements more than the Christ congregations, may have distracted the Jesus movements from fully participating in discussions with the Christ congregations in the "apostolic authority" question. In short, it appears that the Christ congregations exercised more influence. In reality it was probably because their writings and the development of their authority structures simply survived. The Jesus movements' didn't.

Their significant writings, notably the Gospels, were not recognized within the Christ congregations at the time as having a differing theology (which, in fact, they did), but in offering a needed sense of "historical context" for the person, Jesus of Nazareth. The Christ congregations, after reading the emerging Gospel accounts from the communities of Mark, Matthew, and John, did not fully grasp that they were in conflict with Pauline/Hellenistic traditions. For example, the "Great

195

Commission," put on the lips of Jesus by Matthew's community (Matt. 28:19), was not a clarion call to go forth and spread Paul's Gospel. It was a call to go and make all Christians become like those in Matthew's community—Jewish Christians who upheld not only the "letter of the Law (Torah)," but upheld it at the level of motivation and intent, which is what they believed Jesus had done.

Pauline theology, Christian behavior, and proper Church administration were becoming the norm among congregations in Asia Minor and Greece—working their way to Rome. Additionally, there were maturing Jesus Movement groups which were beginning to redefine themselves in light of the Jewish War. Many had become isolated and almost communal in nature. Some of these groups were aware of Christ congregations. Some were still closely associated with synagogues. These Jewish Christian groups found voices, other than Paul's, in authors whose works we recognize as the Gospels.

While these Gospel accounts were being discussed, written, rewritten, and fine-tuned within the communal Jewish Christian groups, the spread of the Hellenistic congregations continued unabated, becoming more organized. Their leadership, men like Ignatius, Clement I, and Polycarp, were writing to each other, as well as to the congregations they were overseeing. They were banding together because as they became more known as a "religion" distinct from Judaism, they were losing their blanket of protection from the Roman authorities.

Christianity had been viewed and tolerated by the Romans as a branch or sect within Judaism proper. As Christians and Christianity began to be seen as a separate religion, the Romans began viewing them with suspicious and hostile eyes. As discussed in earlier chapters, the Romans had valued the Jewish sense of justice, mercy, and care for the unfortunate that the religion exhibited. As long as the Jews opened any of their ceremonies with a prayer for the Roman authorities, the civil government left them alone, including their ability to collect and disburse temple taxes. That sense of admiration no longer was afforded to these new emerging Christians.

These Christ congregations were viewed "... with contempt as a *religio* of fanatics who had committed the cardinal sin of impiety by breaking with the parent faith. The Roman ethos was strictly

196

conservative: it valued the authority of the *paterfamilias* and ancient custom. 'Progress' was seen as a return to a golden age, not as a fearless march forward into the future. A deliberate break with the past was not seen as potentially creative, as in our society, which has institutionalized change. Innovation was regarded as dangerous and subversive. Romans were highly suspicious of mass movements that threw off the restraints of tradition and were on their guard to protect their citizens from religious 'quackery'."[44]

We have discussed how the Roman Empire of the first century—a huge, international empire—had inaugurated an overall spirit of a general restlessness and anxiety. The populace was always looking for new spiritual solutions, whether Egyptian, Jewish, or Oriental, that could be worshipped along with the traditional Greco-Roman gods. A Roman citizen could join as many associations or mystery cults as they wanted, as long as their associations didn't threaten the overall order of the society.

"Nobody expected religion to be a challenge or to provide an answer to the meaning of life. People turned to philosophy for that kind of enlightenment. In the Roman Empire of late antiquity people worshipped the gods to ask for help during a crisis, to secure a divine blessing for the state, and to experience a healing sense of continuity with the past. Religion was a matter of cult and ritual rather than ideas; it was based on emotion, not on ideology or consciously adopted theory. This is not an unfamiliar attitude today: many of the people who attend religious services in our society are not interested in theology, want nothing too exotic, and dislike the idea of change. They find that the established rituals provide them with a link with tradition and give them a sense of security. They do not expect brilliant ideas from the sermon and are disturbed by changes in liturgy. In rather the same way many of the pagans of late antiquity loved to worship the ancestral gods, as generations had done before them. The old rituals gave them a sense of identity, celebrated local traditions, and seemed an assurance that things would continue as they were. Civilization seemed a fragile achievement and should not be threatened by wantonly disregarding the patronal gods, who would ensure its survival. They would feel obscurely threatened if a new cult set out to abolish the faith of their fathers. Christianity, therefore, had the worst of both worlds. It lacked the venerable antiquity of Judaism and had none of the attractive rituals of paganism which everybody could see and appreciate. It was also a potential threat, since Christians insisted that theirs was the *only* God and that all other deities were delusions."[45]

Writings in our New Testament that occurred during this time were the Gospels, the Revelation of John, many anonymous letters attributed to early apostles, and essays and letters from the earliest Church Fathers. The Roman Empire was stretched to its limit and "religious" or cultural conflicts were something that it could not tolerate. As practical as Roman law was, as soon as a religious movement got big enough to exercise real influence, it would be accommodated, not fought. This practice was culminated when Constantine (circa 320 C.E.) finally declared Christianity the official religion of the Roman Empire and convened the Council of Nicaea in 325 C.E. to settle, once and for all, any remaining religious controversies. This resulted in the Nicene Creed. A byproduct of the Council was a definition of the official content of the Christian Bible, which was finally ratified at the Council of Hippo in 393 C.E..

The loosely connected Christ congregations continued to become more and more organized in similar ways and became more coherent as well, as a network of like-minded Christians. Persecutions from the Roman authorities waxed and waned, depending on the emperor. The Jews tried one last time, around 130 C.E., to assert themselves against the might of Rome. Once again they lost.

The growing tendency to focus on the Christ of theology continued to do just that—grow. Creeds, confessions, and hymns were argued, debated, fine-tuned, and became more or less finalized. Faith was not what one had experienced. Faith was now synonymous with what one rationally believed and espoused.

Voices of the Gospel writers

Paul had been trying to use the Jewish scriptures to undergird the existence of Christian congregations. In Galatians he tried to revise the epic history of Israel in order to "claim" the promise of God's covenant without acknowledging the Torah in the five

Books of the Law. Apparently he was dissatisfied with it and he later tried using another tack in his letter to the Romans.

Try as they might, all the various Christian groups, during the forty years immediately following Jesus' death, could not really dislodge or usurp the Scriptures from the epic of Israel—the epic that pointed over and over to its conclusion: What God really wanted was a Jewish theocracy in second-temple Jerusalem. Then the temple was destroyed and Jerusalem was declared off-limits to the Jews. As the Jews had to wrestle with this and attempt to revise their own history, it opened the doors for the Christians to use Jewish Scripture to begin creating their own epic history. The idea began to float around that the temple was destroyed because this anticipated Jewish theocracy wasn't what God wanted at all. What he wanted was summed up in the man, Jesus. Jesus, not the temple-state, that's what God had intended. Mark, Matthew, John, members of the Pauline School, and Luke all had different images of what/who Jesus was, taught, and accomplished.

The Gospels of Mark, Matthew, and Luke emerged during the end of the first century and the beginning of the second, and are referred to as the Synoptic Gospels (Greek: *Synopsis*) because they are so similar and contain a great deal of common material. Literally, they could be placed side by side and viewed together. The Gospel of John is different and has always been acknowledged as such.

However, in many ways the Gospels were simply more voices or more attempts Hellenized Jesus Movement groups were making to put into words that reality that is really beyond words. There was an immense unsettling following the Jewish uprising and the destruction of Jerusalem and her temple. Floundering for their identity, the Gospels of Mark, Mathew, and John—each of whom was part of an identified "community" rather than a congregation, per se—documented realities their respective communities had come to believe. Mark was the first to incorporate Jesus' teachings from the sayings-based Jesus groups, put it all within the "setting" of a historical biography, and make the case that God's intention, through Jesus, was to establish communities of faith like Mark's. Matthew picked up on this, but concluded that God's intention was to establish communities like Matthew's—communities that used the Torah as a guide to personal piety, just as they thought Jesus did. John's community also followed Mark's lead but

Donald L. O'Dell

focused on a more Gnostic-like message. Luke focused on the grand historical scheme of God's involvement in the life of mankind—using prophets and teachers (of whom Jesus was preeminent) to nudge us along.

The Christ congregations saw no need and thus did not pay much attention to the life and teachings of Jesus. On the other hand, the Jesus movements saw little need to focus on the meaning of Jesus' death since, as we have discussed, they were familiar with other teachers and prophets who had been executed. To tell his community's story, Mark was able to bring together these two elements for the first time. It was extraordinary.

In the following discussion of the Gospels, I am greatly indebted to three of Burton Mack's works: *The Lost Gospel of Q; Who Wrote the New Testament;* and *A Myth of Innocence: Mark and the Beginnings of Christianity.*

The Voice of the Community of Mark

The Gospel According to Mark is the earliest surviving Gospel account we have. It is normally dated around 70 C.E. The unknown author wrote his Gospel shortly following the destruction of the Jerusalem temple. According to internal evidence, the author was a Christian Jew. He was acquainted with Jewish life and thought. He had knowledge of the Jewish Scriptures. He incorporated—thus understood—Aramaic phrases within his account. He was familiar with the overall geography of Palestine. He was from a Jesus Movement Group, probably communal, that was still associated with a Diaspora synagogue. His point of view was that of a Hellenistic Jew. He endorsed the Gentile mission, although he was unaware of Paul's letters that had been in circulation in Asia Minor for about fifteen years. He disapproved of the strict Sabbath observance, as well as the purity codes relating to foods. He used Hellenistic terms throughout his text and quoted from the Greek *Septuagint.*

There was a young man named Mark (Marcus) who was a relative of Barnabas and accompanied him and Paul on their first missionary journey. There was also another young man named Marcus who attended to Peter (and perhaps Paul) while imprisoned in Rome. Early tradition (the first half of the second century), especially from Papias, Bishop of Hieropolis, links this second Marcus to this Gospel account. Some traditions believe both Marks to be the same person. Bottom line: we don't know who Mark was.

"Mark's story was what the Greeks would have called a "life" (*bios*). It was a biography. Just as the Greeks would have done, Mark took the many little sayings and stories of Jesus that were available to him from earlier traditions and used them to create an image of Jesus."[46]

As time elapsed following Jesus' death, Mark's community had slowly evolved its thinking to reflect their understanding that communities like theirs were to be the recipient of YHWH's original covenant. As their storytelling evolved, their tale became more and more cohesive, finally taking the form of a biographical novel. It was a natural way to tell their story and interweave remembrances from various personal recollections and messages from the Pronouncements and Miracle Collections. It was a natural way to express their belief that Jesus was God's destined agent of change—the goal of which was to create more communities like theirs. This "historical" context that Mark used in order to frame his account as a "biography" created a framework that was never altered.

Since all Jewish Christians in the Diaspora were experiencing and witnessing very bitter and nasty problems with Judaism, Mark's framework was accepted by Matthew, John, and Luke, even though they added to or embellished his account to serve their own purposes. Most importantly, from my perspective, it recorded some of the Jesus Movement material that might otherwise have been lost to us forever. Later, when both Matthew and Luke incorporated material from Q to strengthen their respective points of view, even more early Jesus Movement material was preserved.[47] However, both in Mark and the later Gospels, some of the "message" of Jesus, as well as its import, was lost. Jesus' emphasis was on the "now-ness" of the Kingdom of God within our midst. *It's here. It's real. It will change your life, if you'll but open your eyes and see. It's a true alternative to "seeing" the world as opposed to the Greco-Roman "reality." Jesus did not envision himself as the culmination of the Old Testament prophecy. He didn't see himself as God's decisive agent of change in terms of Israel's epic history. He didn't see himself as God in the flesh.* That message wasn't translated into Mark's *bios.*

The following exhibit, Timelines of Major Material from 70–120 C.E.[48] visually tries to capture the importance of Mark in the development of the New Testament.

Mark's community, like so many others, had been expelled or shunned by a Diaspora synagogue following the fall of Jerusalem. Believing that maybe the fall of the city and the destruction of the temple was a failure of Judaism in the eyes of God, Mark's community began to see some logic in that line of reasoning, as their view of history evolved. Perhaps they, under Jesus, were the "new" Israel after all! Clearly, this kind of message had not fallen on sympathetic ears within a synagogue. No wonder they were expelled. This kind of "spin" on Israel's history would have worn out their welcome. Feeling the sting of the synagogue's ire suddenly made the fear and anger come alive that must have been exhibited by the Sadducees and high priests toward Jesus after the incident at the temple. I can just see the wheels turning in their heads: *"If these neighborly members of 'our' synagogue can get so upset as to expel us—Jew and God-fearing Gentile alike—then we can now understand how Jesus' reported denunciation of the temple would have driven the high priest and Sadducees to want to get rid of him, much like they worked with Herod to get rid of John the Baptist."*

The Markan community began their story with Jesus' baptism by John the Baptist and his recognition that Jesus was the Son of God. He merged some of the pronouncements of Jesus with some of the traditions from the miracle stories. This combining of two sets of collections portrayed Jesus as having a very distinctive power: his very words could make miracles happen. This kind of power would have been recognized as an open challenge to the authority of Jewish Law and ritual embodied by the Saducees, High Priests, and Pharisees.   From the very beginning of his narrative, Mark builds in this tension between these Jewish authorities and Jesus. The stage for an eventual crucifixion was set.

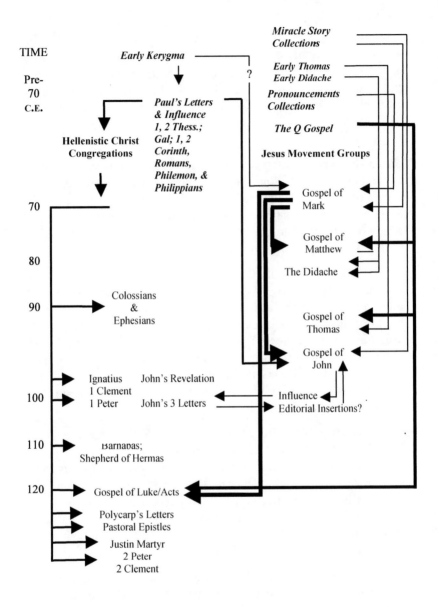

Exhibit 3. *Timeline of Major Material from 70–120 C.E.* The Influence
of Paul, the Q Gospel, and the Gospel of Mark on the writings of the New
Testament are significant.

Mark used the Greco-Roman idea of the noble death—a common theme within Hellenistic Christ congregations. The formula for a noble death was to postulate a righteous man who had been wrongly accused. As the story would unfold, the righteous man would eventually be vindicated, either before or after his death. That would become the framework for Mark's biography.

As Mark told of the events of the Lord's Supper (Mark 14: 22–25) he was not interested in the growing aura of some kind of cultic "presence" of the Lord. He simply wanted to relate the events of Jesus' last supper. Consistent with the noble death motif, Mark saw the last supper as the beginning of Jesus' departure, which would lead to an eventual victorious return. This gave Mark's Gospel an unmistakable ring of the apocalyptic.

Mark's use of the disciples in his narrative is for instructional purposes. The disciples are not apostles; they are often portrayed almost as buffoon-like. The Greek word Mark uses often for the disciples is *teknon*, which means "little children." He uses discourses between Jesus and the disciples as a way to ask rather "dumb" questions or make incredulous statements so Jesus can provide the answers and make his point. This image of the disciples is successively softened by the Gospel accounts of Matthew, John, and Luke.

Mark's community had scoured the *Septuagint* (the Greek Old Testament) to find scriptural references from the prophets. The collections of miracle stories from the Jesus movements quite often had references that likened Jesus to Moses and Elijah. The community that produced the Q Gospel suggested Jesus words were similar to Scripture's wisdom and prophetic traditions. However, to Mark, Jesus was more than just a continuation of these traditions. He replaced them.

"If Mark's overbold strokes fail to startle us, it is because Christians have become so accustomed to the logic of his story line. Without this story, one would have to say, the emergence of Christianity as we know it would not have happened."

49

The Voice of the Community of Matthew

All we really know about Matthew is that he described himself as "… a scribe trained for the kingdom" (Matt. 13:52). Scholars estimate his Gospel was written in the late 80s. The destruction of Jerusalem and Mark's Gospel account had occurred almost twenty years earlier. Almost a generation had passed. Some of the bitter and nasty "edge" had been softened between mainstream Judaism and Jewish Christians in the Diaspora. The Q community was focused on a cultural critique of Judaism. The Markan community, whose Gospel account was now fifteen to twenty years old, focused on the pending (and imminent) apocalyptic vindication that would show, to Judaism's consternation, Mark's community was the rightful heir of Israel's grand tradition. Rather than align themselves with the more radical fringe, Matthew found that—at the level of motive and attitude—all factions could benefit from their community's perceived teachings of Jesus.

Like Mark, Matthew was part of a community of Jewish Christians in the Diaspora. As well, he didn't seem to be aware of Paul's letters circulating in Asia Minor. His community seemed to have learned, by focusing on the intent and personal meaning of the Jewish Torah, that they were able to avoid the divisive rhetoric from the Diaspora synagogue, the Markan community, and the Q community.

Matthew's community used Mark's framework, inserted Jesus' teachings from the Q Gospel, and added some stories of its own. The Gospel account of Matthew's community rearranged much of the Q material by organizing it into five sermons Jesus delivered, the most well-recognized of which is the Sermon on the Mount (Matthew 5–7). The material of Matthew that was added to Mark's framework were the stories of Jesus' birth and childhood, several additional parables, and some post-Resurrection appearances. Even though it is basically Mark's Gospel account with Q teachings inserted, the portrait of Jesus painted by Matthew's community is entirely different from the portrait painted by Mark's. This "softer" image of Jesus as the embodiment of the wisdom and spirit of essential Torah-based Judaism no longer needed to depict the Pharisees as an enemy. They may have been hypocritical, but who of us hasn't? Tension still existed between Jesus and the Pharisees, to be sure, but it was now over a question of the "proper" observance of the Torah, not one of authority and power.

Essentially the Matthean community believed that their understanding of Jesus was as the personification of the spirit of Moses and the Torah. The apocalyptic nature of Mark's Gospel was either ignored or played down. Mark had pictured Jesus as a man of mystery, using parables, for example, so that the general public would not understand his real message. Matthew, by incorporating almost all of the Q Gospel, portrayed Jesus as a man of the people whose message was simple, straightforward, and for the people. It was a message that could be accepted by all who heard it. His portrayal of the disciples is toned down as well. Unlike Mark's portrayal, Matthew's disciples do understand what Jesus is saying. Peter is not a blustering almost-buffoon, but is nicknamed "the Rock" by Jesus and given the keys to the Kingdom.

The Matthean community knew of Jesus' association with Nazareth and of probable efforts to place him in Bethlehem to coincide with Micah's prophecy. I am sure they were aware of the stories of Herod's supposed fear of a coming Messiah. There were probably other stories circulating—similar to our own "George Washington slept here" markers. Perhaps members of the Matthean Community had been perplexed, just as I was, over the facts that none of the High Priests or Saducees had seen the star and, knowing of Micah's prophecy, had made the trip to Bethlehem. Consequently, somewhere in the early tale-telling of the community, arose the notion that Joseph, Mary, and their young family left the area and went to Egypt.

For Jesus to be similar to Moses, the community told stories of Jesus' birth. The initial stories were probably ones of Moses' birth. As the stories grew, honest confusion, misunderstandings, and mistakes occurred. Within several generations, other rumors may have been heard, other assumptions been made, other stories been told, and the birth became more and more magical. Who wouldn't believe stories that were told to them at their youth by their parents, who in turn had heard them from their parents? The tale telling of these stories was recited, refined, mulled over, rehearsed, refined some more, and finally reduce to writing.

As for the Virgin Birth itself, we have to ask ourselves, "What difference does it make?" If I go to Heaven and find out that it really didn't happen that way, will I be terribly upset? I don't think so. The earliest writings we have (Paul and Mark's Gospel) don't mention it. Neither does the later Gospel account of John's community. It's only mentioned by Matthew and later by Luke. Why then has it become so important? Two reasons: (1) It is such a beautiful story. The imagery, the art, and the music it has inspired are truly wonderful and ageless. (2) As the Church Fathers later wrestled with the exact legalistic definition of who Jesus really was—God? Man? Some form of God-Man?—the issue of human sinfulness arose. How could Jesus be "as God," if he were born in a natural way conceived by natural, albeit sinful, parents? The stories of the virgin birth provided a needed solution to get around the theological (not biblical) issue of Original Sin.

As for the post-Resurrection stories Matthew's community added, they knew of the empty tomb stories (perhaps from eyewitness laments), the credibility problems with them, and their personal experiences of the spirit of the Lord that had transcended death. So the community told stories of Jesus' body being stolen and bribes paid to the guards. Another added story—the Great Commission—once again allowed the community to reemphasize the teachings of Jesus: "... make disciples of all men, teaching them to obey everything I have commanded you" (Matthew 28:19). According to Matthew's community, what did Jesus command? He certainly didn't command a theology of the Atonement or Incarnation. He didn't command a Pauline penal-substitutionary doctrine of salvation or a doctrine of the Trinity. What did he command? Obey the requirements of the Torah in external actions as well as in terms of internal motives and intentions.

The Voice of the Community of John

Compared to the three Synoptic Gospels, the Gospel according to John is strikingly different—historical facts are blended in it with distinctive religious interpretations, vivid dramatic narratives, and a profound theology. Since the beginning, Church Fathers had recognized that John's Gospel was more of a spiritual Gospel, different from the synoptic Gospels.

The Gospel of John begins with the familiar statement: "In the beginning was the Word, and the Word was with God, and the Word was God. ... And the Word became flesh and dwelt among us" (John 1:1–14). The Greek term for "word" is *logos*. The community of John and its great doctrine of the *logos*, provide an important key to this Gospel account. Its Gnostic aspects of truth, light, and life pervade the work. In this doctrine John's community took the Hebrew concept of a personal God, illuminated by seventy-five years of Christian experience, and interprets it in terms of Greek philosophy.

In the Johannine community that produced this Gospel the structure of the cosmos is alluded to as Jesus is described as the Son and the *logos* of God. The Pauline school, developed after Paul's death, discussed the cosmos in the letters to Colossians and Ephesians as the wisdom of God inviting all to praise the cosmic Christ. The anonymous author of the Letter to the Hebrews depicts Jesus as the great high priest exercising authority in the cosmic temple of God. The Revelation of John of Patmos visualizes the cosmic City of God. Behind all these visions or descriptions lies the unmistakable influence of current Greek thought that imagined a dualistic universe—a world dominated by powers that could tear it apart or pull it back together.

Tradition names the author of this Gospel as John and points to Ephesus as the city from which it originated. There was a prominent leader in Ephesus (circa 100 C.E.) known as John the Elder, who is cited in the works of Papias (circa 150 C.E.). Current scholarship points to the community of John the Elder as the source of the Gospel and the three epistles of John. It is evident that the three epistles drew on the Gospel from John's community and it is quite probable that community members, as they wrote the three epistles, were the ones who added the Appendix to the Gospel (John Chapter 21) and made several editorial changes to the original text.

Although tinged with Gnosticism itself, John's Gospel went far in meeting the challenge of a particular type of contemporary thinking called Docetism (from Greek: to seem). Docetic thinking posited that Christ only "seemed" to be human—he was really a divine being. John's answer: "The Word was made flesh and lived among us" (John 1:14). However, his Gospel reflects the heavy Greek philosophical influence of the dualistic nature of the universe: light and darkness, spirit and flesh, children of God and children of the Devil, the Church and the world. The community was also familiar with the Greek standard of the descent-ascent pattern of god stories: A god comes down from Heaven with a mission or a message to proclaim and then returns to Heaven when completed. Jesus' mission or message is complete and it's time for him to go home. This is the Johannine community's cosmic view of the universe—the descent of the *logos* and Jesus' return to the Father.

John's community—though quite distinct—was not completely isolated from other Jesus groups or Christ congregations. His use of miracle stories as "signs sources" indicates their involvement early on with those early Jesus movement groups in the 30s and 40s that had centered their communities around the Miracle Collections. Now, some sixty years later (circa 95 C.E.), the miracles had evolved to become signs of something else. Each miracle story was followed by a speech placed on the lips of Jesus to denote some special revelation of truth or enlightenment.

When compared closely with the Synoptic Gospels, John's dependence on Mark becomes rather clear. He follows Mark's basic chronology. When the Synoptic Gospels differ among themselves, the Johannine community usually follows Mark's account. However, one aspect of his Gospel that is probably more historically accurate than the Synoptic's is his treatment of the setting of the Passion narrative. According to Mark's chronological timeline, followed by Matthew and, eventually, Luke as well, the Last Supper is the Passover meal. If this were the case, then the arrest, trial, and crucifixion would have occurred during the most sacred hours of the Passover festival—an absolute abomination of Jewish law. John's account places the Last Supper on the evening before Passover and the Crucifixion on the day of preparation—the day when the paschal lambs were prepared for slaughter for the Passover meal (John 18:28; 19:14).

The overall structure of the Gospel is rather simple. It is built around seven miracles or signs. Following each miracle, there is an opportunity for John's community to "let" Jesus explain what the miracle really meant about himself. Often, during this explanation, Jews within the crowd would object, ask questions, or ask for clarification. This device of attempted dialogue created another situation to "let" Jesus speak on two other important themes scattered throughout the Gospel: those of witness and judgment. Consistent with the Torah, Jews always wanted a second witness. Jesus explained there was none, which mystified them and eventually led to another miracle/sign and continued self-revelation on the part of Jesus. For the Johannine community this mystification on the part of the Jews was merely the conflict between those that understand (are enlightened) and those that don't.

The emphasis on enlightenment in John's Gospel is similar to much of the material in the Gospel of Thomas. However, the Johannine community valued the heritage of Israel more than the Thomas people. The Johannine community had long roots to the same early Christianity as those groups founded on the Pronouncements collections or the Markan and Matthean communities. But the Johannine community did not assume the aura of an exclusive community awaiting the last days like Mark's people. Neither did they move to become a sub-sect of Jewish culture as Matthew's people had done. Similar to Mark, however, they did not want to become a wholesale Christ congregation, which had developed on the model of a Hellenistic mystery cult.

"They apparently were not interested in baptism and memorial rituals, but they may have met for meals, washed one another's feet, prayed together, and sung hymns to the *logos* and to Jesus as the Son of God. The monologue material, famous for its repetitious 'I am' sayings, is suspiciously poetic in ways similar to the opening poem [John, Chapter 1] in praise of the *logos*. Interlocking lines pick up on a term just used, add it to another, then circle back in a rhythmic pattern that overloads the meaning of terms and frustrates clear, conceptual definitions. It gives one the impression of having been produced by collective chanting, and, as a matter of fact, one is not always sure where the voice of Jesus leaves off and the voice of the Johannine community takes over. For John, the 'I' of the mythological Jesus, the light of the world, and the 'I' of the Johannine Christian, the enlightened one who 'abides in Jesus' and 'in whom Jesus abides,' are, in the last analysis, one and the same."[50]

An Aside: The Voice and Revelations of John of Patmos

Perhaps a decade following the Gospel produced by the Johannine community, another John—John of Patmos—wrote to seven churches in Asia Minor: Ephesus, Smyrna, Pergamum, Thyatira, Sardis, Philadelphia, and Laodica. What was the concern of this John? Some (or all?) of these churches were not taking their Christian vows as seriously as John thought they should. Some of the congregations were eating food sacrificed to idols. Some were practicing fornication. Some were paying attention to false teachings. Scholars do not know what these false teachings were, but John references Jezebel the Prophetess, Balaam, the "synagogues" of Satan, and the Nicolaitans. What John wrote to these churches was about a blood-curdling "vision" he had had of the impending end of the world.

By the beginning of the second century two independent changes were occurring in the Roman Empire. First, the Romans were considering or contemplating a cult of a divine emperor. It came to pass. With its passing, public tests of loyalty to this new emperor-god and, as well, to the Empire itself, came into being. Secondly, Christian congregations had come into full view within the Empire, at least in Greece and Asia Minor. These changes were on a collision course with each other.

We know this was occurring during the first decade of the second century from Roman literature, including an exchange of letters (circa 112 C.E.) between Pliny, the governor of Bithynia in northern Asia Minor and the Roman Emperor Trajan.[51] Pliny recounts how local temples and related commerce were suffering because the network of Christian congregations no longer supported them. Also, Pliny noted, they exhibited practices that disrupted the general tranquility of the communities. As a result, non-Christians were charging that Christians were being disloyal to the Roman Empire, certain they would refuse to offer incense to an image of the now divine emperor. Pliny noted that a public refusal to offer incense would have to be punishable by execution. But otherwise, he commented, the Christians were quiet, law-abiding, hard-working members of their communities. What should he do? Trajan responded by cautioning Pliny not to actively seek out Christians and to demand a loyalty test. He also cautioned him not to take evidence second- or third-hand or from anonymous pamphlets as solid proof of suspected disloyalty. Of course, if

Christians were to be brought in and they publicly refused to perform the loyalty test, then they must be punished.

As has been mentioned, the Romans had exempted the Jews, since the time of Julius Caesar, from loyalty rites. Judaism was highly respected within the Empire because of its roots in antiquity and emphasis on social justice. The newly budding Christian groups—be they Jesus movement groups or Christ congregations—fell under Judaism's "umbrella" of protection because they were viewed as simply being a sect within Judaism. Now identified as a distinctly new religion separate from the Jews, Christians could no longer count on that protection.

The vision recounted by John of Patmos essentially tells the reader that the Lord Jesus is coming very soon "… to repay according to one's work" (Rev. 22:12). Consequently, the faithful need to remain faithful until the "City of God" appears, regardless what the "whore of Babylon" (Rome) suggests.

Perhaps the "food sacrificed to idols" was a reference to loyalty tests for the emperor. Perhaps the "synagogues of Satan" referenced Judaism or to clusters of Jewish Christians of the Matthean type. Historians are unsure. Whatever it was, John was angry and very scared.

Tests of loyalty for these seven congregations were becoming a real problem. Potential accommodations that congregations might allow members to make in order to "pass" the loyalty test were becoming a thorny issue. Since John is on the Isle of Patmos, perhaps as a form of exile (Rev. 1:9), he would have been extremely sensitive to the issue of loyalty tests. His use of the phrase "whore of Babylon," rather than openly referring to Rome, might have been a form of code designed to protect any who might be apprehended carrying or reading his letter.

The Revelation of John planted the seed of the image of martyrdom as the ultimate in an expression of Christian faith. According to Burton Mack, this seed would continue to grow until it flourished as a romantic myth of martyrdom during the last half of the second century. Derived from the Greek word *martyria*, Christians coined the term "martyr." *Martyria* means "witness." "It was the curious situation of being on trial before the Romans and having to 'witness' to one's loyalty to Christ, with the consequence of being executed, understood as an imitation of Christ's own martyrdom, that gave the term *martyria* its peculiar

Christian connotation. From this time onward, the true 'confessor' of the Christian faith would be the martyr for Christ."[52] Literal readers of Revelations generally miss this altogether.

The End of Days

Congregations today that interpret the Bible literally make Revelations, the End of Times, the Eschaton, the Last Days, or the Rapture a very big deal. Why the obsession to find concrete current events that will underscore a literal reading of John's apocalyptic visions? Grocery store tabloids consistently have headlines, usually quoting some writing of Nostradamus, about the End of Days. Why is that?

This emphasis seems to occur every time there's a massive social, economic, and political upheaval. We are now in the midst of the Information Age—global communications, global economy, instant messaging, reality TV, CNN (which makes the whole world our community), fads, music stars, athletes, movie-star gossip, political scandals—happen too quickly, get too much coverage, change overnight. Parents can't keep up with what's going on. Fear, concern, worry, generalized angst—all this pervades our collective psyche. The result? A yearning to go back to simpler times. *"I want to go back to a time where there was some predictability about morals, mores, pensions, retirements, diets; where there was some sense of trust in your neighbor, in the ingredients in your food, in your medical professionals, in the political process, or in the educational system."*

The more scared, frustrated, confused, anxious, befuddled, and disappointed people become, the harder they hold on to anything that still makes sense to them. One of those things that always seems to make sense is the adage "He'll get his due" or "They'll get theirs in the end." Why? I believe it is because we cannot conceive of the true, unconditional love that is God. It just doesn't make any sense to us. We cannot conceive of Adolf Hitler, or Josef Stalin, or Jeffrey Dahmer, or a pedophile being forgiven by God and ending up in Heaven. It simply offends our sense of fairness. So we believe God will come back and put these evil, selfish, power-hungry, greedy, have-more-than-I-can-ever-imagine-having people in their place. "They'll get theirs in the end," we say. "Finally I'll be vindicated and will sing and dance for all eternity while they scream in agony."

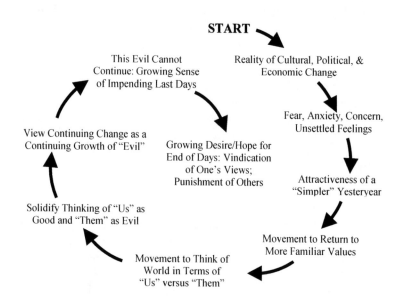

Exhibit 4. *The Anxiety Spiral.* *Anxiety, fear, and loss of control lead to desires to turn back the clock to "simpler" times. Following continued frustrations, hopes build and focus on an eventual vindication of "us" and punishment of "them" at the "End of Times."*

As people begin to feel they cannot cope, the emphasis begins to shift to a focus on the uncontrollability of a non-understood world—and soon that world becomes defined as a "bad" world. *This kind of reaction is a fear-based response and, as I learned, fear is the opposite of faith. When fear is the predominant emotion in a ministry, the more the Old Testament (an eye for an eye, etc.) and the Book of Revelations will be quoted/invoked (in spite of Jesus' commandments), the more secular humanism and situational ethics will be vilified, and the more the Bible will become some kind of literal, magic, holy textbook.*

The Voice of Luke the Physician—Luke/Acts

Recent scholarship places the two-volume work of Luke-Acts around 120 C.E. in a clearly Greek setting. The role and centrality of Jesus of Nazareth is no longer the central focus of the emerging Church. There are congregations scattered throughout the Aegean in Asia Minor, Greece, and toward Rome. Bishops such as

Clement I of Rome, Ignatius of Antioch, and Polycarp of Smyrna held esteemed influence and wrote extensively to congregations and to each other. It is unclear exactly how or when they rose in prominence or how they came to be "bishops." But the embryonic Church, as an organization, was in place, growing and becoming an interconnected support system.

Issues in this early Church were no longer centered on Jesus. The focus was on the role of the apostles, who provided some sort of imagined link between Jesus and these emerging bishops, or overseers, who were responsible for the "correct' instruction of their congregations. This was the time of the writer of the Gospel according to Luke and its follow-on volume, the Acts of the Apostles.

Luke's theme throughout both volumes was that God—first as Yahweh of Israel, then as the God of Jesus—had always used prophet-teachers to chastise, correct, and instruct his people in the ways of righteousness. These prophet-teachers throughout history had been moved by God's spirit. Initially, they were the prophets of the Jewish scriptures, then Jesus of Nazareth, followed by his disciples/apostles. Now that mantle of prophet-teacher fell on the shoulders of the emerging bishops.

As these prophet-teachers proclaimed God's message, via his spirit, there were always those that listened and those that persecuted them. Over and over this theme had played itself out in Jewish history. Looking back, one could see it in Jesus and the disciples/apostles, as well. Luke constructed his story of Jesus within this grand framework: the history of salvation. Beginning with Adam, this theme of the spirit of God using prophet-teachers, coursed through the history of Israel and culminated in Jesus of Nazareth. Later this spirit, at Pentecost, filled the disciples, made them apostles, accounted for the spread of God's grace to all nations beginning in Jerusalem, and now found it centered in Rome.

Luke is different from the other Gospels in this respect. Some of the difference is attributed to the fact that his account was written as the initial part of a two-part history of the development of this embryonic Christian movement as it migrated from Jerusalem to Rome. The second part of this history is the New Testament book, the Acts of the Apostles (or Acts). Nearly one-third of Luke's Gospel relies on the basic chronology of Mark. Not quite a third is very similar to Matthew and can be attributed to Luke's independent use of the Q Gospel or to his use of Matthew's incorporation of Q. The remainder of Luke is unique to Luke (often referred to as "L"). Some of this unique material contains some of Jesus' most memorable parables (including the Good Samaritan), Jesus' interest in the Samaritans, his teachings on the right use of wealth, his emphasis on prayer, his understanding of women, and his graciousness to the penitent.

Tradition has attributed the Gospel (or at least much of the "L" material) to Luke the physician, mentioned in several of Paul's letters (e.g., Philem 24). His purpose in developing this "history" from existing available records was to:

- Compile an account of Christian beginnings that would be accurate and well-arranged;

- Present this account to an esteemed Roman official named Theopolis, in order to allay existing suspicions about Christianity;

- Recommend Christianity to intelligent Gentiles (Greeks), which explained why often, Hebrew words are explained (e.g., Luke 6:15) and geographical sites in Palestine were specifically located (e.g., Luke 4:31; 8:26).

However, overarching themes that truly distinguish Luke's efforts were his emphasis on the role of the Holy Spirit, the elevated status of the disciples, and his distinct "sense" of history.

Mark's community had portrayed Jesus and his teachings in a personal, confronting manner—as if his voice were speaking directly to the reader. The community of Matthew had envisioned Jesus as laying down the law for all time. The Torah was no longer simply for external rituals, rites, and behavior. It was, under Jesus, to be a guide for personal piety at the level of intention or motive. Luke, on the other hand, portrayed Jesus as that "... of an irenic, popular philosopher with his disciples, making their way through village marketplaces, stopping here and there to accept an invitation to a meal. He was, as Peter will later be heard to say, a man 'who went about doing good' (Acts 10:38), or as Luke has the Roman centurion say at the crucifixion, 'This man was surely a righteous person' (Luke 23:47). The way Luke's Jesus appears in the world is quite a contrast to the sense of confrontation in Mark or the serious tone of the instructional speeches in Matthew."[53]

God's spirit is a decisive discriminator of Luke's history in his Gospel and follow-on volume of Acts. To Luke, Jesus was the perfect image of a man in full obedience to God's spirit. During the life of Jesus, however, this spirit became available to everyone, not just the Jews. The spirit descends not only on Mary, Jesus' mother, but on Elizabeth, the mother of John the Baptist (Luke 1:5–24). Even though Luke, in closing his Gospel account, cites a nonexistent scriptural reference to the fact that the Messiah must die, the image of Jesus as the spirit-filled man that death cannot touch has remained unchallenged.

In focusing on a historical sweep of the growth of Christianity in the Roman Empire, Luke wanted to develop the case for Christianity as a religion of the Empire. To do this he needed to demonstrate from the standpoint of a non-threatening religion within the Empire, not how different Christianity was from Judaism, but some of their critical similarities. His history of the Church in Acts creates an image of a sort of "Apostolic Age." The Acts of the Apostles shifts the focus away from Jesus toward the apostles, emphasizes the role of the Holy Spirit of God, and blurs the distinctions between:

- Paul's passionate arguments for freedom from the law, justification by faith, obedience to the spirit, the ethic of suffering for the new Body of Christ;

- Peter's Jewish-Christian Gospel for the "circumcised";

- "Enlightened" teachings of Jesus in any number of Jesus movement groups.

Consequently, the Acts of the Apostles is structured in a way to place Peter, then Stephen, and finally Paul in positions to make speeches or preach sermons. There are about fifteen major speeches in Acts. These fifteen are almost split evenly between sermons that rehearse the Gospel and speeches that defend the speaker's Gospel. To accomplish his aim, Luke could not have Peter and Paul saying things that would resurrect the more divisive features of their convictions. As Mack put it, Luke had to develop some sort of "common denominator gospel."[54] This common denominator went like this: Jesus was the kind of man Yahweh had always had in mind; his life was all about doing good; Judaism rejected him and had him executed; death couldn't hold him; the twelve disciples/apostles witnessed all this; and therefore the hearers should repent, be baptized, and receive the Holy Spirit. Whose authority and importance is at the core of every one of these sermons/speeches? Jesus? No. The apostles.

Luke was able to tie Judaism and Christianity together in a positive way by emphasizing how each relied on the role of the prophet-teacher who appears at the opportune time to correct God's people, call them to repent, and teach them how to be righteous the way God wants them to be righteous—in terms of personal righteousness and piety as well as in terms of social justice for the "little guy."

Luke closes the story of the Apostolic Age with Paul's speeches to the Roman authorities Felix, Festus, and Drusilla, a Jewess and Festus' wife. In none of the language of the Paul we met through his letters, Luke has Paul commend the Church to the elders, who wept at his departure. "It was Luke's way of forging the link to the [emerging] next chapter of church history, the time of the elders, overseers, shepherds, and bishops. ... Luke's point [in Paul's last speeches] was to position Paul clearly as a Christian, distance him from Jews who made trouble for the Romans [like Simeon bar Cocheba, who had recently led a rebellion in Jerusalem], and depict him as a loyal citizen, one whose exemplary life and character were no threat to the peace and order of Roman society."[55]

Summary

Paul, Mark, Matthew, John, Luke—different voices trying to find the words to express a reality that may very well be beyond verbalization. Paul, Mark, Matthew, John, Luke—different people with different spiritual experiences expressing themselves in different ways.

Paul was consumed trying to integrate his Jewish background and reverence for the Law with his newfound sense of freedom in the grace he experienced among the Jewish Christian congregations, which included Gentiles, around Damascus and his hometown of Tarsus.

Mark was integrating, via a setting much like a historical novel, material his community had believed to be very important—information from Hellenistic congregations as well as sayings-based material from various Jesus groups. His Gospel was the first and set the standard format that all subsequent writings would follow. Because of his belief that the return of the Lord was just around the corner, his Gospel was apocalyptic in tone.

Matthew's community correctly saw that many of Jesus' teachings were aimed at the level of motive, rather than the act. It was as if Jesus were saying "Thou shalt not intend ..." as opposed to the Old Testament commandments of "Thou shalt not do ..." Consequently, Jesus' teachings were a redefinition of the Torah—at the level of motive. The Matthean community believed that a new Jewish community, which could include Gentiles, would carry forward this new definition of Israel's heritage.

The Johannine community was the first to place Jesus within a cosmic worldview. The Gnostic-flavored Gospel was quite different from the other, Synoptic, Gospels. It offered a unique blend of Jewish wisdom tradition, Greek philosophical thought, and prevailing Gnostic concepts—all of which were becoming prevalent by the beginning of the second century.

Finally, Luke wrote his two-volume work to place the emerging Christian congregations within the broadest arena of God's history. He was able to tie Judaism and Christianity together in a positive way by emphasizing how each relied on the role of the prophet-teacher. He also was able to elevate the status of the role of the Holy Spirit and the apostles, thus the emerging notion of apostolic succession, which aided these early congregations in establishing a needed sense of orderliness via accepted authority figures.

Paul, Mark, Matthew, John, Luke—people just like you; just like me; with honest intentions, who wrote to further their spiritual perceptions. To portray them as real people with real "agendas" does not disrespect them. Rather, it means we are just like they are, looking for words or searching for images that help verbalize the reality of our spiritual experience. If we don't believe that, then we are left only to believe that these sources of the New

Testament were really different from us, which makes it impossible to relate to them as people. This position leaves us no other option but to deal only with their texts or imagery, which is the seed that often matures into an unhealthy worship of the biblical words themselves. This is an idolization of Scripture. This is faith in the words. This idolization is bibliolatry. As we'll see, this is what began taking place over the next several centuries.

Chapter 10 Notes

[44] Armstrong, *History of God*, p 91

[45] *Ibid.*, pp 91, 92

[46] Mack, *Who Wrote the New Testament*, p 152

[47] This statement remains valid whether you believe, as Spong, that Mark wrote first, then Matthew used Mark and Q, then Luke used Mark and Matthew and Q, or whether you believe that Matthew and Luke independently used Mark and Q.

[48] Much of the material for this exhibit is from Mack, *The Lost Gospel*, Appendix A.

[49] Mack, *Who Wrote the New Testament*, p 161

[50] *Ibid.*, p 183

[51] As quoted in Crossan, *The Birth of Christianity*, pp 5, 6

[52] Mack, *Who Wrote the New Testament*, p 197

[53] *Ibid.*, p 169

[54] *Ibid.*, p 232

[55] *Ibid.*, p 237

Chapter 11

Formalizing the Doctrine and Finalizing
the New Testament

In 115–116 C.E. the Jews of Cyrene, Egypt, Cyprus, and Mesopotamia rose again against Rome. Jews killed Gentiles and Gentiles slaughtered Jews. The uprisings were physically suppressed, but surviving Jews kept their hope alive of a Messiah who would rebuild the Temple and restore them to triumph in Jerusalem.

Judaism-Roman Conflict: 115–135 C.E.

To kill this Jewish spirit, Hadrian declared his intention in 130 C.E., to put a shrine to the Roman god Jupiter on the site of the former Temple in Jerusalem. In 131 C.E. Hadrian issued a decree forbidding circumcision and public instruction in Jewish Law. One man, Simeon bar Cocheba, claimed to be the Messiah, rallied the Jews, and made the last effort in antiquity to recover their homeland and their freedom. For three years the rebels fought against the Roman legions until, finally, they were beaten back by lack of food and supplies. So many Jews were sold into slavery that their price fell to that of a horse.

Hadrian went on to forbid the observance of the Sabbath or any Jewish holiday, as well as the public performance of any Hebrew ritual. A heavier poll tax was placed on all the Jews. They were allowed into Jerusalem each year to weep on the ruins of the Temple.

The pagan city of Aelia Capitolina had been built on the site of Jerusalem's ruins and it now included shrines to Venus and

Jupiter. The long-running Council of Jamnia (where Jewish leaders had been finalizing their canon and wrestling with Judaism without the Temple-State) was dissolved and outlawed. It took centuries for the Jews to recover from the disaster of bar Cocheba's revolt. Will Durant stated, quite simply, the Jews entered their version of the Dark Ages beginning with Hadrian's crushing defeat of Simeon bar Cocheba.[56]

During and throughout these rising tensions with the Roman authorities, the Jews were also focused on distancing and distinguishing themselves from the growing "sect" of Jewish Christians. They were tired of being proselytized, of having their Jewishness watered down by increasingly Jewish-Gentile congregations of Christians, and of having their Scriptures "confused" with emerging Christian versions of Jewish texts. Between 70–90 C.E., Jews passed ordinances against the use of "Christian" writings in synagogues. Between 100–130 C.E., Jewish leaders wrote vehemently against heretical books, which included "Christian" literature. However, by the second half of the second century (150–200 C.E.) these polemical attacks simply ceased. Why? The "state" of Judaism was severely crippled following the devastation of the bar Cocheba revolt, and the distinction between Jewish and Christian literature was clear enough that Christian writings no longer posed a threat to the Jewish community.[57]

The Later Years (150–400 C.E.)

By 150 C.E. the four Gospels, then called the "Memoirs of the Apostles," were being read in Christian worship services along with the "official" Scriptures (i.e., the Septuagint), especially the Prophets. About this same time an energetic layman from Sinope in Pontus, named Marcion, anxious to shake off the association with Judaism, once and for all, and unite the scattered Christian congregations, published a collection of Christian Scripture that contained his edited version of the Gospel of Luke and ten letters of Paul.[58] Although the Marcionite Bible was rejected, the letters of Paul came to hold a place side by side with the Gospel of Luke and, eventually, the other three Gospels. Marcion had selected only Luke because it had the fewest references to the Hebrew Scriptures. A critically important byproduct of the official rejection of Marcion's work was twofold. The controversy over

Marcion's version of an official body of Christian Scripture stimulated a great deal of interest in and an acknowledged value in having an "accepted" body of Christian literature. Secondly, the convened councils, critical debates, circulation of letters (for or against) Marcion's views established a process that would become more and more formalized for the next several hundred years, culminating in the Councils of Nicaea (325 C.E.) and Hippo (393 C.E.). These two councils hammered out the initial accepted creed by which the Church would live (the Nicene Creed) and finalized the accepted list of the contents of the New Testament.

The leaders, or bishops, of the more established congregations had developed over time a growing body of loose theology defending and describing what has been called the "centrist" position of the early Church. It wasn't really formalized, having been developed through letter writing and sermons, but it buttressed the growing overarching belief system of these established churches. In short it was a theology that was evolving to support the essential claim(s)—not about Jesus and who he was—but about how the Christian Church, following Jesus, was the legitimate, institutional heir to the grand history of Israel and her Temple. Jesus and his Church, not Jews and Israel, were the legitimate progeny of Abraham. That's what God had had in mind all along.

Sometime around 145–150 C.E., Marcion was in Rome promoting his body of Christian Writings, the thrust of which was that the Epic history of Israel didn't really matter. Valentinius of Alexandria in Egypt, and a leader of a school of Gnostic thought there, went to Rome about the same time as Marcion to try in vain to win acceptance and leadership. It is rather widely thought that he (or one of his disciples) wrote the Gnostic work, *The Gospel of Truth*. It would appear that Valentinius was the successor to a long line of Gnostic writers that grew from the Thomas and Johannine groups that had migrated or fled to Egypt during the initial rebellion of the Jews in 70 C.E.

Although Justin Martyr was born near Shechem in Samaria, he was a well-educated and wealthy Roman citizen. After converting to Christianity he became engrossed in developing philosophical arguments proclaiming that the ancient wisdom of Moses was fully revealed in the Gospel of Jesus Christ. As a philosopher, he also was in Rome at the time both Marcion and Valentinius were there. Arguing against both men's positions, Justin soon found himself not only a philosopher, but a theologian, championing centrist Christianity as well.

Marcion, Valentinius, and Justin Martyr—all in Rome at the same time—precipitated quite a showdown. The "centrist" position of the established Church Fathers, rooted in a rather self-serving form of apostolic succession, stood over and against both Marcion (on the one hand) and Valentinius (on the other). We have already discussed how the early Fathers circulated letters among themselves and then eventually used the criteria of "often-circulated" as a primary means of determining what set of writings were "orthodox" or heretical. Since the primary centers of the budding Christian Church were in major Hellenistic metropolitan areas, including Rome, they had worked hard to ease tensions and avoid persecution by developing decent relations with the established Roman political power structure. It was working. Their accommodating centrist position was becoming more and more acceptable within the Roman Empire. In other words it was becoming less and less threatening. It extolled:

- The God of Israel, creator of the world, and the God of Christianity—the Father of Jesus—were one and the same. The Romans could appreciate the antiquity. The penchant for Greek (Platonic) philosophy could be integrated. God's creation could be equated with the Platonic concept of archetype or Perfect Mind of Being.

- The Christian life, modeled on the life of Christ, was what God had had in mind all along—for all people. Theirs wasn't an "exclusive" religious cult that could threaten Rome's power, authority, or sense of order.

- It encouraged stable families, high moral standards, social concerns, and a sense of justice that was reminiscent of Judaism. It encouraged virtue, a prized possession of the Greco-Roman culture.

Christian leaders had fought long and hard within the various Christian communities and within the Empire itself to establish this nonthreatening persona. To suddenly adopt Marcionite views or Valentinius' Gnosticism would upset that "okay by me" tolerance from the Roman authorities and start the cycle of distrust and persecution all over again.

The Centrists had a lot to fight for and so they fought. They wrote and argued with Docetism, with Marcionites, with Gnostics. To an outsider in the Roman Empire, the theological arguments they created began to look a lot like a philosophical system. The theological treatises of the early Church Fathers for the next several hundred years were structured as the literature of debates, following the rules of classical rhetoric. The Romans had no difficulty accepting philosophical debates.

By the time of Theophilus of Antioch (circa 180–190 C.E.), a collection of writings was on the threshold of the New Testament as we know it today. Theophilus esteemed the four Gospels and highly valued the ten letters of Paul in Marcion's canon. Although Theophilus still believed the Greek Septuagint was preeminent as the Scriptures, the Gospels were considered inspired, and, to a lesser degree, so also the ten selected letters of Paul.

During the same time these various lists of Scripture were being developed, there were significant movements into the development of doctrine. The process was very similar to the Old Testament priests who developed a manmade and logically thought out set of doctrines from the stuff of early, simple cultic law. For example, from the theophany of early tribal worship came the well-developed set of theories about how people all owed "rent" to God, thus the whole system of offerings, tithes, and taxes. The Old Testament theology was being shaped and developed in order to support and justify the growing institution of the formal priesthood. Unfortunately, early church leaders began following the same process.

It began innocently enough.

If Paul were to be talking in the Greek marketplaces, then he'd have to sound like a Greek and argue like one. He needed to construct a mental or intellectual proclamation whose logic would stand up under scrutiny. That proclamation was perhaps Paul's greatest gift. In the end, Christ Congregations had the last say, not necessarily because they were more correct, but because they had survived. The Jesus movements had emphasized his life. The Christ congregations had emphasized his death and transformed it into a cosmic event because that was the only way it made any sense to their Hellenistic mindset. From 70 C.E. onward, both outlooks continued moving to the extreme. The realities of the transformations that were occurring in individual lives were being overshadowed by the uncontrollable urge to rationally explain what was happening. About 100 C.E., letters from early Church Fathers were beginning to discuss questions like: The "fact" and importance of apostolic succession; What is the relationship of Jesus, the son, to the father; and How does the Holy Spirit play into all this. Later New Testament writings also began stressing these themes, as well as themes that undergirded the emerging administrative structure of the Church. The Jesus of history that had touched and transformed lives was becoming a Christ of theological doctrine that had to make sense in a Judaistic/Hellenistic philosophical argument.

This led to rather intellectually absurd positions. For instance, the Jesus Movement's focus on Jesus' life and teachings relative to the "… new kingdom is now, all around you, if you will but open your eyes to see" led to a theology/philosophy that ended up worshipping *gnosis* (wisdom) to the point that many Gnostics simply proclaimed that Jesus never really existed. It was the *gnosis,* not Jesus, that mattered. The Hellenistic communities where the Gospel of Paul was predominant (and the notion of Jesus rested only in the "something like magic" legal satisfaction God received from Jesus' horrible death) moved on to intellectually construct the theologies of the Incarnation (Jesus had to be as pure as God while being a complete human, therefore was some kind of God-Man), the Trinity (to include the Holy Spirit as an equal partner), the Church as the new body of Christ (with appropriate demands to support the existing clerical hierarchy), and the importance of apostolic succession, which gave the authors of these writings the cloak of respectability. In isolation the Q and Thomas groups eventually went to the extreme—gnosticizing to the extreme—but based on some of the actual words of Jesus. Paul did much the same—go to extremes—to justify his authority and to find in the Old Testament Scriptures, regardless of how he had to "spin" it, God's promise to include Gentiles.

Somewhere in between these two extremes probably lies the truth: less Gnostic than the Gnostics, but more Gnostic than Paul.

The institutionalization of the Christian faith was beginning. The Jesus of Nazareth had become the Christ of faith; the Christ of faith now was becoming the Christ of theology and doctrine. We talked in the Old Testament about codification or institutionalization as a desire used by the priests to be as right and powerful as God by controlling the knowledge of good and evil.

Another form of control, of codification, is to institutionalize. Fear of the unknown, or the uncontrolled, is the driver to create institutions and the predictability that goes with them. Control, then, becomes a matter of protecting the institutions spawned from institutionalization. In our case, the control of institutions came through the development of a manmade logical theology.

Around the turn of the century (200 C.E.), we have evidence from Bishop Irenaeus of Lyons and Turtullian of Carthage concerning the "state" of accepted New Testament writings. They now included the four Gospels, Acts, the ten letters of Paul, and 1 Peter, 1 John, Jude, the Shepherd of Hermas, the Revelation of John, and the Revelation of Peter.

By the end of the second century, Clement of Alexandria, head of the famous school there, had accepted four additional "Pauline" letters, attributed to Paul but known to have been written by the Pauline school to discredit Marcion: 1–2 Timothy, Titus, and the Epistle to the Hebrews. This raised Paul's letters to fourteen. Clement also accepted 2 John, 1 Clement (of Rome), and Barnabas as being works of apostolic authority. During the mid-third century, Origen developed his list of the canon, including writings he considered to be "disputed"—accepted by some congregations but not by others.

During these several centuries of debate, definition, and defense of the centrist position, the Roman Empire was beginning to decline. Into this political climate came the new Emperor Constantine. He possessed an intense desire to rid the Empire of all internal religious squabbles. These squabbles and skirmishes constituted an expense of energy that the Empire simply could not tolerate. After surveying the religious landscape he determined that Christianity would be the eventual successor to the alive but waning Greco-Roman system of pagan gods and emperor worship.

He converted to Christianity and made it the official religion of the empire. He wanted to convene a supreme council of Church leaders as quickly as possible after his coronation. What he wanted was straightforward: a common, easy-to-learn creed (or statement of faith) and a common, accepted body of approved literature. [*By the middle of the second century, probably around Rome, there had developed the core of what we have come to know as the Apostles' Creed.*] Additionally, Constantine asked Eusibius, the

Bishop of Caesarea, to put together a list of writings to be discussed and finalized. In Constantine's mind, future religious tensions could be resolved more quickly if there were some accepted standards by which to judge them.

Council of Nicaea

The initial emphasis, and indeed the primary outcome, of the Council of Nicaea (325 C.E.) was the development of the Nicene Creed. *[The Creed is reproduced in Appendix C.]* A quick reading shows the inordinate amount of verbiage that is spent on the definition of Jesus Christ, as opposed to God the Father. Why? As myths and legends about the Virgin Mary continued to grow, almost to a level of semi-goddess, so did the doctrine of Original Sin. By the fourth century it was essentially accepted as a theological tenet. Original Sin, which is not a biblical doctrine but a theological extrapolation, demanded that Jesus had to be more than a mere man to be able to satisfy God so God could forgive this native sin. Paul's initial writings about the Law had now blossomed into a full-blown penal-substitutionary theology: God made us. God loves us. But we sinned and that sin permeates our being and is passed on generation after generation. God cannot forgive us that sin because we can never be good enough. Both God and mankind are trapped by the Law. However, God finds a way out. He sacrifices himself, in the form of his son, as atonement for us. His son will endure our punishment as a substitute for us. His son had to be a man, so he was born of a woman. But he had to be more than a mere man as well, thus the special circumstances of his birth. Now, God can forgive us by overlooking our innate sinful being, but only if we'll try to be like Jesus.

So, is God equal to Jesus? Is Jesus equal to God? Is Jesus some sort of lesser God, greater man, or some form of God-Man? Was Jesus the man who, at his baptism, became the divine Christ? Much of the argument was centered around which of two Greek words best described Jesus when compared to God the Father: *homoousia* and *homoiousia*. One means "like" and the other means "similar to." East and West split over these definitions. *A split we still see today—the Roman Catholic Church as opposed to the Greek Orthodox Church.* The doctrine of the Trinity also had to be fully defined as well, to include the Holy Spirit. Without the Trinity—the triune Godhead—there would be a natural hierarchy to the source of a revelation. A revelation from God the Father would "count" more than one from Jesus, the son. A revelation from the Holy Spirit would run a distant third. As silly as that sounds, that kind of instance and debate had already occurred. The doctrine of the Incarnation (the "enfleshment" of God) had to be developed to coincide with the doctrine of the Trinity. To buttress the doctrine of the Incarnation, the nature of the Immaculate Conception really took hold. Now it was mandatory to believe in the Virgin Birth because it underscored the separate but equal nature of Jesus.

So the Nicene Creed was hammered out and accepted. But for our purposes here, a byproduct of the Council of Nicaea was the development of a list of definitive writings that would be designated as "official" Christian Scripture. Constantine had asked Eusibius, the Bishop of Caesarea, to draw up a straw-man list of writings.

Origen's list was revisited by Eusebius, who attended the Council of Nicaea in 325 C.E. At this Council, as well as at the Synod of Laodicea (363 C.E.), the twenty-seven books of our New Testament were listed with notations of the "disputed" texts. Finally, at the Council of Hippo (393 C.E.), the twenty-seven books of our New Testament were listed, with no alternative comments. However, as late as the sixth century, the Syrian canon had only twenty-two books, while the Ethiopian canon had thirty-five books. The writings that caused the most problems, in terms of whether or not they should be included, were 2–3 John, 2 Peter, Jude, James, the Revelation of John, 1 Clement, Barnabas, the Shepherd of Hermas, and the Revelation of Peter.

The following table summarizes this discussion:

Our New Testament Writings	(c. 150) Marcion	(c. 200) Irenaeus, et al.	(c. 250) Origen	(c. 300) Eusebius	(393) Council of Hippo
4 Gospels	Luke	4 Gospels	4 Gospels	4 Gospels	4 Gospels
Acts of the Apostles		Acts	Acts	Acts	Acts
8 Letters of Paul (1-2 Thess.; Gal.; 1-2 Cor.; Rom.; Philemon; Philippians)	1-2 Thess. Galatians 1-2 Cor. Romans Philemon Philippians	1-2 Thess. Galatians 1-2 Cor. Romans Philemon Philippians	1-2 Thess. Galatians 1-2 Cor. Romans Philemon Philippians	1-2 Thess. Galatians 1-2 Cor. Romans Philemon Philippians	1-2 Thess. Galatians 1-2 Cor. Romans Philemon Philippians

Our New Testament Writings	(c. 150) Marcion	(c. 200) Irenaeus, et al.	(c. 250) Origen	(c. 300) Eusebius	(393) Council of Hippo
Disputed Letters of Paul (Ephesians; Colossians; Hebrews)	Ephesians Colossians	Ephesians Colossians	Ephesians Colossians Hebrews	Ephesians Colossians Hebrews**	Ephesians Colossians Hebrews
Pastoral Epistles (1-2 Timothy; Titus)			1-2 Timothy Titus	1-2 Timothy Titus	1-2 Timothy Titus
Catholic Epistles (1-2 Peter; Jude)		1 Peter Jude	1 Peter 2 Peter** Jude**	1 Peter 2 Peter** Jude**	1 Peter 2 Peter Jude
Johannine Letters (1-3 John)		1 John	1 John 2 John** 3 John**	1 John 2 John** 3 John**	1 John 2 John 3 John
James				James**	James
Revelation of John		Revela-tion	Revelation**	Revelation **	Revelation
		Shepherd of Hermes	Shepherd of Hermes **	Shepherd of Hermes ***	
			1-2 Clement (of Rome)		
			Letter of Barnabus**	Letter of Barnabus** *	
		Revela-tion of Peter		Revelation of Peter***	
				Acts of Paul***	
TOTAL = 27	11	21	29	31	27
			**Disputed but prob. OK	**Disputed -OK;*** Disputed- NO	

Table 9. *Summary of the Canonization of the Books of the New Testament. In Eastern (Greek) congregations the Revelation of John was the most troublesome. In Greek Orthodox Churches today there still are no readings from this in Church lessons. In the Latinized Western congregations the Letter to the Hebrews was most troublesome, with 2 Peter, 2–3 John, Jude, and James running a close second.*

This chapter may seem rather sketchy. Why? Because we simply don't have much information. There are no records available as to what the rationale was to include or exclude a writing from the canon. For example, why did the small book of James suddenly "appear" on the list of accepted scriptural writings in Eusibius' list? We don't know. What was going on with the writing called Shepherd of Hermes? Irenaeus included it. Origen thought it was okay and included it, although he noted some congregations didn't recognize it. Eusibius recommended it not be included and also noted it was disputed by some congregations. The Council of Hippo rejected it. What was the problem? Why was it disputed? Who was doing the disputing? We don't know.

Understanding why some writings were found attractive and helpful sometimes is rather intuitively obvious. The three Pastoral Epistles (1–2 Timothy, Titus) are a good example. They very much support the emerging institution of the centrist Church. It is easy to understand why Church leaders would find them attractive and why congregations would find them instructive. Written much later but in the name of Paul, they exhort the congregation members to revere their leaders—referred to as *presbyteroi* (elders) or *episkopoi* (bishops or overseers)—in order to preserve stability and order.

Understanding why other writings were included remains rather mysterious. When examined more closely, the letter of 2 Peter incorporates virtually all the Letter of Jude within it. Why? Since Jude was already on the list, why add 2 Peter? If it is important to add 2 Peter, maybe Jude is no longer necessary. We simply do not have information as to the rationale.

There is very little discussion associated with these lists of the canon. So we don't know the specific arguments as to why something was included, disputed, or excluded. For all those who believe the Bible has been pretty much "dictated" to mankind by God, I wish we did know the rationale or thinking of these early Church Fathers. Nevertheless, by the end of the fourth century, the New Testament, as we know it, was pretty well fixed. We must keep in mind that this timeframe, from Jesus to the Council of Hippo, is roughly the same timeframe as from the Pilgrims at Plymouth to today.

233

Although we do not have detailed accounts of specific arguments, we can make some general assumptions. As the Council of Hippo (393 C.E.) reaffirmed the New Testament selections made by the Council of Nicaea in 325 C.E., the Council issued statements to the effect that there was no longer a necessity to consider other writings that might be included in the New Testament canon. About a century later, Gregory the Great (Pope from 590–604 C.E.) declared the writings of Holy Scripture to be the writings of the Holy Spirit and infallible as the collection of "sacred writings" or "divine law," the two terms that had been used more and more often by the Church Fathers during the third, fourth, and fifth centuries.

As the canon of Scripture was being hammered out during the controversies with the Gnostics, the process had involved asserting the principle of tradition or authenticity as the basis of selection of writings to be included. Simultaneously, the embryonic Christian theology was also being hammered out: The *Incarnation* (the "enfleshment" of God), the *Atonement* (defining mankind's reconciliation to God), the *Trinity* (Father, Son, and Holy Spirit), *Christology* (defining Jesus), the *Eucharist* (Holy Communion or the Lord's Supper), *Baptism*, and *Soteriology* (the theology of salvation). Writings that supported those general tenets were favorably received. Those that didn't were rejected. During this same time, the evolving Church administrative structure was solidifying: Bishops, elders, synods or general councils, the use of creedal statements, the role (or lack) of women, and the acceptance of annual festivals/rites (Christmas, Easter, Pentecost, Baptism, the Eucharist). Writings that supported this evolving Church structure were favorably received. Those that didn't were rejected.

As the test of canonicity during this period, tradition or authenticity had assumed an authority superior to that of the Scriptures. However, once the canon was accepted, the accepted Books began to be held in a special reverence. The shift in emphasis began to favor the use of these accepted texts in and of themselves. The tradition or authenticity argument was used less and less. The developing theology and creedal statements, now supported by Scripture, were used, in return, to interpret and define Scripture. This trend has continued, pretty much, to today. The primacy of Scripture is certainly asserted, but it needs to be interpreted in accordance with accepted Church tradition and teachings.

The tension that existed then, even within Pope Gregory's own allegorical writings, still exists today. From the time of early great preachers there were those that asserted the Scriptures were infallible, which meant that any one, individual textual reference was inherently true. Others preferred a more allegorical approach, such as Saint Augustine, Jerome, Ambrose of Milan, Chrysostom of Antioch, and even Gregory himself. They asserted that the Scriptures were infallible, which meant that, taken as a whole, the Scriptures provided divine inspiration. Those that fell in this allegorical camp often cited Jesus' own use of his Scriptures (our Old Testament). On the one hand Jesus takes the Old Testament as it stands and insists on its authority. (*I have come to fulfill the Law and the Prophets.*) On the other he ventures to criticize it, reinterpret it, and attack traditional interpretations. (*You have heard it said ... but I say to you ....*)

This same tension exists today.

To most conservative Christians, Biblical inspiration is infallible and inerrant. Their whole foundation of religious belief will crumble if the entire Bible is not considered to be the authoritative Word of God. If the Bible contains some errors and irrelevancies, then there is no firm basis on which to base beliefs, morality, and personal practices. For the conservative Christian it is a purely black-and-white issue—either the Bible must be inerrant as the Word of God or it must be devoid of all authority.

To more liberal Christians the Bible is not inerrant. The writings that comprise the Bible were authored by human beings whose scientific point of view skewed their thinking, whose specific belief systems were promoted, who attributed anthropomorphic qualities of God that reflected themselves (many of which would be considered immoral by our standards), who incorporated material and ideas from other cultures, and who disagreed with other biblical authors. The task of the liberal Christian is to separate the wheat from the chaff, to concentrate on the true ideas and statements by Jesus, the prophets or the apostles, and leave behind those elements that solely belong in earlier, biblical centuries.

Donald L. O'Dell

Is the Bible *the Word of God*?

The phrase *the Word of God* was always used to refer to Jesus Christ, in the same vein as was used by the writers of the Gospel of John, e.g., the *Living Word*. The use of the phrase *the Word of God* as a description of the Bible did not come into play until after the Protestant Reformation (in the 1500s). Neither Martin Luther nor John Calvin, the two pillars of Protestant theology, referred to the Scriptures as *the Word of God*. That was a phrase reserved only as a description of Jesus. When viewed within the timeframe of the last 2,000 years, the phenomenon of referring to the Bible as *the Word of God* occurred rather recently.

Coming from a Reformed Protestant theological background, my perspective is admittedly "tinted." Traditional reformed theology has declared that the only final authority for faith is not the Bible but the Holy Spirit making the love of God in Christ come alive in a person. To attribute the term, *the Word of God*, to the Bible has been a relatively recent phenomenon.

In our contemporary society, *the Word of God* means one of two things:

- If the Scriptures are regarded as literally inerrant, then the writers or sources are but transparent beings through which God himself wrote the Bible. In this manner the Scriptures have become the "final authority" in matters of faith and practice. The Scriptures are *the Word of God*.

- If the Holy Spirit aids us in exercising discriminatory judgment when reading the Scriptures, then the ability to think of the biblical sources as real people becomes absolutely critical in the process of making their faith, belief, and practices our own. The Bible, then, tells the story of God's revealing activity in and through men and women, which enables God's spirit to reveal his activity in and through you.

I believe the historical and literary evidence supports the second viewpoint.

Summary

In Part 2 we've covered four hundred years from the time of Jesus to the Council of Hippo.

The journey began as Jewish Christians gathered for a meal—eating together as a sign and symbol of the new kingdom of God that was being lived and experienced in Jesus of Nazareth. It was a reality that transformed the lives of those who were there. They truly understood what Jesus had meant when he talked of the kingdom being like leaven to dough—the reign of God is invisible, but powerful. They understood the parable of the treasure buried in the vineyard—God is like this same buried treasure in each of us. Whether we follow that reality through various synagogue-based Jesus movements in and around Jerusalem, through various Hellenistic Jewish-based communities like Mark's, Matthew's, or John's, or whether we follow the reality of the kingdom through the Christ Congregations, we've discovered all shared some form of the common meal tradition. But as this movement began to get organized, the institutions that arose took on a life of their own. The same pattern we saw in the Old Testament began to happen again—different players, different circumstances, different environment—but the same tune all over again. In the Old Testament, acts of purification and sacrifice initially were acts of faith and belief. We saw how the priestly class began codifying and institutionalizing these rites and rituals to the point that they became more critical than the faith behind them. As the institution of the Church began to gel, faith became focused on the words of "accepted" Scripture and on the theology and doctrine that had been rationally developed by early Church Fathers. Faith in the transforming spirit of a living Jesus began to take a distant back seat.

Hear the words of this same Eusebius, as he described the imperial banquet celebrating the conclusion of the Council of Nicaea (as quoted by Crossan):

"Detachments of the body-guard and troops surrounded the entrance of the palace with drawn swords, and through the midst of them the men of God proceeded without fear into the innermost of the Imperial apartments, in which some were the Emperor's companions at table, while others reclined on couches arranged on either side. One might have thought that a picture of Christ's kingdom was thus shadowed forth, and a dream rather than reality."

[Crossan goes on]: "The meal and the kingdom still come together, but now the participants are the male bishops, and they recline, with the Emperor himself, to be served by others. Maybe, Christianity is an inevitable and absolutely necessary 'betrayal' of Jesus, else it might have died among the hills of Lower Galilee. But did that 'betrayal' have to happen so swiftly, succeed so fully, and be enjoyed so thoroughly?"[59]

Chapter 11 Notes

[56] Durant, *The Story of Civilization*, Vol. 3, pp 548, 549

[57] For these early Christians the term "scripture" meant the *Septuagint*, the Greek translation of Hebrew writings, which contained the thirty-nine books of our Old Testament plus the books of the Apocrapha—exactly as the Roman Catholic Old Testament does today.

[58] 1-2 Thess., Galatians, 1-2 Corinth., Romans, Philemon, Philippians, Ephesians, and Colossians

[59] Both Eusebius' quote and Crossan's commentary are from Crossan, *The Historical Jesus*, p 424

Chapter 12

New Testament Themes to Remember

It may seem rather pretentious to try to summarize the New Testament—and it is. However, in light of the broad brushstrokes discussed in Part II, I will focus on five areas:

- The difference between general guidelines and literal instruction;

- The recognition and danger of bibliolatry;

- Understanding the dangers of institutionalization;

- Acknowledging who Jesus is; and

- Understanding how powerfully seductive fear can be.

These five areas are not independent, stand-alone issues or ideas. Think of them as overlapping circles—they touch and influence each other. Jiggle one and all the others will wiggle as well.

Guidance Versus Literal Instruction

In light of all the evidence at hand, it appears that Jesus' own teachings were rather introspective in that they required some judgment and common sense to make them "real" for a hearer. His teachings were parables about the nature of the new Kingdom of God. They were short, punchy, cynic-like one-liners that seemed to poke holes in the logic of institutionalized religiosity. They were metaphors from the life and times of his listeners and of him—wineskins, lost coins, trees and their fruit (or lack of fruit), leaven in dough, harvests, and laborers. His commandments remained vague. Love your neighbor as yourself. Who is my neighbor? One in need. Love God with all your heart, soul, mind, and strength. Love each other.

But we don't like vague instructions that have to be interpreted, depending on the situation, on a personal level. We don't like commandments that instruct us to "... do justice, love righteousness, and walk humbly with [our] God." We like things that are concrete, black-and-white, easy to remember, easy to quote, easy to understand—even if it means we have eventually handcuffed God himself. As the Church grew and matured, it succumbed to that urge to make things of the Spirit concrete and easy to discern. Within fifty years of Jesus' death the reality of his Spirit was being subjected to the accepted standards of Greco-Roman philosophical debate and polemic. As the Church moved through the second and third centuries, it became clear that the reality of the philosophical polemic had become more of a reality than the reality of the Spirit. That significant shift played a tremendous role in the development of what we understand as the New Testament. This development took place, of course, within the venue of the Christ congregations. The writings, remembrances, and communal spirit of the various Jesus movements pretty much dissolved during this time.

Doesn't all this information simply "ruin" the beauty of the New Testament? Absolutely not. It puts the focus where it should have been all along—on the Self. We are still able to use the Scriptures just as the initial Jewish Christians used their Scriptures (our current Old Testament). We can either start with an experience or we can start with Scripture. Early Christians had a transforming, spiritual experience and looked through their familiar Scriptures to find something similar that would assist them in verbalizing the reality of that sense of spirituality. Sometimes they came at this from the reverse, starting with Scripture. They would read something in their Scripture and upon reflection realize that something very similar had happened to them. This second way of using Scripture is very similar to what I experienced in my early AA meetings. I heard things from old-timers that described how I felt, although I didn't know I felt that way until I heard it—and then I knew, and I knew I knew, and it was exhilarating. We are to do the same kinds of things with the New Testament.

But, once again, we don't like vague instructions that have to be interpreted. We want things concrete. We want to know—*have to know*—we are right in order to quell our fear. This whole issue of having to be right is disturbing. When we are talking politics, we succumb to the pressure to be "right"—even though our attempt to be "right" is generally confused with making the opponent look "wrong." That's just lazy. It's lazy reporting on the part of print/media journalists or talk radio hosts, and it's lazy reading/listening on our part. It's just not helpful. This same desire to ritualize, legalize, get it down on paper, black and white, cut and dried, no bones about it, "We are Right!" was tried during the Crusades. It was tried again during the Inquisition as an equal and opposite reaction to the Protestant Reformation and its attempt to establish "perfect" religious communities such as Salem, Massachusetts, in the United States.

We've tried it in our contemporary culture. We've translated our religious convictions—convictions we now know were based on misunderstandings of what the Old Testament was trying to communicate—into laws to keep African Americans "in their place," keep women from voting, keep labor from organizing, keep alcohol off the streets. It didn't work then. Not only haven't we learned, we still are trying—only now it's with drugs, with soft, victimless vice, with anti-gay sentiment, with condemning people who want to choose when to die, or with abortion rights and stem cell research.

We have all seen bumper stickers that proclaim: "God Is Pro-Life." We understand what that means in the context of being either anti-abortion or pro-choice. However, we all need to be careful about statements like that. God is pro-life but not in the strict Roe v. Wade context. God values all life. But that applies to the thousands of children that die monthly from malnourishment and abuse. If indeed God is going to be as judgmental as evangelicals seem to believe, then he'll judge/forgive us just as we judge/forgive, which is what we have prayed, over and over, in the Lord's Prayer: "… forgive us our debts AS we forgive our debtors …." If you condemn a pro-choice person as a baby killer, then God will judge you accordingly: *"You gave your money to your church to build a sanctuary, or buy new choir robes, or purchase new curriculum*

243

materials for Sunday school, or refurbish a sponsored summer campground while my children starved to death. You and your congregation participated in pro-life rallies and raised money for the pro-life cause but you never adopted one unwanted child, nor gave money to help someone else in your community adopt, nor gave money to provide support to an adopted child of mine. Many who want to terminate a pregnancy are educated, have money, have means, and will take care of themselves regardless of the law. However, many people who want to exercise freedom of choice are already poor, on federal assistance, underage, and undereducated, and they want to terminate a pregnancy as an act of desperation. Your actions to withhold this from them perpetuates their cycle of poverty and ignorance. How could you possibly do that to one of these little ones who are my beloved?"

Becoming a Christian or believing in Jesus is not about supporting the Church or having the Church provide society with a code of ethics or morals literally quoted from the New Testament. It's about finding the Kingdom of God right now for you in the here and now. It's letting people see God in you and training yourself to see God in them. It's fuzzy. It requires thought and decisions—not all of which are going to be correct. It's responding to Jesus' commandments: Love God and love your neighbor. Well, okay, but how do I do that? He responded with the parable of the Good Samaritan (Luke 10:25–37). That's called "guidance" rather than a cut-and-dried "formula" for successful God-pleasing. That's about as good as it gets.

Recognizing the Danger of Bibliolatry

Righteousness and faith are not equivalent to some form of purity of belief about what's in the New Testament. To believe something literally happened, just because it's in the Bible, is not the mark of a true Christian. Biblical literalism does not equate to faithfulness. Rather, we are to open our eyes and begin to see the new Kingdom all around us—the events and miracles in our lives. Scripture will guide us. How do we do this? The same way early Christians did it. Through eating together, serving each other, healing each other, sharing with each other in trust and honesty about the signs, wonders, and miracles that are occurring in our own lives right now.

Crossan paints a wonderful verbal image concerning Luke's allegory of the appearance of Jesus to the couple on the road to Emmaus (Luke 24:13–32).

> "Jesus' own followers ... talked eventually of the resurrection. They tried to express what they meant by telling, for example, about the journey to Emmaus undertaken by two Jesus followers, one named and clearly male, one unnamed and probably female. The couple were leaving Jerusalem in disappointed and dejected sorrow. Jesus joined them on the road and, unknown and unrecognized, explained how the Hebrew Scriptures should have prepared them for his fate. Later that evening they invited him to join them for their evening meal, and finally they recognized him when once again he served the meal to them as of old beside the lake. And then, only then, they started back to Jerusalem in high spirits. The symbolism is obvious, as is the metaphoric condensation of the first years of Christian thought and practice into one parabolic afternoon. Emmaus never happened. Emmaus always happens."[60]

I love those sentences: "Emmaus never happened. Emmaus always happens." For me that pretty much says it all. That is why it is desperately important to me that we begin to see the New Testament authors as real people struggling with the real difficulty of putting words to a spiritual experience. Without this ability to visualize real people, we're left with finding the New Testament characters archaic and irrelevant or finding ourselves idolizing the very words simply because—well, it's in the Bible.

Some have made the Bible an idol—*bibliolatry*—treating the very words of the Bible in the same manner as the priestly class treated the rites and rituals in the Old Testament. It's as if they don't have any personal experience of the transforming nature of the new Kingdom within their midst, so they try to fake it by vicariously believing, with all the fervor they can muster, in the stories in the Holy Book. Challenge the Bible or question its historicity and they will summarily damn you because if any one little part of the Bible is shown to be incorrect, their whole faith-system crumbles.

There is always a tension between the faith itself and our attempt to communicate it in a rational language at a given historical period. A relatively static authoritarianism, either of the Roman Catholic type or fundamentalist/evangelical type, so confuses the authority of the Church, the Bible, the creeds, and the faith of the people that the tension which is between God, as we understand God, and our human understanding, is removed. Without that tension the doors are opened to idolatry—in this case a blind worship of the Bible itself—or bibliolatry. *Appendix D contains a current and well-written example of biblical literalism that comes very close to what I mean by bibliolatry.*

One could make a case that the Old Testament priestly class made an "idol" out of the Law. Similarly, the emerging Church made an "idol" out of theological nit-picking that allowed the reality of the living Lord in people's lives to play second fiddle to the rationality of theology. Today we see the Christian Right making an "idol" out of the Bible—worshipping (i.e., pronouncing, defending, promulgating, promoting) their interpretation of it more than the spirit of the living Lord that moves through it.

It seems that as God reveals himself through history, "truth" consistently has been incorporated from other cultures: Babylonian, Persian, Egyptian, Greek, Roman. Karl Barth, the Reformed theologian, often has been quoted as saying that the only proper way to study the Bible is to keep it in one hand while keeping the daily newspaper in the other. The two need to be read together. After the New Testament was declared "complete" by the Council of Hippo, the prevailing sense of bibliolatry would begin to posit that there is no more "truth," from other cultures or from anywhere. In fact other cultures now became threatening. I think that is uncharacteristically unbiblical. Ideas from other cultures have always impacted the Bible.

Idea	Culture
Purification/sacrifice as basis for worship	Consistent with surrounding cultures of Babylon and Egypt
Eternal-ness	Babylon, Persia, Egypt
Immortality	Greek and Roman philosophies
"Biographical" format of the Gospels	Greek tragedy format—the "Hero-is-finally-vindicated"
Concept of Fate	Greek and Roman philosophies
Resurrection	Babylon, Persia, Egypt, and consistent Greco/Roman concepts of deities
Concepts of God/Man interaction and Incarnation	Consistent with antiquity, as well as Greco/Roman concepts of deities

Table 10 *Examples of Cultural Influence on New Testament writers. The cultural exchange of ideas is found throughout the Bible.*

Bibliolatry—Most dangerous, indeed! How does it express itself?

- In fierce defense of the Scriptures—one cannot doubt, challenge, or question without incurring the wrath of those who believe that the Bible (and their view of the God behind it) somehow needs their protection. It's almost as if the perception of God by those who must defend the Scriptures is as one who is needy and helpless, and who requires all the assistance possible to defend his truth and his "honor."

- In the reasonable assertion that history and its influences are almost impossible to deal with. Those who must defend the Scriptures cannot conceive that I experience and think about God differently than they, which may be different than Abraham experienced as a middle Bronze Age nomad, or Paul experienced as a first-century Jewish-Roman citizen. They seem to be saying, basically, that believing in the Bible the way they believe in the Bible is the essence of being a Christian. For them, one cannot believe in nor interpret the Bible any other way.

- In the children's ditty: "Jesus loves me this I know, 'cause the Bible tells me so." This is fine for children, although I suspect there are too many adults whose personal experience of God has never matured beyond the message of that song.

So what can we say when confronted by one who idolizes the New Testament? When someone quotes Scripture to you—ask them for their version. They probably won't understand. Using Luke's Emmaus story as an example, tell them, *"I'm not interested in the Emmaus version Luke created. Tell me about the times you've had a spiritual insight on your journeys to your Emmaus. I'd be interested in that."* If someone quotes to you from one of the many lists Paul gives us about sinful behavior (fornication, adultery, greed, homosexuality, etc.), ask them which compulsions have left them since they became a Christian. *"How does it now feel to be free from that? How did it happen? I'd be interested in that."* When Paul talks about the gifts of the spirit—the chief of which is Love, followed by Faith and Hope (1 Cor. 12–13)—ask, *"Describe those gifts that have been given to you.*

How have those gifts matured in you? What difference has that made in your life? I'd be interested in that."

This is how we use the New Testament. Just like the earliest of Christians used their Scriptures. Generations of others have experienced a spiritual awakening before we've come along. That experience includes grappling with the difficulty of recognizing the awakening when it happens as well as the difficulty in verbalizing it after it's been recognized. Just as the initial Christians used their Scriptures to help them, we can do the same. That's the timeless value of the New Testament.

Institutionalization

As the embryonic Christ congregations grew, they became organized in part because their Greco-Roman milieu was steeped in a culture of authority and orderliness. As their sense of orderliness matured, their communications with each other began building a dogma that reinforced their views and values. These communications, or letters, became much of what we now recognize as Books of the New Testament. Simultaneously, the sayings-based Jewish groups were either still clinging onto the organizational model of the synagogue or they were leaving the Palestinian arena (including Jerusalem) altogether, fleeing from the impending Roman onslaught. What influence they might have had on the prevailing, circulating correspondence left with them.

It is the nature of institutions that they begin to take on a life of their own. The emerging Christian Church was no different. More and more the Church began to solidify its theological positions in ways that bolstered their established institutional structure. The early and important authority, role, and status of women went downhill, the original Jewish sayings-based groups had become more communal, isolated, and out of the mainstream. From these communal settings came the Gospels of Mark, Matthew, and John—each of which was promulgating their communal group as *the* group God had had in mind. As such, they did not participate in the congregational give-and-take of the Christ congregations. As far as the Christ congregations were concerned, the sayings-based groups had become a classic case of "out of sight, out of mind." As a result, the unadorned true import and impact of Jesus' teachings, known most specifically in these Jesus groups, never reached the pages of our New Testament.

Overreacting, Israel of the Old Testament got it wrong despite the prophets. They moved to create a strict theological system of external behavior and activities that was specific in terms of what one needed to do or not do. This institutionalization or theocracy of morality and worship sort of "guaranteed" that God would be pleased. It's the same old "wanting to be as God" idea first recorded by the Yahwist. But God doesn't want a codified, sterile, here's-the-right-formula kind of society. He wants a community of people who can be still and hear him, who will seek justice, who will watch out for the little man, and who will walk humbly with him.

It appears the "Church" got it wrong, too, making the same kind of mistake as post-exilic Judaism. The basic message of Jesus—"The Kingdom of God is now—in your heart. Just open your eyes and you will see it"—got left behind or reinterpreted by Mark, Matthew, John, and Luke. By focusing on Pauline theology and embellishing it with all sorts of mental and philosophical gymnastics—rebaptism, Incarnation, the Trinity, the nature of Christ (*homoousia* versus *homoiousia*.)—the Christ congregations innocently began building a self-serving set of doctrines that were used, in turn and not so innocently, as a method of self-justification.

With our manmade theologies we have developed a faith in our theology—not in the living Spirit of God who is all around us all the time. Most often we don't see the Spirit because we're conditioned to look only at our theology. But that's not where we'll find the Spirit. We'll find it in the ordinary. If the only thing that's "real" is the theology—the words, the phrases, the biblical idiom—then that's where we'll look, and that's dangerous. That's why it's so sad to remember the evangelical who couldn't stand the thought of people having their lives changed by their Higher Power, when he desperately wanted them to acknowledge that their Higher Power was Jesus Christ. Without that acknowledgment and naming, he could do no less than condemn. That's how he was conditioned. God was looking him right in the face and he couldn't see him. The "correct" trigger words weren't being used.

We can see a great parallel within our own Congress. The early framers of the Constitution had envisioned a Congress that would consist of part-time, expenses-only citizens performing their civic duty. Politics was not a profession. Politics hadn't been institutionalized. The framers couldn't conceive of today's full-time, career politicians. Now, as we know, the fully institutionalized career path begins as a State Representative, moves to the State Senate, and on to the U.S. House of Representatives, and finally to the U.S. Senate. The whole process will consume a forty-year career. Just as Benjamin Franklin or Thomas Jefferson would be appalled at our career politicians, so the early Christians would have been appalled at the theological infighting and hair-splitting that was going on in order to preserve the emerging institution of the Church. The timeframe from the birth of our Constitution to now is about the same timeframe we're talking about here—two or three hundred years.

We get all twisted around. I know; I have been twisted around. You'll recall I believed I had to have alcohol in my system twenty-four hours a day in order to feel normal, and it never occurred to me that that was abnormal. So I know what tricks my mental capacities can play on me. I still don't fully trust what I've figured out. I still get reality checks on all my major decisions. However, I trust in my infant baptism. I trust it primarily because I didn't have anything to do with it. I trust that my image of what God wants and what God is like is that Spirit of God that caused the knot in my stomach to disappear when I touched the doorknob of St. Timothy's Episcopal Church in Reston, Virginia. I trust the Spirit that enabled me to find Maureen's telephone number and allowed her to say "yes" when she had just decided to say "no."

In that light I can know that God is like Jesus Christ—not the magical, biblically romantic vision of Jesus in the Gospels or the overarching cosmic vision in Paul's later letters, but in the eyes of my "trusting" and "knowing." In this way I understand Paul. He wasn't laying down a theology for all of us to follow. *I still believe that Paul has rolled over in his grave hundreds of times upon learning that we were squabbling over words he dashed off in a letter.* Paul was working out—integrating—his Jewishness with what he'd experienced on the way to Damascus. Similarly, I am working to integrate the spirituality I came to trust while working the suggested 12 Steps of Alcoholics Anonymous with my formal education in a "proper" Reformed theology. I'm not Paul—don't misunderstand me. But I can "sense" how he wrestled to find the right words.

Who Is Jesus?

Does it matter how you experience Jesus the Christ? Does it matter if you experience him as the Divine Son of God or as a man who, more than anyone else, lived the life of God's love? Does it matter?

If you think like Paul, a Pharisaic Jew and first-century Roman citizen who believed that Yahweh

- Responds to purification and sacrifice,

- Created us to praise and adore him,

- Gets angry and punishes,

- Believes he must be placated before he can relent or rewrite his rules,

then, yes, it matters very much.

For you, Jesus Christ is the Son of God who has absorbed all the sins of mankind so he can offer a new redemption, a new covenant. Understanding the person, Jesus, this way certainly does help "explain" things. However, I have learned to be cautious about the necessity of having to be able to "explain" things. I remember a biology professor telling our class that a baby doesn't need to understand all the nutritional value of mother's milk in order for it to work very well.

I also remember when my professor of Systematic Theology at Princeton, Dr. George Hendry, drove this same point home to me in a personal way. Since our son was about to be born, I had requested and received permission from Dr. Hendry to get a deadline extended for an assignment. Shortly after Christopher was born, I was back in class. Dr. Hendry was lecturing on baptism and the theological principle that infant baptism (as opposed to Confirmation) doesn't require that the child acknowledge the import of the rite. He acknowledged my return to class and asked me to stand. He then said to me: "Mr. O'Dell, isn't it correct that you and your wife just had a son?" "Yes," I replied. He went on: "And when they first brought your son to you to hold, did you and your wife count his toes and fingers and look at his tiny fingernails?" "Yes, we did," I answered—wondering where he was going with this. "Did you, at some point during this initial inspection of your child, give the wee lad a kiss on his cheek or forehead?" "Yes. I kissed him on his fingertips and his forehead," I replied. "Well then, Mr. O'Dell, would you please face the class and explain to your colleagues the meaninglessness of your kiss since the wee one was obviously too young to comprehend it."

Does it really matter?

- If you believe in the message of the prophets and you believe that the sayings of Jesus of Nazareth continued the message of the prophets—not only that—but that he was the embodiment of the message;

- If you believe he proclaimed "I have fulfilled the spirit of the Law and the message of the prophets," that the Kingdom of God is here, is now, and in its now-ness is forever, and that Yahweh is not an angry, jealous, prideful God who will protect, love, and lift to victory his people only when they do as he wishes;

- If you believe he is like the love lived in Jesus—a God that is here and now and is love and mercy and kindness and healing in the hearts of people now.

Then no, it doesn't matter. Dr. Hendry, in his book *The Gospel of the Incarnation,* says of the life, teaching, Crucifixion, and empty tomb—the love of God met the sin of mankind, and love won. The sin of mankind is that incessant egoism that wants to be as right as God, wants to have things explained, wants to be in control, wants to have figured out God, wants to be as God.

Love always wins. Righteousness always wins. Truth and mercy always win. They win in the here and now. They may not win in ways we expect or would like. But they win—how else can we explain the hope or optimism that simply will not die within the human breast? God is love and love won! Jesus of Nazareth was the living embodiment—the incarnation—of the message of the prophets. Seeing Jesus is seeing the face of God. What's God like? Look at Jesus. The prophets were right in their time. Jesus was right in his time. His spirit could not be killed. His spirit confronted Paul and Paul was changed forever. But Paul's message—freedom from the law and justification by faith alone—

got all bogged down and twisted around like all our messages get. Like we get. Like Paul's exhortations to behave correctly as an expression of gratitude to God for the freedom of his grace became twisted to mean rigid, almost pharisaical, codes of ritual behavior. And in the end the later New Testament writers and early Church leaders began the cycle of the Old Testament dance all over—codifying, intellectualizing, institutionalizing—to rationalize the spirit in a way that made it predictable, that put it in a theological straitjacket unable to do anything but what mankind had predicted it will do.

Isn't this what happened to the Pilgrims that settled New England? They fled the British Empire and other parts of Europe to find religious freedom—to develop and live by their own set of moral laws based on their understanding of Christianity. Once here they established communities based on their (now freely) defined versions of Christian law and moral behavior. Life was hard but wonderful. Then they began persecuting those that disagreed with them. They persecuted as fiercely as the English or French Catholics had persecuted them. One needs only to recall the Salem witch trials. So, what had changed? Nothing, except those that had been persecuted became the persecutors.

Why did I say it "appears" the Church got it wrong? Because there is a lot we simply don't know. The New Testament of the Bible we all swear by and swear on is a book we know precious little about—in terms of how it came to be. We cannot answer how and why this biblical book was included or excluded from the Bible's New Testament. We cannot answer how and why this apostle's letters were included and that apostle's letters weren't. People went through this process, but we don't understand how they made their decisions and what the criteria were by which they decided. Maybe there weren't many criteria at all. Maybe, like the character Topsy in the book/movie *Gone with the Wind*, "It jes growed up all by itself."

I doubt it. There were criteria. We just don't have records.

Fear is Seductive

We began this book with a discussion of the temptation in the Garden of Eden, and we have seen the desire to be in possession of the knowledge of good and evil as a powerfully seductive force.

After all, who doesn't want to be right? But that's not exactly what we're talking about here, is it? We're talking about a desire to know the mind of God, to know what, exactly, he wants us to do. We're talking about the same desire that drove the Deuteronomic reformers to put a theological straightjacket on God.

All this is tempting because this powerfully seductive force quells our fears. What are we afraid of? We're afraid of going to Hell and we're afraid of death—all kinds of death: changes to that which is known, predictable, and comfortable; financial lack; failure; being exposed; being ugly; being wrong; losing. Our fear-based institutionalized religiosity assuages these fears. But at the same time it works diligently to keep those fears inflamed—to keep them real so the Church can continue to assuage them.

I have learned that fear is the lack of faith. More precisely, I learned that faith is nothing but fear that has said its prayers. Fear and faith are contradictory terms. I remember the slogan I quoted earlier: "Religion is for those that are afraid of going to Hell. Spirituality is for those who have been to Hell and don't want to go back." Rather than discussing the fruits of the Tree of Knowledge of Good and Evil, Jesus talked simply of judging a tree by the quality of its fruit (Matt. 7:16–20). Where there are good fruits we will find a good tree. Where the fruits of the Spirit are, we will find a good, godly Spirit. As Paul enumerated the gifts of the Spirit in the twelfth and thirteenth chapters of 1 Corinthians, he concluded that the three greatest gifts (or fruits) of the Spirit are faith, hope, and love, and the greatest of these gifts is love. The desire to "button down" and explicitly define these gifts/fruits and their expressions is to succumb to fear.

To understand the Incarnation (or enfleshment) of God is to understand that it doesn't simply apply to Jesus. Each of us is an incarnation of the Spirit of God and that incarnation is the beginning of the journey from fear to freedom—the freedom of the Kingdom of God as fully lived in the message of the life and death of Jesus. But to live the message of the life and death of Jesus is to live the life of being guided. It is to live the life of shades of gray—there are no cut-and-dried absolutes. It can be scary. "What if I'm wrong or mistaken?" It can produce doubt, which produces fear. To begin to assuage the fear is to begin to move away from the message of the life and death of Jesus.

Look for the fruits of love, acceptance, inclusiveness, tolerance, empathy, encouragement, and honesty. Where we find these fruits we find God's Spirit—even if the proper religious language of the New Testament isn't being used in just the "right" way.

Summary

It seems to me that the Bible tells the simple story of the constant tension between mankind's desire for a didactic, explicit, prescribed set of approved behaviors that God will (purportedly) bless as opposed to God's issuance of "fuzzy" moral instructions. We don't like "fuzzy" instructions or suggestions. We want assurances—almost guarantees. We want teachers to tell us if we do A, B, and C, we'll get a "gold star." We want to know, beyond the shadow of a doubt, that if we save this much, invest it this way, we'll be assured we'll have enough to live comfortably in our retirement. We like things explicit, cut and dried, predictable. We also enjoy being in a position of being able to be condescending in our graciousness. We like the reassurance we get from sermons that focus on all the evil occurring in the world "out there." Whew! We may be selfish, fearful of change, non-trusting, judgmental, and mean spirited, but at least we aren't communists, or drug addicts, or sexual perverts, or abortionists, or whatever.

In the Old Testament this tension bubbled to the surface early: As the covenant with Yahweh was being given its first shape under Moses during the Exodus, the populace continually wanted to create and worship idols. This was followed by the continuing struggle between the organized priesthood and the prophets.

In the New Testament it took only one hundred years for Jesus' "fuzzy" message of the Kingdom of God to be institutionalized by various Jesus groups as a newer form of Judaism, and by Paul as a message that the Kingdom incorporated both Jews and non-Jews. So far so good. But then the Jesus groups dissolved and Paul's message was overcome with administrative issues of appropriate first-century behavior and got bogged down over how, theologically, to "get" from a Jews-only historic tradition to one of "well, 'Jews-only' really meant everyone." As he tried to rationally justify his insight, he moved from the Christ of faith to the Christ of theology. The early church fathers picked up on the Christ of theology and continued the construction of an elaborate, unified dogma. So now the words of Jesus had morphed into the doctrines of Salvation (soteriology), Christology, Trinity, Atonement, Incarnation, and Apostolic Succession.

Paul experienced the freedom he found in the message of the Damascus/Antioch Christ congregations. It was exhilarating and life-changing. He began to understand that these Christ congregations, which he once loathed because they undercut his beloved Pharisaic Judaism, had stumbled on to something truly revolutionary: God's love and presence was not reserved for Jews alone—but included all of mankind. Nevertheless, he was a Pharisee. He knew the Law (Torah) as well as the oral interpretations (the embryonic Midrash) and he just couldn't let that go. So he became preoccupied with integrating this new thought with his knowledge of the Law. He also had the same problem with his new spirituality that I had trying to explain or verbalize my spiritual experience. He verbalized his sense of this new reality in terms of redefining Israel's history and thus the meaning of the Law. At the same time behavioral abuses in his congregations surfaced, which seemed—at least to him—to threaten his authority. These abuses also pricked his sense of orderliness and accompanying codes of behavior—something familiar to his Pharisaical upbringing. The Pharisees after all were fastidious in their observance of behavioral/purity codes: what to eat, how to prepare it, what ingredients to use, what prayers to repeat, and how to serve it.

As a result, Paul's surviving messages began to be transformed by church fathers, slowly but surely, in "new" behaviors befitting a "new" Gospel that was a result of a "new" sense of history. Lost was the sense of freedom that had so influenced Paul. The "fuzzy" was being replaced once again with the "explicit."

Paul had it right simply as a revelation: God's plan was for Jews and Gentiles alike. He said so and then maybe he should've stopped. But he asked himself a fateful question—posited a thoroughly Pharisaic assumption: It must have been this way since the beginning, and since Judaism was so steeped in its sense of God's revelation in history (and the interpretation of the history couldn't have been incomplete or in error), then he was compelled by his own sense of Roman and Pharisaic senses of orderliness, completeness, and legal precedence to develop an interpretation of

Old Testament history that would work. This interpretation, in turn, got sidetracked by issues of "proper" congregational behavior, and *voila*—the original message of freedom from the Law that he had personally experienced began to get lost in the shuffle. Later writers, either biblical or non-biblical (Justin, Clement, Ignatius, et al.) began picking up on his themes—not themes of freedom and grace, but of orderliness, behavior, rational (neat) explanations—and continued to expand, getting further and further away from his Gospel of Freedom.

Concluding Remarks

Jesus' message was such a simple, powerful one. It still is. It doesn't save us. It transforms us. Over the four centuries after his death it got garbled, complicated, and twisted. It still is.

"The significance of our self
cannot be measured by the fame and
glory of this world or the material
things we have,

But

By the love and compassion we
have shown to others every day of our
life—without fame or glory or
thanks—just in the name of love,

And

Maybe all the little things we do
for one another is the most significant
thing you and I might do in our
lifetime."

—Mi Sun

Although I remain unsure of the spiritual persuasion of this Oriental philosopher, I believe I can hear Jesus clapping his hands and shouting: *"Hallelujah, brother! Amen! To live this way is to be in the reality of the eternal here and now of the new Kingdom of God I came to proclaim."*

If you've had my experience or experienced your own version of Emmaus, then we can be put in a room and we'll all be able to identify, talk, and laugh at our foolishness, as well as cry with joy and sadness. Some of us in the room will call this Spirit that changed our lives Jesus Christ, or the Holy Spirit, or God, or the Universal Consciousness, or the Great Spirit, or our Higher Power, or the Mind of God, or Universal Truth. The reality we've all experienced, however, will be recognized and honored. The terminology won't really matter.

That is, it won't really matter until …

- Some of us make the words that make sense to us—become the only words that anyone can use;

- Some of us institutionalize those words into verbal formulas;

- Some of us institutionalize the verbal formulas into an organizational model;

- Then, we'll fear, distrust, and eventually hate each other for not agreeing about how we've institutionalized the reality of the Lord of Love.

Rather ironic, isn't it? At least now we know it isn't really a new story, so we can have hope. It's the same tension that's exhibited throughout the Old Testament. It's the same tension that was instrumental in the development and selection of the contents of the New Testament. Read or reread the prophet Hosea in the Old Testament (discussed in Chapter 4). It's the same old tension. Yet the prophet Hosea out-loved his wife's (Gomer) rejection of him; the love of God out-loved the sin and egoism of mankind at Jesus' Crucifixion. The priests really didn't win out over the prophets. I don't believe the biblical literalists will win out over the reality of the Spirit of Love and Truth.

As I stated in the Introduction: I believe it will make a significant difference if people simply begin to say, "This is the path I have chosen in order to know and experience God, as I understand God" rather than "This is the only path to God."

I hope you have enjoyed this book.

I hope it has made you think.

Even if you have disagreed, I hope it has helped you grow.

I hope you are continuing to walk with God, as you understand God, in a manner that disciplines you to see the love of God in others and allows others to see the love of God in you.

Namaste. Shalom. Peace.

Donald L. O'Dell

Chapter 12 Notes

[60] Crossan, *The Historical Jesus, p. xiii.*

Afterword

About the Author

How did the Bible become the Bible? How did the historical context and purposes of the emerging authors who produced most of the text we know as the Scriptures evolve into the Bible? The sources of our Biblical texts were people of their times. Using incidents from my own personal experience and a down-to-earth approach to history, I hope I have made these people "come alive" for you. After reading the book, my hope is that you will be in a better position to use the Bible as a spiritual, albeit non-literal, reference.

I have made a case that our human nature has always had a strong desire for simplistic biblical beliefs and practices. We know this is really a desire to feel in control of the knowledge of good and evil and therefore to be absolutely certain about what it is God wants. It's a desire to believe that you're right, which quells doubts and, as such, is fear-based. This inclination had its beginnings in the Old Testament, led to abuses in Israel's Temple-State system, and influenced what was included and excluded from the New Testament. These are the same fear-based "religious" forces that dominate the beliefs of today's fundamental and evangelical churches, leading them to *mis*use the Bible.

Why should you consider my point of view?

- I am a graduate from Princeton Theological Seminary with a Master of Divinity. Also, I graduated (High Honors) from North Texas State University (now the University of North Texas) with a bachelor's degree in history along with a double minor in philosophy and psychology.

- I was a full-time Presbyterian minister for over five years, where I developed a "street gang" ministry in Trenton, NJ. Later, I moved to Oklahoma where I served two small congregations and also functioned as the chaplain of a county hospital. Although I joined the business world, I continued to work with small congregations on a part-time basis for another twelve years.

- I had a visceral spiritual experience during my recovery from alcoholism and, for the first time in my life, came face-to-face with the difference between being spiritual and being religious. As a result, I haven't had a drink for almost nineteen years.

- I am active in a congregation of the New Thought Religion.

"Nice resume," you say. But you still may be thinking, "Why have you written this book?"

My sister is one of the sweetest people you could ever know. She's an evangelical Christian, interprets the Bible pretty literally, uses the Bible to authenticate itself, and admits she doesn't know very much about how the Bible became the Bible. She constantly sprinkles quotations from the Bible throughout her conversations. However, her zealous expression of faith is not apparent to the average observer because her genuine love of life and people shines through—there's not a fake bone in her body. You couldn't cover her faith with a blanket nor could you beat it off with a stick. She had a spiritual encounter while trying to quit smoking. That experience made God very real for her in a similar way that becoming sober made God very real for me. Her spiritual life began to grow from that point on. She's wonderful, and I love her more than life.

Shortly before I stopped drinking, she and I were talking about the sense of spiritual reality in our society. She was concerned about me. Of course I was using "street" language and she was using "religious" language. There were naturally a few odd moments——but nothing that our fondness for each other couldn't handle.

During our conversation she looked at me with a serious expression on her face and told me of a vision she had experienced on several occasions. According to my sister, in that vision I would become a modern-day Jonah. What a jolt to my system! She didn't explain any more than that and I was too stunned to ask any specific questions.

The story of Jonah is part of the writings in the Old Testament referred to as Wisdom Literature. It was written as a severe criticism of the existing Jewish priestly class, the religious leaders of the day, for wanting to turn Judaism into a "gated community" of God's people. No one could be a part of that community except good, strict Jews. Jonah's message, in essence, was that God loved all people.

The *Book of Jonah* is in the Old Testament and is estimated to have been written sometime between 600 B.C.E. and 200 B.C.E. It is about a reluctant prophet, Jonah. God wants him to preach repentance and salvation to the citizens of a large city named Nineveh. But Jonah doesn't want to do it. He doesn't like Nineveh and doesn't want the population saved. He runs away and wherever he goes, bad things happen to him. Finally, while on board a ship, the sailors throw him overboard to get rid of him and his bad "karma," which they believe has caused all sorts of storms, high waves, and rough weather. Of course, we all remember how a large fish swallowed Jonah. After a while the fish threw him up, Jonah swam ashore, and agreed to preach to the city of Nineveh, urging them to repent. They did and were saved from destruction by God. Jonah was angry that God saved them.

The moral of the story? Jonah was avoiding his duty to preach to the city of Nineveh, just as the priests were avoiding their duty. They were determined to build an exclusive community of God's people that consisted only of devout and observant Jews. They wanted to hoard all of God's mercy and love for themselves. All the rest of the world, the non-Jews, could be damned.

This conversation with my sister was a long time ago, but I've never forgotten it. The thought of Jonah has since lain dormant in my mind. Maybe twice a year it pops up and reminds me of the conversation with my sister. (Because of this, the initial working title of this book was *A visit with Jonah.*)

Within the context of her vision, I certainly can relate to Jonah's reluctance to engage people with a message to change their ways. Since I've been sober, I've avoided a lot of old hurts, old behavior, old drinking habits, and old tendencies to become a "champion" for some cause. Whenever I am involved in some cause, I can get very frustrated and angry. Often, it's a form of righteous anger. According to AA, the emotions that come with a good dose of righteous anger always seem to trigger thoughts of drinking within recovering alcoholics. This certainly has been true for me. Righteous anger is, in short, an emotion that I can ill afford, and I've used that knowledge as a shield to protect myself. So, for almost nineteen years I've avoided religious issues or causes, even though I feel strongly about them.

Until now.

I've noticed that when someone in the room begins to quote or "spout" biblical messages, everyone else gets quiet. Sometimes the outburst embarrasses us. Sometimes it scares us a little. Other times we're afraid to say something, lest we reveal our ignorance. Mostly we don't say anything because it's been ingrained in us that religion is a private thing, not something to be discussed in public. We remember the sage advice to avoid discussing politics and religion.

Whatever the reason, for the last twenty years, while those of us who don't normally go around spouting Bible quotes have been quiet, Protestant fundamentalist denominations have seen enormous increases in attendance. So has the very literal Opus Dei organization of the Roman Catholic Church. These groups have spawned an assortment of conservative religious groups that have become more and more active in our communities and nation. The longer we stay quiet, the louder their voices seem.

Because most of us don't trust our knowledge of the Bible, we've stayed quiet and let the biblical fundamentalists get away with it. But they are *mis*using the Bible to exclude others, to build fortresses against "evil" (as they perceive it), to develop a national moral consensus for targeted behaviors, and to condemn or attack any who disagree with them. Their *misguided* use feeds their confidence in the rightness of their interpretation of Scripture because they use other Bible texts to authenticate that very same text. "If it's in the Bible, then it's absolutely true." This literal *mis*use of the Bible supports their fundamental views on society and together those forces have become loud and repetitive: anti-abortion, anti-gay, anti-Middle Eastern, anti-alternative lifestyles, anti-non-evangelical religion, anti-sex, and anti-stem cell research. And people are listening!

Their behavior contributes a lot to the sense of divisiveness or polarization we feel all around us. On matters of belief, we are seeing more books, radio or TV talk shows, letters to newspapers or magazine articles that seem to be saying, regardless of the topic, "I'm right!" or "It's my way or the highway!" Every issue is a very big deal. Every issue is cast in terms of black or white, right or wrong, good or bad. The Bible is either wholly accurate in every way or it isn't. There seems to be no middle. That's an indication people are *mis*reading the Bible. That's an indication that people have begun to idolize the Bible—and people traditionally fight to protect that which they worship and adore.

This kind of polarizing divisiveness has never been healthy and right now, with radical, militant Islamists, Palestinian-hating Jewish extremists, and Christian fundamentalists all running around proclaiming they're right—well, it's downright scary.

I'm confident this book is not what my sister envisioned I might write as a modern-day Jonah. The story of Jonah pointed out that the leaders of Judaism wanted to hoard all of God's mercy and love for themselves. All the rest of the world, the non-Jews, could be damned. Jonah's message pronounced that was not what God wanted at all. The Religious Right, the Christian Coalition, or any other evangelical group is attempting to place limits and strict legalistic parameters on the definition of being a true believer. This is the same mistake the priestly class made during the times of the prophets in the Old Testament. This is also the same mistake the emerging Church made in the centuries immediately following the life and death of Jesus of Nazareth

Appendixes

Appendix A

Historical Overview of the Bible

Note: NAME* = Individual; <u>Name</u> = Title of Writing

Date	Event(s)
2,000 – 1,700 BC	**1**. The Patriarchs (ABRAHAM*, ISAAC*, JACOB*). **2**. Habiru (Israelites, Moabites, Amorites, Edomites, Horites, etc.) migrate to Egypt. **3**. Hyksos invasion of Egypt **4**. Hyksos move Egyptian capitol from Thebes to Avaris (Tanis)
1,600 – 1,300 BC	**1**. Hebrews in Egypt **2**. Pharoah Ahmose I overthrows Hyksos **3**. Capitol returns to Thebes **4**. Hebrew oppression in Egypt begins **5**. Believed that some portions of the House of Joseph (Ephraim and Manasseh) return to Palestine with the Hyksos
1,300 – 1,250 BC	**1**. MOSES* **2**. The Exodus (c. 1,290 BC) **3**. Rameses II is the probable Pharoah at the the time of the Exodus **4**. The formation of "religious" Israel through the 10 Commandments and Moses' interpretation of the Exodus events, i.e., the Covenant relationship between YHWH (Yahweh or God) and the people of Israel. **5**. <u>Recitations and Poetry/Songs</u>: Song of Miriam (Ex. 15:21); Deut 6:20-24; Deut 26: 5-10
1,250 – 1,200 BC	**1**. JOSHUA* **2**. Conquest of Canaan (known destruction of Jericho, Bethel, Lachish, Eglin, Debir, and Hazor) **3**. Joshua forms the 12 Tribes of Israel at Shechem **4**. <u>Recitations and Poetry/Songs</u>: Taunt song over the Amorites (Num. 21:27-30); Eternal war with Amalek (Ex. 17:16); Joshua's renewal of the initial covenant with Yahweh (Josh. 24: 2-15); Song of Lamech (Gen. 4:23-24); Incantations to the Ark (Num. 10: 35-36); Joshua's appeal to the Sun and Moon (Josh. 10: 12); Oracles of Balaam (portions: Num. 23-24)
1,200 – 1,020 BC	**1**. Period of the Judges **2**. Sea People (among whom are the Philistines) invade Egypt **3**. Sea People defeated by Ramses III and Philistines settle on the southern coastal plain of Palestine (Gaza) **4**. Battle of Megiddo (c. 1,125 BC) **5**. Death of Eli (c. 1,050 BC) **6**. Rise of Saul in popularity **7**. <u>Recitations and Poetry/Songs</u>: Song of Deborah (Judges 5); Song of the Well (Num. 21: 17-18); Samson's Riddle (Judges 14: 14, 18); God's blessing that favored Israel (Gen. 9: 25-27); Jacob's Blessing (Gen. 44: 1-27)

Date	Event(s)
1,020 – 922 BC	1. The Monarchy (Israel is now a "political" nation) under 3 kings: SAUL*, DAVID*, and SOLOMON.* The prophet SAMUEL*. 2. Saul (ruled 1,020 – 1,000) 3. David (ruled 1,000 – 961) 4. David captures Jerusalem and makes it his political capitol of Israel 5. Solomon (ruled 961 – 922) 6. YAHWIST* (J Document) <u>National Epic of Israel</u> – found in portions of Genesis, Exodus, Numbers, Joshua, and Judges. 7. <u>Other Writings:</u> David's UNKNOWN COURT HISTORIAN* - some scholars suspect it may have been the Yahwist (cf, Burton Mack); most believe it was Ahimaaz, son of Zadok: This material is considered to be among the oldest near eye-witness history ever recorded! It includes I Sam. 4-6, 9-11, 14-16, 20, 26-31; II Sam 1-6, 9-20, 24; and I Kings 1-2; Book of Jasher (extinct – cf. Josh 1-:13); Book of "The Wars of the Lord" (extinct – cf. Num 21: 14-18); <u>Proverbs</u> (22:17 – 24: 22); <u>Psalm</u> 24: 7-10; <u>David's Proverb</u> (I Sam. 24:13); <u>Psalms by David</u> (Psalms 18, 29, 88, 89)
922 BC	*** * * * S C H I S M * * * * ***

	Kingdom of Judah (922 – 587)	Kingdom of Israel (922 – 721)
922 – 850 BC	Rehoboam (922-915)	Jeroboam I (922-901)
	Jehoshaphat (873–849); Coalition against Assyri of Karkar (853)	Omri (876-869); Ahab (869-850); ELIJAH* (890-850?); Syrian coalition against Assyria: Battle of Karkar (853)
850 – 800 BC		Jehu (842-815); ELISHA* (850-801)
800 – 750 BC	Uzziah (783 – 742)	Jeroboam II (786-746); AMOS* (c. 780's); <u>Amos;</u> I Kings 16:29–19; 21; <u>II Kings</u> 1-10
750 – 700 BC	ISAIAH* (760-700); <u>Isaiah 1-39</u>; MICAH* (742-687); <u>Micah</u> 1:2 – 2:10; 4 –5	HOSEA* (C. 730'S) <u>Hosea</u>
	Ahaz (735-715); Hezekiah (715-687) Judah, under Hezekiah, is trapped	Fall of Damascus and Samaria by Assyria under Tiglath-Pileser III in 732. Israel is a "client-state" of Assyria. Israel begins to rebel and

Date	Event(s)
	between Assyria (under Sennacherib) and Egypt. Hezekiah joins Egypt & other Palestinian states to oppose Sennacherib. By 701 Sennacerib advances to Jerusalem but has to withdraw because of troubles back home and plagues within his troops.	Assyria, now under Shalmaneser V (727-722) carries 27,290 leading citizens into exile. *Israel, as an independent country, ends in 722.* The ELOHIST* (E) Writer(s): presumed priests at Bethel (c. 750) write portions of Genesis, Exodus, Numbers, and Joshua. The tribal cult, disregarded (or ignored) by the Yahwist is stressed by E, whose masterpiece is the story of the sacrifice of Isaac (Gen 22:1-13, 19) * * * * * * * * * *
	Judah, Only
700 – 650 BC	Manasseh (687 – 642); Assyria conquers Egypt (c. 663)
650 – 600 BC	Josiah (640 – 609); JEREMIAH* (640-587); Jeremiah 1-45; **1.** The Deuteronomic Reforms (aka D WRITER*) (c. 620); **2.** Josiah attempts to reform Judah according to the new-found "Book of the Law" (cf. II Kings 22: 8-10; 23: 1-3). Scholars believe the "Book of the Law" was Deuteronomy 12-26; 28. It was written by the Deuteronomic Historian (aka D WRITER*). NAHUM*; ZEPHANIAH*; HABAKKUK* **3.** Assyria is in decline; the Fall of Ashur and] Ninevah to the Babylonians (c. 614-612). **4.** Egypt (Pharoah Necho) tries to recapture lost land in Palestine. He defeats and kills Josiah (609) but is defeated by the Babylonians at Haran in the same year. He is decisively beaten by the Babylonians, who are now under Nebuchadnezzar, at Carchemish in 605. Nebuchadnezzar controls Syria-Palestine and leaves Judah as a "client-state."
600 – 550 BC	Zedekiah (597-587); EZEKIEL* (620-571); OBADIAH*; Esekiel (c. 580s); II Kings 24-25; Obadiah; **The Exile**. Under Nebuchadnezzar's orders,

Date	Event(s)
	leading Judean citizens were exiled from the country in 598 and again in 587. Among the exiles is Ezekiel, who became a preacher to the exiled "congregations."
587 BC	***Jerusalem was burned and the Kingdom of Judah ended (587).*** * * * * * * * * During the Exile (587-520) Isaiah 40-66 and Lamentations 2; 4 were written.
550 – 500 BC	Remnant of Judah remains in exile. HAGGAI*; ZECHARIAH* Haggai; Zechariah; **1.** Cyrus unites Persia and Media and conquers Babylon in 539. **2.** Cyrus liberates the Jews and they (The Remnant) Return to Jerusalem. **3.** The Temple is rebuilt by Zerubbabel (c. 520 –515). **4.** The Deuteronomic Redactor (550-520) completed Deuteronomy and adds edits to Joshua, Judges, I-II Samuel and I-II Kings. **5.** Palestine is under Persian control during the Darius/Xerxes Dynasties (539-323).
500 – 450 BC	Israel (Judah) is becoming a kingdom controlled by priests. The Synagogue and the TORAH are becoming more important than Temple ritual. MALACHI* Job (Job can be placed anytime between 600 – 400 and defended. Job is the longest-sustained and finest poetic composition in the Hebrew canon. Its author is unknown but is probably a priest dealing with the basic theological problem – evil – of the Deuteronomic school); Malachi. The PRIESTLY* Writers (P) compose Leviticus and edit Genesis, Exodus, Numbers, as well as some of the "histories." The Pentateuch (Genesis through Deuteronomy) is now close to its current form and is attributed to Moses.
450 – 400 BC	Israel (Judah) remains under Persian control. EZRA* is the supreme religious leader and NEHEMIAH* is the civil governor. Ezra (5:3 – 6:13; 7:27 – 9:6) and Nehemiah (1-6; 8-10; 13:6-31) were written during this period. Ezra is often called the Father of modern Judaism. The Jews are beginning to speak more in Aramaic. Hebrew is becoming the "classical" or "literary" language of the

Date	Event(s)
	Jews. In Greece it was the Golden Age of Pericles (460 – 429); Socrates (470 – 399).
400 – 350 BC	JOEL*; <u>Ruth</u> (c. 400); <u>Joel</u>; <u>Jonah</u> (Probable – Jonah can be placed anytime between 600 – 200 and defended); <u>Proverbs</u> (probable: c. 400 - 300). Greece's Golden Age continues: Plato (428 – 348); Aristotle (384 – 322).
350 – 250 BC	The Greeks defeat Persia and Hellenistic control over Palestine begins. This is the Age of the rulers Phillip (359 – 336) and Alexander the Great (336 – 323). After Alexander's death competition for his throne resulted in 3 empires emerging: (1) Macedonia (301 – 168); (2) Egypt under the Ptolemies (323 – 180); and (3) Syria under the Seleucids (312 – 64). Palestine was under the control of the Ptolemies of Egypt (323 – 200). This was the time of THE CHRONICLER* (c. 350), who writes <u>I-II Chronicles</u> and edits/completes <u>Ezra</u> and <u>Nehemiah</u> (c. 350).
250 – 200 BC	Rome's Punic Wars (264 – 156); <u>Song of Songs</u> (c. 250) a collection of love and marriage lyrics; <u>Ecclesiastes</u> (c. 200); <u>Psalms</u> (c. 200) — Much like our Hymnbooks, Psalms probably took its final form during this period.
200 – 150 BC	Syria (Seleucids) wrestles Palestine from Egypt (Ptolemies) and Palestine is under the Seleucids (200 – 63). Judas Maccabaeus (166 – 160) leads Judah in revolt in 167 against the Seleucids. The Maccabean period lasts until 63 as a "vassal" state under Syria. Including Judas Maccabaeus there were 8 "kings" or procurators of the House of Maccabaeus. The Temple was destroyed during the revolt (dates uncertain – c. 165). <u>Daniel</u> (c. 165) was written during the Maccabean revolt.
150 – 100 BC	<u>Esther</u> (c. 125) was written during the Maccabean Period.
100 – 50 BC	Pompey captures Palestine from Syria and Israel (Judah) is under Roman control from 63 BC. Rome's first Triumvirate (60): Pompey, Caesar, Crassus. Caesar's Gallic Wars (58-51).
50 – 0 BC	Assassination of Julius Caesar (44); Second Triumvirate (43): Antony, Octavian, Lepidus. Brutus and Cassius defeated by 2nd Triumvirate at Phillipi (42). Antony forges an alliance with Cleopatra (Egypt) only to be defeated by

Donald L. O'Dell

Date	Event(s)
	Octavian (later called Augustus) who became sole ruler (31) and ruled until 14 CE. It was the Golden Age of Latin literature, e.g., Virgil.
	Herod the Great, Idumaean King of Judah (under Rome) ruled from 37 – 4). He began to rebuild the Temple in 19 BCE). **Birth of JESUS* of Nazareth (c. 7 - 4).**
0 – 50 CE	Tiberius rules Rome (14 – 37); Herod Antipas, Tetrarch of Galilee (4 BCE – 39 CE); Herod Agrippa I, King of Judah (41 – 44); Pontius Pilate, Procurator from Rome (26 – 36). Ministry of JOHN THE BAPTIST*; Ministry of Jesus; Jesus' crucifixion (29); Pentecost (c. 30/1); the stoning of Stephen (31); The beginnings of various JESUS MOVEMENTS — focused on lore teachings, miracle stories, pronouncement stories, or other oral teaching through itinerant preachers; Initial writings of Q-type remembrances based on the sayings of Jesus; The beginnings of home-based CHRIST CONGREGATIONS in the Jewish Diaspora in Northern Syria, Asia Minor, and Greece; PAUL (Saul of Tarsus) is converted (c. 32-35) near Damascus in Northern Syria. Paul stays and studies 13 years with the Damascus congregation; Jerusalem Council "authorizes" Paul's ministry to Gentiles (c. 47/8); Paul's second missionary journey (49 – 52). Writings; 45 – 50: Galatians; Sayings-based Collections; Q-type collections
50 – 100 CE	Paul's third missionary journey (52-56); Paul in Rome (62-64); Martyrdom of James (the brother of Jesus) (61/2); Paul's death (64/5); Peter's death (64/5); Nero burns Rome and blames the Christians (64) and the first organized persecutions of Christians begin; Jerusalem revolts against Rome and the brief rebellion is crushed in 70. Many Jewish Christians flee to Pella. The Temple is destroyed for the last time; Persecutions under Emperor Domitian. **Writings** 50 – 55: I-II Thessalonians; First letter to Corinth (extinct – cf. I Cor 5:9-11)

Date	Event(s)
	55 – 60: I-II Corinthians; Philippians; Philemon; Early Q-Writing 60 – 65: Romans 65 – 70: Q-Writings Expanded 70 – 80: Mark; Colossians; Q-Writings Expanded; Josephus' Jewish War 80 – 90: Ephesians; Gospel of Thomas; Matthew 90 – 100: John; *The Didache*; Jude; I Peter; Ignatius (of Antioch) Letters; Josephus' *Antiquities*; Clement (of Rome) writes to Corinth (*I Clement*); Jews finalize their canon of Scriptures and Apochrypha at Jamnia
100 – 150 CE	There are still strong communities of Jewish Christians in southern Syria and northern Egypt. Their foundations rest on early Jesus Movements and are sayings-based, e.g., the *Didache*, the *Gospel of Thomas, and the Q Document*. However, Christianity is rapidly becoming essentially a Gentile religion centered in Asia Minor and Greece. Although Clement is in Rome, he has not been referred to as a "Bishop." Ignatius is commonly called Bishop of Antioch as is Polycarp referred to as Bishop of Smyrna. In the 130s there is one last gasp by the Jewish community to regain their independence. Led by Bar-Cochba, the revolt is crushed in 135, along with the last and final Jewish hope of an actual Temple. Marcion attempts to establish a canon: It included Luke plus 10 Letters of Paul. Marcion had severely edited them to remove references to the Old Testament or to rewrite passages that showed close ties to writings of the Old Testament. Letters from prominent leaders are beginning to focus on the authority of those in charge and their right to determine what is valid to be believed. The Pauline emphasis to replace the Christian congregation as the rightful heir of the Old Testament Covenant — as opposed to the now temple-less Jews — is gathering political momentum. Writers are beginning to scour the Old Testament to find proof-texts that justify the concept that Jesus and the emerging Gentile Christian congregations are, in fact, the "New Jerusalem" or the "New Israel." **Writings** 100 – 120: I, II, III John; II Peter; Revelation, Luke/Acts; Ploycarp's *Letter to the Philippians*;

Date	Event(s)
	Hebrews; Pastoral Letters (I-II Timothy; Titus) 120 – 150: James(?); *Martyrdom of Polycarp* is written; Justin Martyr writes his *Apology* and *Dialogues*; Marcion vs. Valentinius correspondence over "gnostic" issues; *Letter of Barnabus*; *Shepherd of Hermas* written
150 – 200 CE	Partly as a reaction to Marcion, the value of the Old Testament was asserted, since many of the current, circulated writings and letters referred to its history, key figures, and concepts. By the latter part of the 2nd Century the four Gospels (Mark, Matthew, John, and Luke) had been grouped as "The Gospels" and were generally recognized as having a basic importance, although debates and discussion would continue for some time relative to John. Acts, which had been separated from Luke, included many references to the Twelve, Paul, and other church leaders (Stephen, Timothy, Barnabus, et.al.). Consequently, writings ascribed to some of these other apostolic leaders — commonly referred to as the "Catholic Letters" (James, I-II Peter, Jude, and I-III John) — along with Paul's basic body of letters (Galatians, I-II Thessalonians, I-II Corinthians, Philippians, Romans, Philemon), plus the four Gospels were beginning to be widely and uniformly known. Lastly, by the end of the 2nd Century these commonly referred to texts began to include the Pastoral Letters (Titus, I-II Timothy) and Revelations although, like the Gospel of John, it was hotly contested well into the 3rd Century. **Writings** 185: Irenaeus writes *Against Heresies* to attack the Gnostics and their concurrent lack of trust in the emerging episcopate, i.e., the authority of bishops and other formal church structure(s). 200: Muratorian canon published

Date	Event(s)
200 – 393 CE	Beginnings of the concept of the Trinity and the embryo of the Apostle's Creed; Conversion of Constantine, first Holy Roman Emperor; Council of Nicea (325); Finalization of the canon and major Christian festivals/holidays at Hippo (393).

Appendix B

The Words of Jesus

John Dominic Crossan, is a Professor of Biblical Studies at DePaul University in Chicago, IL. In his Introduction to The Historical Jesus[1] he outlines his three-tiered methodology (pp. xxviii - xxxiv) for evaluating textual references as to their inclusion in an inventory of words that were probably spoken by Jesus. The sources for his inventory are both from Biblical and extra-Biblical writings.

"If we ask, however, which of all the words placed on his lips actually go back to the historical Jesus, it is possible to offer at least a reconstructed inventory. But, as you read them, recall that ... these words are not a list to be read. They are not even a sermon to be preached. They are a score to be played and a program to be enacted."[2]

His reconstructed inventory of sayings (pp. xiii – xxvi) is as follows:

Carry no purse, no bag, no sandals, nor two tunics. Whatever house you enter, eat what is set before you; heal the sick in it and say to them, "The kingdom of God has come upon you."

Ask, and it will be given to you; seek, and you will find; knock, and it will be opened for you.

The kingdom of God will not come with signs that can be checked beforehand; nor will they say, "Here it is!" or "There!" because the kingdom of God is already among you.

You have ears, use them!

Whoever receives you, receives not you but me; whoever receives me, receives not me but the one who sent me.

---

[1] Crossan, John Dominic, The Historical Jesus, Harper San Francisco, 1992.

[2] Ibid., p. xiii.

Whoever divorces his wife and marries another commits adultery, and whoever marries a woman divorced from her husband commits adultery.

What goes into your mouth will not defile you, but what comes out of your mouth, that will defile you.

Those who enter the kingdom of God are like infants still being suckled.

You are the light of the world!

No prophet is acceptable in his village; no physician heals those who know him.

Human beings will be forgiven all their sins.

A woman in the crowd raised her voice and said to him, "Blessed is the womb that bore you, and the breasts that you sucked!" But he said, "Blessed rather are those who hear the word of God and keep it!"

Forgive, and you will be forgiven.

The first will be last and the last first.

Whatever is hidden will be made manifest, whatever is covered up will be uncovered.

A sower went out to sow. And as he sowed, some seed fell along the path, and the birds came and devoured it. Other seed fell on rocky ground, where it had not much soil, and since it had no root it withered away. Other seed fell among thorns and the thorns grew up and chocked it, and it yielded no grain. And other seeds fell into good soil and brought forth grain, growing up and increasing and yielding thirtyfold and sixtyfold, and hundredfold.

The kingdom of God is like a mustard seed, the smallest of all seeds. But when it falls on tilled ground, it produces a great plant and becomes a shelter for birds of the sky.

No one after lighting a lamp puts it in a cellar or under a bushel, but on a stand, that those who enter may see the light.

Be wise as serpents and innocent as doves.

To one who has will more be given; from one who has not, it will be taken away.

Blessed are the destitute.

If you follow me, you carry a cross.

A man planted a vineyard, and let it out to tenants, and went into another country. When the time came, he sent a servant to the tenants, that they should give him some of the fruit of the vineyard; but the tenants beat him, and sent him away empty-handed. And he sent another servant; him also they beat and treated shamefully, and sent him away empty-handed. And he sent a third; this one they wounded and cast out. Then the owner of the vineyard said, "What shall I do? I will send my beloved son; it may be they will respect him." But when the tenants saw him, they said to themselves, "This is the heir; let us kill him, that the inheritance may be ours."

Blessed are the reviled.

I will destroy this Temple and no one will be able to rebuild it.

The harvest is great but the laborers are few. Pray the Lord of the harvest to send out laborers.

Why have you come out into the desert? To see a reed shaken by the wind? To see a man clothed in soft clothing? Those who are gorgeously appareled and live in luxury are in kings' courts. What then did you come out to see? A prophet? Yes, I tell you, and more than a prophet.

When you see a cloud rising in the west, you say at once, "A shower is coming;" and so it happens. And when you see the south wind blowing, you say, "There will be scorching heat," and it happens. You know how to interpret the appearance of earth and sky; but why do you not know how to interpret the present time?

They showed Jesus a gold coin and said to him, "Caesar's men demand taxes from us." He said to them, "Give Caesar what belongs to Caesar, give God what belongs to God."

Blessed are those who weep.

Who is not against you is for you.

It is like a fisherman who cast his net into the sea and drew it up from the sea full of small fish. Among them he found a fine large fish. He threw all the small fish back into the sea and chose the large fish without difficulty.

I have cast fire upon the world, and see, I am guarding it until it blazes.

Do you think that I have come to give peace on earth? No, I tell you, but rather division; for henceforth in one house there will be five divided, three against two and two against three; they will be divided, father against son and son against father, mother against daughter and daughter against her mother, mother-in-law against her daughter-in-law and daughter-in-law against her mother-in-law.

It is as if a man should scatter seed upon the ground, and should sleep and rise night and day, and the seed should sprout and grow, he knows not how. The earth produces of itself, first the blade, then the ear, then the full grain in the ear. But when the grain is ripe, at once he puts the sickle, because the harvest has come.

You see the mote in your brother's eye, but do not see the beam in your own eye. When you cast the beam out of your own eye, then you will see clearly to cast the mote from your brother's eye.

A city built on a high mountain and fortified cannot fall, nor can it be hidden.

What I tell you in the dark, utter in the light; and what you hear whispered, proclaim upon ther housetops.

If a blind man leads a blind man, both will fall into a pit.

It is not possible for anyone to enter the house of a strong man and take it by force unless he binds his hands; then he will be able to ransack his house.

Do not be anxious about your life, what you shall eat, nor about your body, what you shall put on. Consider the ravens; they neither sow nor reap, they have neither storehouse nor barn, and yet God feeds them. Consider the lilies, how they grow; they neither toil nor spin; yet I tell you, even Solomon in all his glory was not arrayed like one of these. Instead, seek his kingdom, and these things shall be yours as well.

Woe to the Pharisees, for they are like a dog sleeping in the manger of oxen, for neither does he eat nor does he let the oxen eat.

Among those born of women, from Adam until John the Baptist, there is no one so superior to John that his eyes should not be lowered before him. Yet, whichever one of you comes to be a child will be acquainted with the kingdom and will become superior to John.

No servant can serve two masters; for either he will hate the one and love the other, or he will be devoted to the one and despise the other.

No one drinks old wine and immediately desires to drink new wine.

No one puts a new patch on an old garment, and no one puts new wine into old wineskins.

Whoever does not hate his father and mother cannot become a disciple to me. And whoever does not hate his brothers and sisters cannot become a disciple to me.

The kingdom may be compared to a man who sowed good seed in his field; but while men were sleeping, his enemy came and sowed weeds among the wheat, and went away. So when the plants came up and bore grain, then the weeds appeared also. And the servants of the householder came and said to him, "Sir, did you not sow good seed in your field? How then has it weeds?" He said to them, "An enemy has done this." The servants said to him, "Then do you want us to go and gather them?" But he said, "No; lest in gathering the weeds you root up the wheat along with them. Let both grow together until the harvest; and at harvest time I will tell the reapers, 'Gather the weeds first and bind them in bundles to be burned, but gather the wheat into my barn.'"

There was a rich man who had much money. He said, "I shall put my money to use so that I may sow, reap, plant, and fill my storehouse with produce, with the result that I shall lack nothing." Such were his intentions, but that same night he died.

There was a man who (wanted) to invite guests and when he had prepared dinner, he sent his servant to invite the guests. He went to the first and said to him, "My master invites you." He said, "I have claims against some merchants. They are coming to me this evening. I must go and give them my orders. I ask to be excused from the dinner." He went to another and said to him, "My master invites you." He said to him, "My friend is going to be married, and I am to prepare the banquet. I shall not be able to come. I ask to be excused from the dinner." He went to another and said to him, "My master invites you." He said to him, "I have just bought a farm, and I am on my way to collect the rent. I shall not be able to come. I ask to be excused." The servant returned and said to his master, "Those whom you invited to the dinner have asked to be excused." The master said to his servant, "Go outside to the streets and bring back those whom you happen to meet, so they may dine."

Blessed are the hungry.

A man said to him, "Tell my brothers to divide my father's possessions with me." He said to him, "O man, who has made me a divider?"

The kingdom is like a merchant who had a consignment of merchandise and who discovered a pearl. The merchant was shrewd. He sold the merchandise and bought the pearl alone for himself.

Foxes have holes, and birds of the air have nests; but the human being has nowhere to lay its head.

Why do you wash the outside of the cup? Do you not realize that the one who make the inside made the outside too?

If you have money, do not lend it at interest, but give it to one from whom you will not get it back.

The kingdom is like a certain woman. She took a little leaven, concealed it in some dough, and made it into large loaves.

The disciples said to him, "Your brothers and your mother are standing outside." He said to them, "Those here who do the will of God are my brothers and my mother."

They said to Jesus, "Come let us pray today and let us fast." Jesus said, What is the sin that I have committed, or wherein have I been defeated? But when the bridegroom leaves the bridal chamber, then let them fast and pray."

The kingdom is like a shepherd who had a hundred sheep. One of them, the largest, went astray. He left the ninety-nine and looked for that one until he found it. When he had gone to such trouble, he said to the sheep, "I care for you more than the ninety-nine."

The kingdom of heaven is like treasure hidden in a field, which a man found and covered up; then in his joy he goes and sells all that he has buys that field.

The scribes and elders and priests were angry because he reclined at table with sinners.

Love your enemies and pray for those who abuse you.

He was casting out a demon that was dumb; when the demon had gone out, the dumb man spoke, and the people marveled. But some of them said, "He casts out demons by Beelzebul, the prince of demons." But he said to them, "Every kingdom divided against itself is laid waste, and a divided household falls. And if Satan also is divided against himself, how will his kingdom stand? For you say that I cast out demons by Beelzebul."

If I cast out demons by Beelzebul, by whom do your sons cast them out? Therefore they shall be your judges. But if it is by the finger of God that I cast out demons, then the kingdom of God has come upon you.

Beware of the scribes, who like to go about in long robes, and to have salutations in the marketplaces and the best seats in the synagogues and the places of honor at feasts.

Salt is good; but if salt has lost its saltness, how will you season it?

If any one strikes you on the right cheek, turn to him the other also; and if any one would sue you and take your coat, let him have your cloak as well; and if any one forces you to go one mile, go with him two miles.

One of the disciples said to him, "Lord, let me go and bury my father." But Jesus said to him, "Follow me, and leave the dead to bury their own dead."

Another said, "I will follow you, Lord; but let me first say farewell to those at my home." Jesus said to him, "No one who puts his hand to the plow and looks back is fit for the kingdom of God."

You are as lambs in the midst of wolves.

What father among you, if his son asks him for bread, will give him a stone? Or if he asks for a fish, will give him a serpent? If you then, who are evil, know how to give good gifts to your children, how much more will your Father who is in heaven give good things to those who ask him!

Are not five sparrows sold for two pennies? And not one of them is forgotten before God. Why, even the hairs of your head are all numbered. Fear not; you are of more value than many sparrows.

Where your treasure is, there will be your heart also.

From the days of John the Baptist until now the kingdom of God has suffered violence, and men of violence take it by force. For all the prophets and the law prophesied until John.

Peter came up and said to him, "Lord, how often shall my brother sin against me, and I forgive him? As many as seven times?" Jesus said to him, "I do not say to you seven times, but seventy times seven."

A man going on a journey called his servants and entrusted to them his property; to one he gave five talents, to another two, to another one, to each according to his ability. Then he went away. He who had received the five talents went at once and traded with them; and he made five talents more. So also, he who had received the two talents made two talents more. But he who had received one talent went and dug in the ground and hid his master's money. Now after a long time the master of those servants came and settled accounts with them. And he who had received the five talents came forward, bringing five talents more, saying, "Master, you delivered to me five talents; here I have made five talents more." His master said to him, "Well done, good and faithful servant; you have been faithful over a little, I will set you over much; enter the joy of your master." And he also who had the two talents came forward, saying, "Master, you delivered to me two talents; here I have made two talents more." His master said to him, "Well done, good and faithful servant; you have been faithful over a little, I will set you over much; enter into the joy of your master." He also who had received the one talent came forward, saying, "Master, I knew you to be a hard man, reaping where you did not sow, and gathering where you did not winnow; so I was afraid, and I went and hid your talent in the ground. Here you have what is yours." But his master answered him, "You wicked and slothful servant! You knew that I reap where I have not sowed, and gather where I have not winnowed? Then you ought to have invested my money with the bankers, and at my coming I should have received what was my own with interest. So take the talent from him, and give it to him who has ten talents."

He said to them, "The kings of the Gentiles exercise lordship over them; and those in authority over them are called benefactors. But not so with you; rather let the greatest among you become as the youngest, and the leader as one who serves. For which is the greater, the one who sits at table, or the one who serves? Is it not the one who sits at table? But I am among you as one who serves."

It is easier for a camel to go through the eye of a needle than for a rich man to enter the kingdom of God.

Love your neighbor like your soul; guard your neighbor like the pupil of your eye.

Become passersby.

It is impossible to mount two horses or to stretch two bows.

Blessed is the one who has suffered.

Split a piece of wood, and I am there. Lift up a stone, and you will find me there.

The kingdom is like a certain woman who was carrying a jar full of meal. While she was walking on the road, still some distance from home, the handle of the jar broke, and the meal emptied out behind her on the road. She did not realize it; she had noticed no accident. When she reached her house, she set down the jar and found it empty.

The kingdom is like a certain man who wanted to kill a powerful man. In his own house he drew his sword and stuck it into the wall in order to find out whether his hand could carry through. Then he slew the powerful man.

If you are offering your gift at the altar, and there remember that your neighbor has something against you, leave your gift there before the altar and go; first be reconciled to your neighbor, and then come and offer your gift.

Do not swear at all, either by heaven, for it is the throne of God, or by the earth, for it is his footstool, or by Jerusalem, for it is the city of the great King. And do not swear by your head, for you cannot make one hair white or black. Let what you say be simply yes or no; anything more than this comes from evil.

Exalt yourself and you will be humbled; humble yourself and you will be exalted.

The kingdom may be compared to a king who wished to settle accounts with his servants. When he began the reckoning, one was brought to him who owed him ten thousand talents; and as he could not pay, his lord ordered him to be sold, with his wife and children and all that he had, and payment to be made. So the servant fell on his knees, imploring him, "Lord, have patience with me, and I will pay you everything." And out of pity for him the lord of that servant released him and forgave him the debt. But that same servant, as he went out, came upon on of his fellow servants who owed him a hundred denarii; and seizing him by the throat he said, "Pay what you owe." So his fellow servant fell down and besought him, "Have patience with me, and I will pay you." He refused and went and put him in prison till he should pay the debt. When his fellow servants saw what had taken place, they were greatly distressed, and they went and reported to their lord all that had taken place. Then his lord summoned him and said to him, "You wicked servant! I forgave you all that debt because you besought me; and should not you have had mercy on your fellow servant, as I had mercy on you?" And in anger his lord delivered him to the jailers, till he should pay all his debt.

The kingdom is like a householder who went out early in the morning to hire laborers for his vineyard. After agreeing with the laborers for a denarius a day, he sent them into his vineyard. And going out about the third hour he saw others standing idle in the marketplace; and to them he said, "you go into the vineyard too, and whatever is right I will give you." So they went. Going out again about the sixth hour and the ninth hour, he did the same. And about the eleventh hour he went out and found others standing; and he said to them, "Why do you stand here idle all day?" They said to him, "Because no one has hired us." He said to them, "You go into the vineyard too." And when evening came, the owner said to his steward, "Call the laborers and pay them their wages, beginning with the last, up to the first." And when those hired about the eleventh hour came, each of them received a denarius. Now when the first came, they thought they would receive more; but each of them also received a denarius. And on receiving it they grumbled at the householder, saying, "These last worked only one hour, and you have made them equal to us who have borne the burden of the day and scorching heat." But he replied to one of them, "Friend, I am doing you no wrong; did you not agree with me for a denarius? Take what belongs to you, and go; I choose to give to this last as I give to you."

There are eunuchs who have been so from birth, and there are eunuchs who have been made eunuchs by men, and there are eunuchs who have made themselves eunuchs for the sake of the kingdom of heaven.

A man had two sons; and he went to the first and said, "Son, go and work in the vineyard today." And he answered, "I will not;" but afterward he repented and went. And he went to the second son and said the same; and he answered, "I go, sir," but did not go. Which of the two did the will of the father?

A man was going down from Jerusalem to Jericho, and he fell among robbers, who stripped him and beat hem, and departed, leaving him half dead. Now by chance a priest was going down the road; and when he saw him he passed by on the other side. So likewise a Levite, when he came to the place and saw him, passed by on the other side. But a Samaritan, as he journeyed, came to where he was; and when he saw him, he had compassion, and went to him and bound up his wounds, pouring on oil and wine; then he set him on his own beast and brought him to an inn, and took care of him. And the next day he took out two denarii and gave them to the innkeeper, saying, "Take care of him; and whatever more you spend, I will repay you when I come back.

Which of you who has a friend will go to him at midnight and say to him, "Friend, lend me three loaves; for a friend of mine has arrived on a journey, and I have nothing to set before him:" and he will answer from within, "Do not bother me; the door is now shut, and my children are with me in bed; I cannot get up and give you anything?" Though he will not get up and give him anything because he is his friend, yet because of his importunity he will rise and give him whatever he needs.

A man had a fig tree planted in his vineyard; and he came seeking fruit on it and found none. And he said to the vinedresser, "Lo, these three years I have come seeking fruit on this fig tree, and I find none. Cut it down; why should it use up the ground?" And he answered him, "Let it alone sir; this year also, till I dig about it and put on some manure. And if it bears fruit next year, well and good; but if not, you can cut it down."

For which of you, desiring to build a tower, does not first sit down and count the cost, whether he has enough to complete it?

Otherwise, when he has laid a foundation, and is not able to finish, all who see it will begin to mock him, saying, "This man began to build, and was not able to finish." Or, what king, going to encounter another king in war, will not sit down first and take counsel whether he is able with ten thousand to meet him who comes against him with twenty thousand? And if not, while the other is yet a great way off, he sends an embassy and asks terms of peace.

What woman, having ten silver coins, if she seeks one coin, does not light a lamp and seep the house and seek diligently until she finds it? And when she has found it, she calls together her friends and neighbors, saying, "Rejoice with me, for I have found the coin which I had lost."

There was a man who had two sons; and the younger of them said to his father, "Father, give me the share of property that falls to me." And he divided his living between them. Not many days later, the younger son gathered all he had and took his journey into a far country, and there squandered his property in loose living. And when he had spent everything, a great famine arose in that country, and he began to be in want. So he went and joined himself to one of the citizens of that country, who sent him into his fields to feed swine. And he would gladly have fed on the pods that the swine ate; and no one gave him anything. But when he came to himself he said, "How many of my father's hired servants have bread enough and to spare, but I perish here with hunger! I will arise and go to my father, and I will say to him, 'Father, I have sinned against heaven and before you; I am no longer worthy to be called you son; treat me as one of your hired servants.'" And he arose and came to his father. But while he was yet at a distance, his father saw him and had compassion, and ran and embraced him and kissed him. And the son said to him, "Father, I have sinned against heaven and before you; I am no longer worthy to be called your son." But the father said to his servants, "Bring quickly the best robe, and put it on him' and put a ring on his hand, and shoes on his feet; and bring the fatted calf and kill it, and let us eat and make merry; for this my son was dead, and is now alive again; he was lost, and is found." And they began to make merry. Now his elder son was in the field; and as he came and drew near to the house, he heard music and dancing. And he called one of the servants and asked what this meant. And he said to hem, "Your brother has come, and you father has killed the fatted calf, because he has received him safe and sound." But he was angry and refused to go in. His father came out and entreated him, but he answered his father, "Lo, these many years I have served you, and I never disobeyed your command; yet you never gave me a kid, that I might make merry with my friends. But when this son of yours came, who has devoured your living with harlots, you killed for him the fatted calf!" And he said to him, "Son, you are always with me, and all that is mine is yours. It was fitting to make merry and be glad, for this your brother was dead, and is alive; he was lost, and is found."

There was a rich man who had a steward, and charges were brought to him that this man was wasting his goods. And he called him and said to him, "What is this that I hear about you? Turn in the account of your stewardship, for you can no longer be steward." And the steward said to himself, "What shall I do, since my master is taking the stewardship away from me? I am not strong enough to dig, and I am ashamed to beg. I have decided what to do, so that people may receive me into their houses when I am put out of the stewardship." So, summoning his master's debtors one by one, he said to the first, "How much do you owe my master?" He said, "A hundred measures of oil." And he said to him, "Take your bill, and sit down quickly and write fifty." Then he said to another, "And how much do you owe?" He said, "A hundred measures of wheat." He said to him, "Take your bill and write eighty."

There was a rich man, who was clothed in purple and fine linen and who feasted sumptuously every day. And at his gate lay a poor man named Lazarus, full of sores, who desired to be fed with what fell from the rich man's table; moreover the dogs came and licked his sores. The poor man died and was carried by the angels to Abraham's bosom. The rich man also died and was buried; and in Hades, being in torment, he lifted up his eyes, and saw Abraham far off and Lazarus in his bosom. And he called out, "Father Abraham, have mercy upon me, and send Lazarus to dip the end of his finger in water and cool my tongue, for I am in anguish in this flame." But Abraham said, "Son, remember that you in your lifetime received your good things, and Lazarus in like manner evil things; but now he is comforted here, and you are in anguish. And besides all this, between us and you a great chasm has been fixed, in order that those who would pass from here to you may not be able, and none may cross from there to us."

In a certain city there was a judge who neither feared God nor regarded man; and there was a widow in that city who kept coming to him and saying, "Vindicate me against my adversary." For a while he refused; but afterward he said to himself, "Though I neither fear God nor regard man, yet because this widow bothers me, I will vindicate her, or she will wear me out by her continual coming."

Two men went up into the Temple to pray, one a Pharisee and other a tax collector. The Pharisee stood and prayed thus with himself, "God, I thank thee that I am not like the other men, extortioners, unjust, adulterers, or even like this tax collector. I fast twice a week, I give tithes of all I get." But the tax collector, standing far off, would not even lift up his eyes to heaven, but beat his breast, saying "God, be merciful to me a sinner!" This man went down to his house justified rather than the other.

Appendix C

The Nicene Creed

We believe in one God, the Father Almighty, Maker of heaven and earth, and of all things visible and invisible.

And in one Lord Jesus Christ, the only-begotten Son of God, begotten of the Father before all worlds, God of God, Light of Light, Very God of Very God, begotten, not made, being of one substance with the Father by whom all things were made; who for us men, and for our salvation, came down from heaven, and was incarnate by the Holy Spirit of the Virgin Mary, and was made man, and was crucified also for us under Pontius Pilate. He arose again according to the Scriptures, and ascended into heaven, and sitteth on the right hand of the Father. And he shall come again with glory to judge both the quick and the dead, whose kingdom shall have no end.

And we believe in the Holy Spirit, the Lord and Giver of Life, who proceedeth from the Father and the Son, who with the Father and the Son together is worshipped and glorified, who spoke by the prophets. And we believe in one holy catholic and apostolic church. We acknowledge one baptism for the remission of sins. And we look for the resurrection of the dead, and the life of the world to come, Amen.

Note: I can still hear my professor of Christian Ethics at Princeton, Dr. Edward A. Downey, comment that these early Church Fathers, in all their great wisdom, were able to summarize all of Jesus' teachings, sermons, and acts of healing into a comma: Jesus "... was made man, [comma] and was crucified..."

293

Appendix D

The Eloquence of Fundamental Literalism

In the process of creating the Bound Galley of the book, this letter was published in a local paper. It so happened that a friend recently had commented that I might have spent more time on the subject of *bibliolatry*.

The following letter is published with the permission of the author and is an excellent example of fundamental literalism – what I refer to as bibliolatry – where one's faith appears to be primarily in the Bible, rather than in the transforming spirit of Jesus Christ.

From the *St. Augustine Record*, One News Place, St. Augustine FL 32086, July 15, 2005, Page 6A, the *Opinion* section of the paper. I have used only the writer's initials.

Word of man should not override the word of God.

The decision by the rule-making body endorsing same-sex marriage is not only a sad day for the Church of Christ* (sic) but for Christianity as a whole. It is but one more example of satanic influences invading the minds and hearts of those charged with governing church affairs.

The Bible, God's Holy Word, is alone the foundation of our faith and must be the incontrovertible truth that guides a Christian's life and the church.

Sadly, the ruling body has ignored this fact.

The scriptures are clear in the condemnation of homosexuality, yet these church leaders have chosen to reject Biblical teaching, and have moved the church on a path alienated from God.

---

* It was not the Church of Christ but the United Church of Christ.

How is it possible for a Christian to receive God's blessings while a member of a church that has alienated itself from Holy Scripture?

What should a church layman do in this case? If this ruling stands, I would run, not walk, to the exit and seek a different church – one that believes the Bible to be God's inerrant word of absolute truth and the final authority in all matters. If a church doesn't adhere to these principals, it has denied the very faith it claims to represent.

When that happens, the church is without biblical guidance and is exposed to other sins and perversions based on the perceived truth of man rather than the absolute truth of Holy Scripture.

Unfortunately, other Christian denominations are considering gay involvement in church affairs, contrary to scriptural teaching which should signal a sense of alarm among all Christians who believe in the absolute truth of the Holy Bible. It is just another prophetic sign that we are fast approaching the end of this age.

D.S., St. Augustine

Bibliography

Anderson, Bernhard W. *Understanding the Old Testament.* Englewood Cliffs, NJ: Prentice-Hall, Inc., 1957.

Armstrong, Karen. *A History of God.* New York: Ballantine Books, 1993.

Crossan, John Dominic. *The Historical Jesus.* New York: HarperCollins Publishers, HarperSanFrancisco, 1991.

Crossan, John Dominic. *The Birth of Christianity.* New York: HarperCollins Publishers, HarperSanFrancisco, 1998.

Didache, *Volume I: The Apostolic Fathers.* Great Britain: Loeb Classical Library, St. Edmundsbury Press, Ltd., 1998.

Durant, Will. *Volume III – Caesar and Christ, The Story of Civilization.* New York: Simon and Schuster, 1944.

Filson, Floyd V. *A New Testament History.* Philadelphia: Westminster Press, 1964.

Harper's Bible Dictionary. 7th Edition. New York: Harper and Brothers, Publishers, 1961. I used this source for correct dates, spelling, geographical locations, etc.

Hendry, George S. *The Gospel of the Incarnation.* Philadelphia: Westminster Press, 1958.

Mack, Burton L. *A Myth of Innocence: Mark and Christian Origins.* Philadelphia: Fortress Press, 1991.

Mack, Burton L. *The Lost Gospel: The Book of Q and Christian Origins.* New York: HarperCollins Publishers, HarperSanFrancisco, 1994.

Mack, Burton L.. *Who Wrote the New Testament.* New York: HarperCollins Publishers, HarperSanFrancisco, 1995.

Meek, Theophile James. *Hebrew Origins.* New York: Harper and Row, Harper Torchbooks, 1960.

Donald L. O'Dell

Metzger, Bruce M. *An Introduction to the Apocrypha.* New York: Oxford University Press, 1957.

Metzger, Bruce M. *The Text of the New Testament.* New York: Oxford University Press, 1964.

Meyer, Marvin (with Harold Bloom). *The Gospel of Thomas.* New York: HarperCollins Publishers, HarperSanFrancisco, 1992.

Muilenberg, James. *The History of Religion in Israel, Interpreter's Bible, Volume I.* Nashville: Abingdon Press, 1952.

Pagels, Elaine. *The Gnostic Gospels.* New York: Vintage Books Edition, 1989.

Rosenberg, David and Harold Bloom. *The Book of J.* New York: Grove Weidenfeld, 1990.

Spong, John Shelby. *Rescuing the Bible from Fundamentalism.* New York: HarperCollins Publishers, HarperSanFrancisco, 1992.

Spong, John Shelby. *This Hebrew Lord.* New York: HarperCollins Publishers, HarperSanFrancisco, 1993.

Spong, John Shelby. *Liberating the Gospels.* New York: HarperCollins Publishers, HarperSanFrancisco, 1996.

Index

A

B

C

D

E

G

Complete Footnotes

[1] Anderson, Bernhard, *Understanding the Old Testament*, pp 3–4

[2] Muilenburg, James, *Interpreter's Bible*, Vol. 1, p 305

[3] Muilenburg, James, *Interpreter's Bible*, Vol. 1, p 298

[4] Bloom, Harold and Rosenberg, David, in *The Book of J*, make the case that the Yahwist may have been a woman.

[5] From Anderson, *Understanding the Old Testament*, p 17

[6] *Harper's Bible Dictionary*, 7th Edition, p. 824

[7] Anderson, *Understanding the Old Testament*, pp 3-4. *Italics are mine.*

[8] Anderson, *Understanding the Old Testament*, p 319

[9] Muilenburg, *Interpreter's Bible, Volume 1*, p 326

[10] Ibid.

[11] Ibid., p 329

[12] Anderson, *Understanding the Old Testament*, p 465

[13] Mack, *Who Wrote the New Testament*, p 26

[14] Ibid., p 32. For an excellent discussion see Chapter 1, "Clashing Cultures"

[15] Crossan, *The Historical Jesus*, p 230, 231

[16] Mack, *Who Wrote the New Testament*, pp 54–56

[17] Crossan, *The Historical Jesus*, pp 45, 46

[18] Mack, *A Myth of Innocence*, p 64

[19] Crossan, *The Historical Jesus*, p 360

[20] Tacitus, *Annals*, 15.44, as reported in Crossan, *The Historical Jesus*, p 374, 375

[21] 1, 2 Thessalonians, Galatians, 1, 2 Corinthians, Romans, Philemon, and Philippians

[22] Mack, *Who Wrote the New Testament*, p 41

[23] One of the oldest documents of Christian antiquity, dated between 75–90 C.E. Author unknown. It was designed for the newly baptized or for those preparing for Christianity. Highly esteemed by Jewish Christians in Palestine, Syria, and Egypt.

[24] Spong's writings, especially "Liberating the Gospels from Fundamentalism," covers this very well.

[25] Mack, *The Lost Gospel: The Book of Q*. Chapter 5 has an English translation of the reconstructed text.

[26] Data for this table is from Mack, *Who Wrote the New Testament*, pp 49-53

[27] Pagels, *The Gnostic Gospels*, pp xix-xx

[28] Mack, *Who Wrote the New Testament*, p. 71.

[29] Source: *The Tampa Tribune*, November 13, 2004, p. 1, "Chaos Engulfs Arafat Burial," byline: Steven Erlanger, *New York Times*.

[30] Crossan, *The Birth of Christianity*, Chapter 26: "Exegesis, Lament, and Biography," pp 527ff

[31] Mack, *Who Wrote the New Testament* p 95

[32] For further reading on these "missing years": John Dominic Crossan: *The Historical Jesus; The Birth of Christianity;* Burton Mack: *The Lost Gospel–The Book of Q; Who Wrote the New Testament; A Myth of Innocence;* Elaine Pagels: *The Gnostic Gospels;* John Shelby Spong: *Liberating the Gospels; Rescuing the Bible from Fundamentalism.*

[33] Mack, *Who Wrote the New Testament*, pp 117-119.

[34] Armstrong, *History of God*, pp 87, 88.

[35] Ibid., p. 89.

[36] Ibid., p. 83.

[37] Ibid., p. 82.

[38] Ephesians, Colossians, 1 & 2 Timothy, Titus, and Hebrews.

[39] In the following discussion I am indebted to my professor of Systematic Theology at Princeton Theological Seminary, George Hendry, and his wonderful book, *The Gospel of the Incarnation*.

[40] Ibid., p 115.

[41] Ibid., pp 141-143. Italics mine.

[42] Mack, *A Myth of Innocence*, p. 129.

[43] The Big Book refers to *Alcoholics Anonymous*, 3rd Edition, 1976, Alcoholics Anonymous World Services, Inc., New York, NY

[44] Armstrong, *History of God*, p 91

[45] *Ibid.*, pp 91, 92

[46] Mack, *Who Wrote the New Testament*, p 152

[47] This statement remains valid whether you believe, as Spong, that Mark wrote first, then Matthew used Mark and Q, then Luke used Mark and Matthew and Q, or whether you believe that Matthew and Luke independently used Mark and Q.

[48] Much of the material for this exhibit is from Mack, *The Lost Gospel*, Appendix A.

[49] Mack, *Who Wrote the New Testament*, p 161

[50] *Ibid.*, p 183

[51] As quoted in Crossan, *The Birth of Christianity*, pp 5, 6

[52] Mack, *Who Wrote the New Testament*, p 197

[53] *Ibid.*, p 169

[54] *Ibid.*, p 232

[55] *Ibid.*, p 237

[56] Durant, *The Story of Civilization*, Vol. 3, pp 548, 549

[57] For these early Christians the term "scripture" meant the *Septuagint*, the Greek translation of Hebrew writings, which contained the thirty-nine books of our Old Testament plus the books of the Apocrapha—exactly as the Roman Catholic Old Testament does today.

[58] 1-2 Thess., Galatians, 1-2 Corinth., Romans, Philemon, Philippians, Ephesians, and Colossians

[59] Both Eusebius' quote and Crossan's commentary are from Crossan, *The Historical Jesus*, p 424

[60] Crossan, *The Historical Jesus, p. xiii.*